Collected Works of Sebastian Kappen
Volume II

Marxian Atheism and Related Essays

Collected Works of Sebastian Kappen

Volume II

Marxian Atheism and Related Essays

Compiled and Edited by

Sebastian Vattamattam

2020

Collected Works of Sebastian Kappen, Volume II: Marxian Atheism and Related Essays, Ed. Sebastian Vattamattam — published by the Indian Society for Promoting Christian Knowledge (ISPCK), Post Box 1585, Kashmere Gate, Delhi-110006.

Online order: http://ispck.org.in/book.php

Also available on amazon.in

ISBN: 978-81-947592-2-5

Cover design: Manush John

Laser typeset by

ISPCK, Post Box 1585, 1654, Madarsa Road, Kashmere Gate, Delhi-110006 • *Tel:* 23866323

e-mail: ashish@ispck.org.in • ella@ispck.org.in
website: www.ispck.org.in

Sebastian Kappen (1924 - 1993)

Sebastian Kappen, an Indian Jesuit theologian, doctored in 1961 from the Gregorian University, Rome, with a thesis on 'Praxis and Religious Alienation according to the Economic and Philosophical Manuscripts of Karl Marx.' His subsequent studies had been geared to the requirements of transformative social action in India. This led him to an investigation into the liberative and humanizing potential of the original teachings of the historical Jesus as well as of Indian religious traditions, particularly the tradition of dissent represented by the Buddha and the medieval Bhakti Movement. He wrote and lectured extensively on the cultural restructuring of Indian society.

In 1977 appeared Kappen's major work in English, *Jesus and Freedom*. It was followed by *Marxian Atheism* (1983), *Jesus and Cultural Revolution - an Asian Perspective* (1983), *Liberation Theology and Marxism* (1986), and *The Future of Socialism and Socialism of the Future* (1992). His posthumous publications are *Tradition Modernity Counterculture* (1994), *Hindutva and Indian Religious Traditions* (2000), *Divine Challenge and Human Response* (2001), *Jesus and Society* (2002), *Jesus and Culture* (2002), *Towards a Holistic Cultural Paradigm* (2003), *Marx Beyond Marxism* (2012), *Ingathering* (2013), *What the Thunder Says* (2013). His books in Malayalam are *From Faith to Revolution* (1972), *A Sexual Morality for Tomorrow* (1973), *Ecology and Culture* (1988), *An Introduction to the Philosophy of Marx* (1989), *Prophecy and Counterculture* (1992), *In Search of the Non-Christian Jesus* (1999), *Liberation of Jesus from the Churches* (2012), and *Death of God and the Birth of the Human - tr. of Marxian Atheism* (2015)

Sebastian Kappen had been visiting professor to the Pontifical Seminary (Pune), Vidyajyoti (Delhi), The Catholic University of Louvain (Belgium) and Maryknoll Seminary (New York). Mother Earth called him back on 30 November 1993.

Contents

Introduction

Communism was taking roots in Kerala, Fr. Kappen's native place, when he was sent to Rome for higher studies in Theology. He was advised to take up Marxism for research, as his superiors thought of making him a crusader in the fight against Communism. But the result was quite different. The title of his first book, in Malayalam, was *From Faith to Revolution*, and that reveals what really happened. That book came out in 1972. Next year, the title of an article he wrote was "The Goals of Revolution" and that is Chapter 13 in this second volume of his collected works.

Kappen's doctoral thesis was on "Praxis and Religious Alienation According to the 'Economic and Philosophical Manuscripts of Karl Marx.'" As Kappen says, "The thesis resulted from an attempt to encounter Marx 'in person', that is, without going through later interpretations." The first part of this volume is his book *Marxian Atheism* based on his doctoral thesis.

Marx helped him understand Jesus and the gospel message of the Kingdom of God, in the historical perspective. On the other hand reading Marx in the light of the bible, Kappen could recapture the original Marxian concerns from the avalanche of later interpretations.

In 1980s, Fr. Kappen edited and published 'Negations – a journal of culture and creative praxis.' This volume contains in the second part a series of six essays (chapters 7 to 12) on Marxian philosophy, and the

Communist movement in India, he wrote in Negations. Chapter 14 is a talk he made in 1981. The remaining three chapters were written before 1983.

Let me express my gratitude to Mercy Kappen, and artist C F John, both closely related to Fr. Kappen, for their consistent support and encouragement in completing this volume. The cover image of this book is John's artistic creation.

Sebastian Vattamattam

Part - I
Marxian Atheism

Preface of the First Edition

The substance of this book goes back to my doctoral thesis on "Praxis and Religious Alienation According to the Economic and Philosophical Manuscripts of Karl Marx." The thesis resulted from an attempt to encounter Marx 'in person', that is, without going through later interpretations. Encumbered as it was with too many references to works in foreign languages and with citations from the German original, the work if published, would have been beyond the ken of the ordinary reader. Nor had I time to revise it in the years that immediately followed. Looking back I realize the delay in publishing has been a blessing in disguise. For in the intervening period I have had the opportunity to delve deeper into the writings of Marx and lecture extensively on the Marxian philosophy of man. In the light of the new insights gained and with a view to greater readability, I have thoroughly revised the text of the dissertation. However, I have not found it necessary to alter my original interpretation, which subsequent studies have only served to confirm.

The book opens with an overview of Marx's criticism of religion as a form of estranged consciousness. The next two chapters describe how he roots religion first in the domain of politics and finally in that of material production. Thus far, it was the descending movement of thought from consciousness to social being, from theory to practice. Now comes the reverse movement from practice to theory. The transformation of economic life through revolutionary practice is discussed in chapter 4, which is followed by an attempt in chapter 5 to delineate the salient features of the New Man and his trans-religious consciousness. The final chapter is devoted to a critical evaluation of Marx's theory of religion.

With Marx, the denial of the existence of God is a vindication of the essential being of man. I have therefore tried to present Marx's criticism of religion in the broader framework of his philosophy as a whole. This procedure reflects also a practical concern. To my knowledge, no book has appeared which seeks to explain Marxian philosophy to the Indian readers. Works published abroad tend to abound in allusions and references to western philosophers little known here. Besides, they are generally addressed to an elitist readership. As for the writings of Indian Marxists, they, by and large, faithfully reproduce the Engelsian interpretation of Marx which is often misleading. Hopefully, the present work will serve as a useful introduction to the philosophy of the founder of Marxism.

To let Marx speak for himself, I have quoted generously from original sources. This will help the reader test the truth of my interpretation against Marx's own formulations. For the same reason, I have avoided inserting my own critical comments in the course of the exposition and have eschewed all polemics. Polemics is the reflection, in the world of writing, of the capitalist value of competition. My concern is not to prove anyone wrong but help the reader gain a fair grasp of Marx's atheistic humanism.

In evaluating the Marxian theory of religion, I proceed from the standpoint of one who believes human existence has a dimension of Transcendence which discloses itself as an unconditional demand to get free of all that debases the human. Belief in this sense involves a stubborn refusal to imprison the Absolute in relative terms and calls for the demolition of all the gods made in the image of estranged humanity. As such, it is closer to atheism than to many forms of historical religion. Conversely, certain varieties of atheism tend to merge into belief. In fact, for all its violent critique of religion, Marxian atheism is not the less instinct with the quest after absolute Transcendence.

Many have helped me in writing this book. But none deserves my thanks more than that philosopher-sage, Joseph de Finance of the Society of Jesus, who way back in 1959-61 directed my research. Had it not been for his guidance and sustained encouragement, I might have got lost in the maze of Marx interpretations. I am also grateful to my niece, Mercy Kappen, who, apart from typing out the manuscript in its many versions, with her perceptive comments helped me in my search for clarity of expression and, what is more, sustained me with her humane and compassionate presence. I must also record my gratitude to 0. V. Usha who painstakingly edited the penultimate version of the text, and to Reliance Printers, Madras, for printing the book promptly and neatly.

The author shall feel amply rewarded if the present work helps Marxists and believers understand where they converge and where they diverge and engage in concerted action for a new social order in which man's greatest need will be for his fellowmen.

S. Kappen

Bangalore December 1983

1

Critique of Heaven

Influences

Karl Marx was born of Jewish parents in 1818 in the historic town of Trier in Germany. His father, Heinrich Marx, was an emancipated Jew, steeped in the free French ideas of the 18th century on politics, religion, life, and art.[1] He shared the faith of the French rationalists in the unbounded capacity of human intelligence to explain and improve the world. However, he maintained till the end a certain belief in God, as may be seen from the advice he gave his son, Karl:

> "A good support of morality is a simple faith in God. You know that I am the last person to be a fanatic. But sooner or later a man has a real need of this faith, and there are moments in life when even the man who denies God is compelled against his will to pray to the Almighty."[2]

A lawyer by profession, Heinrich Marx accepted the Protestant faith in 1817. Had he not done so, he would have found it impossible to carry on with his profession, because of the discriminatory policy of the government to members of his community. His wife, Henrietta, however, held firmly to orthodox Jewish beliefs and practices. Through her, something of the Jewish ethos and aspirations persisted in the family. Religion was also very much a part of Marx's environment. In school, he had to attend classes on religion. The essay he composed for his school-leaving certificate was on "the reason, nature, necessity, and effects of the union of believers with Christ." There he wrote:

> "Thus the history of mankind teaches us the necessity of union with Christ. Also when we consider the history of individuals and the nature of man, we immediately see a spark of the divine in his breast, an enthusiasm for the good, a striving after knowledge, a desire for truth."[3]

How deep was the faith that underlay these words we have no means to ascertain. In any case, whatever faith he had was lost during his student days, when he came into contact with radical thinkers who questioned the very foundation of religion.

The foremost among these was Hegel. A brief resume of his thought is in order here.[4] According to Hegel, the ultimate reason for all that is and becomes is the Idea. The Idea externalizes itself in Nature, the visible material universe. At a certain stage in the evolution of Nature, the Idea, hitherto latent in it, becomes conscious of itself in individual human beings as the subjective Spirit. The subjective Spirit then proceeds to enflesh itself in the world around, assuming the form of law, morality, family, civil society, and the state, all of which together constitute the objective Spirit. The tension between the subjective and objective Spirit is overcome at a higher level of synthesis which Hegel calls the absolute Spirit. The further self-unveiling of the absolute Spirit takes place in three stages, one more perfect than the other, namely, in art, religion, and philosophy. In art, the Spirit is revealed in the form of beautiful objects perceived by the senses. In religion, man strives to realize unity with the absolute Spirit using representations like symbols, images, hymns, and forms of worship. Worship is an attempt on the part of man to reach out to God and be united with him. It is also conceived as capable of effecting God's coming down to man. A still more adequate representation of the unity of the human and the divine is the Christian dogma of the Incarnation which teaches that God himself has become man.

None of these representations, however, is capable of bringing about the complete unity of the finite and the infinite. Man continues to experience the otherness of 'the other' and, consequently, feels doomed to what Hegel calls 'unhappy consciousness'. The chasm between the finite and the infinite can be bridged only if man leaves religion behind and attains to true philosophical knowledge. What religion expresses figuratively, philosophy expresses conceptually. But what Hegel has in mind is not any philosophy but his philosophy. Whoever has reached philosophical knowledge in this sense knows that the infinite 'Other' is nothing but his self-consciousness.

The judgment Hegel passes on religion is at once positive and negative: positive, because religion expresses the fundamental truth of the unity of the finite and the infinite; negative, because the concrete forms in which that unity is represented are inadequate. No less inadequate are the institutions embodying religious faith. Religion, therefore, is a mode of human alienation to be superseded. This evaluation of religion had a profound impact on Marx. He acknowledged in so many words that the Phenomenology of Hegel contained many elements for valid criticism of religion, though clothed in mystified terms.[5] He, however, could not subscribe to Hegel's idealism and subsequently parted company with him. The one thinker who, more than anybody else, set him on the road to a critical reappraisal of Hegel was Ludwig Feuerbach.

Feuerbach objected to Hegel's setting up the Idea as the point of departure of the world process and his philosophical system. He maintained that all thinking must start from below, i. e. from nature which, for him, also included man. Regarding religion, his central thesis was that it is not God who creates man, but man who creates God in his own image. Belief in God arises when man projects his own essential qualities outside himself on to the realm of illusion. Religion is nothing but man's relationship with his true essence as though it were an alien essence. What he worships are but his attributes, shorn of their limitations. Religion makes these attributes into a subject and reduces him to its predicate. But what is it that enables the human being to project his true essence in the shape of an infinite being? The answer lies in the distinction Feuerbach makes between man's individual and social essence. As an individual, each person is limited and imperfect, but as a member of the species, he is universal, potentially infinite. This is what makes it possible for him to think of an Infinite Being transcending the universe. Religion, therefore, is man's indirect consciousness of himself, indirect in so far as it is mediated by the consciousness of a creator. To become fully human, man has to transform this indirect self-consciousness into direct self-consciousness. He must transcend his limitations by enfolding the whole of mankind in his thinking, willing, and loving. The love of God must give way to the love of humanity. Thus Feuerbach reduces religion to humanism, theology to anthropology. He wrote:

> "We have reduced the supermundane, supernatural, and superhuman nature of God to the elements of human nature as its fundamental elements. Our process of analysis has brought us again to the position with which we set out: The beginning, middle and end of religion is man."[6]

Marx responded enthusiastically to the call to denounce all idealism and start thinking from the real world. He compliments Feuerbach for having founded "genuine materialism and positive science by making the social relationship of man to man the basic principle of history."[7] He appropriated the Feuerbachian reversal of subject and predicate and extended its application to the study of society as a whole. He would show that under capitalism economic, political, and ideological structures assume the role of subjects degrading human beings to mere predicates and that only in a socialist society would man be restored to his position as the real subject of history.

Further reflection led Marx a year later to a more critical assessment of Feuerbach, and that on the following grounds: First, in Feuerbach's view, the believer is an isolated individual. But such an individual is a fiction of the mind. Real men and women find themselves inserted into a closely-knit web of social relations. Secondly, the social essence into which the idea of God is reduced is an abstraction, being no more than a biological quality inherent in each individual as a member of the species. As a result, Feuerbach failed to see "that the 'religious sentiment' is itself a social product."[8] Thirdly, he represents a kind of contemplative materialism "which only observes the world' i. e. which does not conceive sensuous existence as practical activity."[9] Marx argued,

"All social life is essentially practical"[10] and it is only through praxis that religious alienation can be eliminated.

> "All the mysteries which lead theory towards mysticism find their rational solution in human practice and the comprehension of this practice."[11]

The Feuerbachian critique of religion was from a standpoint essentially opposed to Hegel, whereas that of David Strauss and Bruno Bauer was, on the whole, in keeping with the idealist tradition. In his Life of Jesus, Strauss tried to show that the Biblical narratives are not philosophical symbols, as Hegel thought, but myths expressing the aspirations of the Jewish people. By thus reducing Christianity to a sum of myths, he denied its historical character. Jesus, for him, was but a moment in the self-revelation of the divine. Only the development of humanity as a whole will reveal the complete image of God. "The man-God is humanity", he wrote.[12]

Bruno Bauer, on the other hand, started as a defender of orthodoxy in the controversies provoked by Strauss' writing. Nevertheless, he too launched a rigorous criticism of Christianity, which he reduced not to myth but to the syncretic tendencies that emerged in the wake of the decadence of political liberty in the Roman empire.[13] He was concerned to highlight not so much the human content of Christianity as its inhumanity. He saw Christian religion as the concentrated expression of the misery of the world.[14] Regarding the different religions that have appeared in history, he was of the view that they were but successive phases in the progress of universal human consciousness, each phase having only a relative significance. He further held that religion had served its purpose and had become an obstacle to mankind's march forward.[15]

Significantly, all the three post-Hegelian thinkers we have considered combine attack on religion with a profound concern for man and his destiny. This holds of Marx as well. But he was not content with repeating what others had said. On his own, he instituted a critique of religion that goes deeper than that of any of his contemporaries.

Religious Alienation: An Overview

By the time Marx wrote his doctoral thesis (1841), his views on religion had crystallized into a definite attitude of defiance against all gods. In his introduction to that work we read the following passage, which sounds like a hymn to philosophy and the supremacy of the human spirit:

> "Philosophy as long as a drop of blood shall pulse in its world-subduing and absolutely free heart, will never grow tired of answering its adversaries with the cry of Epicurus: Not the man who denies the gods worshipped by the multitude, but he who affirms of the gods what the multitude believes about them, is truly impious. Philosophy makes no secret of it. The confession of Prometheus, in simple words, I hate the pack of gods' is its own confession, its own aphorism against all heavenly and earthly gods who do not acknowledge human self-consciousness as the highest divinity. It will have none other besides."[16]

These words clearly show that Marx had become an atheist much before he turned 'Marxist'. They also tell us that he saw the denial of God as an essential prerequisite for safeguarding the dignity of man. The character of his humanism as the reverse side of atheism comes into fuller relief in the critical evaluation of the Hegelian dialectic, which he undertook in the year 1884.

As pointed out earlier, Hegel conceived religion as a form of human striving to realize union with the Absolute. If man longs for the Absolute, it is because he is in a sense already the Absolute. His consciousness of God is nothing but God's consciousness of himself. In other words, religion represents that stage in the self-manifestation of the Spirit where, in and through man, the same Spirit projects an infinite Other, so that, by uniting with it, it may attain to self-consciousness.

Marx concurred with the view that when man thinks about God he is but thinking of himself. But he disagreed with Hegel on several counts. He argued that the subject of religious awareness is not abstract self-consciousness but "a human and natural subject, with eyes, ears, etc, living in society, in the world and nature"[17] Seen with concrete individuals, even Hegel's absolute spirit is no different from the God of religion, as the former is the real subject of history, working, as it were, behind the back of individuals.[18] Put differently, after banishing God from history, Hegel reintroduces the same God, this time under the guise of the absolute Spirit. What is more, since the subject of history is the absolute Spirit, conceived as abstract self-consciousness, the process of alienation and its supersession remains abstract, merely conceptual, with no impact on the real world.[19] Consequently, the overcoming of religion takes place only in thought; in reality, religion continues just as before. The dialectic even legitimates religion. For, in the Hegelian scheme, the absolute Spirit is not only the end-result of the dialectical movement of nature and history but also all the phases of the same movement. Thus every human alienation in the course of history is restored as a necessary moment in the Spirit's march towards total self-realization.[20]

After demolishing Hegel's conception of religion and its supersession, Marx states his own position: Religion is alienated human self-consciousness. What the believer, as such, thinks is not his true self but his alienated self. Hence his true self as a conscious being is affirmed not in religion but in the abolition and supersession of religion.[21]

Grappling with the dialectic of Hegel helped Marx to further radicalize his atheism. He rejected not only the God of popular religion, located outside man and nature, but also the absolute Spirit at work in man and nature. He could not brook any manner of transcendence, not even the immanent transcendence of the Hegelian Absolute. Nor could he concede that religion represents a stage in the development of man's genuine self-consciousness. This radicalization of atheism goes hand in hand with an equally radical affirmation of man's total immanence and self-sufficiency.

Though Marx was convinced early enough that religion is an alienation to be done away with, it took him some time to arrive at a clearer perception of its nature and origin. He came to the conclusion that the roots of religion are to be sought in society. The following passage gives us an eloquent formulation of his thinking:

"The basis of irreligious criticism is this: man makes religion; religion does not make man. Religion is indeed man's self-consciousness and self-awareness so long as he has not found himself or has lost himself again. But man is not an abstract being, squatting outside the world. Man is the human world, the state, society. This state, this society, produces religion which is an inverted world consciousness because they are an inverted world. Religion is the general theory of this world, its encyclopedic compendium, its logic in popular form, its spiritual point d'honneur, its enthusiasm, its moral sanction, its solemn complement, its general basis of consolation and justification. It is the fantastic realization of the human being since the human being possesses no true reality. The struggle against religion is, therefore, indirectly a struggle against that world whose spiritual aroma is religion. Religious suffering is at the same time an expression of real suffering and a protest against real suffering. Religion is the sigh of the oppressed creature, the sentiment of a heartless world, and the soul of soulless conditions. It is the opium of the people."[22]

The basic structure and movement of Marx's thinking on religion are evident here. He starts with the Feuerbachian assumption that it is man who makes religion, not religion that makes man. Religion has no autonomous existence of its own. Neither does it exercise any independent action on society. Man alone exists and acts on his own. But the man who produces religion is neither the isolated individual nor the abstract human nature common to all men but the concrete man inserted in a particular state, living in a specific society.

But why does he make religion at all? Because the world he inhabits is an inverted (the German original could equally mean 'perverted') world. This perversion is described as consisting of loss of being, in suffering, lovelessness, soullessness, and oppression. Religion is man's protest against the lived perversion of this world. He protests by projecting a world of illusion where he can lead an ideal existence. The heaven of religious hope is everything that this world is not. If here below man is like one who has lost himself, in the world above he will be restored to fullness of being. If here life is misery, there it will be joy abounding. If here his existence is impoverished and fragmented, there it will correspond to his true universal essence.

Then, religious consciousness is not merely one of passive acquiescence; it is also creative in its own way. It conjures up an other world of perfect happiness where man can find compensation for all the indignities he suffers on earth. Thus consoled and comforted, he will reconcile himself to the evils of society. But in fashioning the deity as the supreme embodiment of all that he is deprived of, the believer is setting up an absolute master to rule over him. Henceforth it is this master who will create or destroy, save or damn him. The same God will also be used by the dominant classes to legitimate systems of exploitation and domination. Thus will come into being beliefs, dogmas, and laws, all calculated to perpetuate the rule of might. In this way, religion, which arose as a protest against the world, will end up by affirming and sanctioning the same world. What was initially a flight from the world will become a return to it to further reinforce it. In consequence, every human alienation in secular life finds its counterpart in the world of religion. Slavery to man is compounded with slavery to God; estrangement from one's kind with estrangement from one's maker, and so on, Thus religion, originally meant to be a source of consolation, becomes, in turn, a source of misery.

The main elements that constitute religious alienation may now be summed up. In the first place, religion is a form of false consciousness, a distorted vision of reality. It is also a form of deprivation in so far as man's true essence is sought not in himself but in God. Again, it causes rupture and disunity within human existence by splitting it into life on earth and life in heaven. More importantly, the believer suffers loss of freedom, not only because he becomes a slave to God but also because the same God strengthens the chains that bind him to his secular masters.

Marx saw this conception of religious alienation verified in historical religions, as may be seen from the following tirade against Christianity:

"The social principles of Christianity justified the slavery of antiquity, glorified the serfdom of the Middle Ages and are capable, in case of need, of defending the oppression of the proletariat, even if with somewhat grimaces. The social principles doleful of Christianity preach the necessity of a ruling and an oppressed class, and for the latter, all they have to offer is the pious wish that the former may be charitable. The social principles of Christianity place the ... compensation for all infamies in heaven, and thereby justify the continuation of these infamies on earth. The social principles of Christianity declare all the vile acts of the oppressors against the oppressed to be either a just punishment for original sin and other sins or trials which the Lord, in His infinite wisdom, ordains for the redeemed. The social principles of Christianity preach cowardice, self-contempt, abasement, submissiveness and humbleness, in short, all the qualities of the rabble, and the proletariat which will not permit itself to be treated as rabble, needs its courage, its self-confidence, its pride and its sense of independence even more than its bread. The social principles of Christianity are sneaking and hypocritical, and the proletariat is revolutionary. So much for the social principles of Christianity."[23]

Passages like this, which are not infrequent in the writings of Marx, have led some to argue that what he attacks is not religion as such but its distorted historical manifestations, not the true God but the God of popular religion. In support of this view, it could be pointed out that the contemporary versions of Christianity he came in contact with tended to exalt God at the expense of man, as though whatever greatness accrues to the latter is so much taken away from the former. Marx was also unsparing in his criticism of Judaism as a religion of money-making. Though the experience of current religious beliefs and practices may have influenced his thinking, it is beyond doubt that his criticism was directed against religion as such. For, the essence of Marxian atheism lies not so much in his denunciation of religion as in his affirmation of the radical autonomy and self-sufficiency of man. His criticism of religion is aimed at making man 'revolve about himself as his own true sun'. Of crucial importance in the present context is the following passage from the Economic and Philosophical Manuscripts of 1844:

"A being does not regard himself as independent unless he is his own master, and he is only his own master when he owes his existence to himself. A man who lives by the favor of another considers himself a dependent being. But I live completely by another person's favor when I owe to him not only the continuance of my life but also its creation; when he is its source. My life necessarily has such a cause outside itself if it is not my own creation. The idea of creation is thus one which it

is difficult to eliminate from popular consciousness. This consciousness
is unable to conceive that nature and man exist on their own account
because such an existence contradicts all tangible facts of practical life."[24]

Underlying these words is a prospective vision of man, of man as he
ought to be. Man is truly human only when he is the source of his
own being, the maker of his own life. Evidently, such a concept of man
rules out belief in a creator. But, is not the total immanence of man a
mere postulate? No doubt it is. Marx himself admits that the notion
of man being his own creator 'contradicts all tangible facts of practical
life'. However, he did attempt to substantiate that notion by appealing
to the scientific data then available.

His argument takes the form of a dialogue with an imagined
adversary. He begins with the statement that the idea of the creation
of the earth has received a severe blow from the science of geogeny, i.e.
from the science which portrays the formation and development of the
earth as a process of spontaneous generation. *Generatio equivoca*, he
says, is the only practical refutation of the theory of creation.[25] Then,
as though dissatisfied with his own logic, he goes on to argue that each
man is engendered by his father and mother and that even in a physical
sense human beings owe their existence to themselves. In considering
the origin of man one should not focus exclusively on the aspect of
infinite regression, and ask. Who engendered my father and mother?
One must also note the circular movement perceivable in that very
regression, whereby man reproduces himself in the act of generation.
Thus man always remains the subject of the process.

This does not satisfy the opponent. While admitting the reality of
the circular movement, he insists on the regressive movement and asks,
Who created the first man and nature as a whole? Marx replies that
the question itself is a product of abstraction, a perverted question. To
inquire into the creation of man and nature amounts to abstracting
from man and nature. It is to suppose them non-existent and then try
to demonstrate their existence. Once the abstraction is given up, the
question becomes meaningless. If the opponent wants, by all means,

to cling to the abstraction, he must be consistent and think himself non-existent. And that would be the end of his questioning as well. At this, the adversary urges that it is not necessary to consider man and nature non-existent to legitimately pose the question of their origin. Marx's final answer bears no continuity with the line of argument he has been pursuing thus far. He says:

> "Since, however, for socialist man, the whole of what is called world history is nothing but the creation of man by human labour, and the emergence of nature for man, he, therefore, has the evident and irrefutable proof of his self-creation, of his own origin. Once the essence of man and nature, man as a natural being and nature as a human reality, has become evident in practical life, in sense experience, the quest for an alien being, a being above man and nature (a quest which is an avowal of the unreality of man and nature) becomes impossible in practice."[26]

There is here a sudden change of focus from the biological to the world-historical, from the standpoint of contemporary man to that of socialist man. Further, the verification of atheism is postponed to a future yet to be made, when man will see in practice that he is his own creator. In this prognosis justified? We shall discuss this question in the concluding chapter devoted to an evaluation of Marxian atheism. In the meanwhile, let us try to gain a deeper understanding of the materialistic conception of religion propounded by Marx.

If belief in a creator arises from the fact that in practical life man does not create himself, the only way to get rid of religion is to change the world. The illusory happiness provided by religion can be abolished only by the promotion of man's real happiness in this world. You cannot require him to shed his other-worldly illusions about the conditions of his existence without at the same time requiring him to eliminate the conditions which beget such illusions. Hence the need for revolutionary praxis, which, in turn, can arise only from a thorough-going critique of society, Writes Marx,

> "It is the task of history, therefore, once the other world of truth has vanished, to establish the truth of this world. The immediate task of philosophy, which is in the service of history, is to unmask human self-

alienation in its secular form now that it has been unmasked in its sacred form. Thus the criticism of heaven is transformed into criticism of earth, the criticism of religion into the criticism of law, and the criticism of theology into the criticism of politics."[27]

The aim of criticism is not merely to lay bare the structures of alienation at the practical level but also to discover how these provide the point of departure for the birth of religious consciousness. In all his subsequent studies Marx strictly adhered to this principle. At every step, he is at pains to point out how economic, social and political conditions form the breeding ground of ideologies. His first attempts in this direction are the two articles he wrote on the Jewish question where he reduces religious alienation to political alienation. To this, we shall address ourselves presently.

The Political Basis of Religion

It was as a journalist that Marx first came into conflict with political power. The Prussian state of his day was a highly authoritarian one, perfected and maintained by government functionaries owing allegiance to their prince and the orthodox Lutheran Church. Its status as a 'Christian State' was provided theoretical underpinning by court theologians in the service of the king. They argued that to unequivocally interpret the will of God, the basis of all morality and justice, there is need for an authority superior to natural law. That authority can be none other than the state, directly or indirectly guaranteed by God himself. Underlying this view is the Lutheran conception of human nature as totally corrupt. Man is a sinner. Left to himself, he can only act according fo the dictates of lust, selfishness, and the craving for power. The state, therefore, is necessary lest human beings should devour one another. The sinfulness of man requires that the state also exercise coercion in meting out punishment. In doing so, it is but representing the supreme lawgiver, God. Since, however, the state, too, is sinful, its jurisdiction is restricted to man's external actions. It has no authority over individual conscience, of which God alone is supreme judge.

In an article published in 1842 Marx attacked the concept of the Christian state. He showed that the 'Christian state' is riddled with an inner contradiction. By calling itself Christian, it recognizes that it must be governed by the teachings of the Gospel; but, in reality, the affairs of the state and the everyday life of citizens are shaped by secular laws founded on reason. In practice, Christians do not consider it wrong to appeal to the couits if they have been cheated, though the Apostle writes that it is wrong. If they are struck on one cheek, they start an action for assault although the Gospel requires them to turn the other cheek also. They demand rational right in this world, grumble at the slightest raising of taxes, and are beside themselves at the least infringement of their liberty. And this against the Gospel teaching that the suffering in this life is not to be compared with the bliss to come. Most of their court cases and most of their civil laws are concerned with property. But they have been told that their treasure is not of this world. Nor can Christians claim innocence on the ground that they are but rendering unto Caesar the things that are Caesar's and to God the things that are God's. If that were the case, they should regard not only golden Mammon but at least as much free reason as the ruler of this world. And what, asks Marx, is the 'action of free reason' but philosophizing?[1]

The Christian state can be rid of this internal contradiction only if it ceases to be Christian and turns secular, founded solely on rational freedom and free reason. The recognition that reason should be the foundation of the state represents, for Marx, a revolution in political thinking.

> "Immediately before and after the time of Copernicus' great discovery of the true solar system, the law of gravitation of the state was discovered, its gravity was found in the state itself."[2]

Where the state revolves around its axis which is reason, it becomes the great organism in which legal, moral and political freedom is realized, and in which "the individual citizen in obeying the laws of the state only obeys the natural laws of his reason, of human reason."[3]

In the article under consideration Marx's concern is to free politics from religion. And in the course of his reflections he was able to develop the concept of an ideal state in which the demands of law and the demands of individual reason will coincide. But of such a perfect state the Prussian state of his day was truly an antithesis, bent as it was upon suppressing every manifestation of individual freedom. The real challenge, therefore, consisted not merely in freeing the state from religion but in freeing human beings from both religion and the state. The opportunity to tackle this problem was provided by the publication of an article by his erstwhile friend, Bruno Bauer, on the emancipation of the Jews.

Bauer argued that the Jews could not be emancipated as citizens so long as they clung to their narrow religious prejudices. Nor could the Christian state confer emancipation so long as it held fast to its narrow Christian prejudices. The Jews have no right to ask the state to give up its religious prejudices when they are not prepared to give up their own. Political emancipation is possible only if Jews and Christians relinquish their respective religions and meet based on common humanity. They should see in their religions nothing more than phases in the development of the human mind. In future, science and the critical attitude should suffice to unite human beings. Marx would, of course, agree that mankind should be freed from the shackles of religion. But he could not see how religion could be criticized away. To effectively abolish the religious illusion there is no other way but to remove the historical conditions that give rise to it; and this can be achieved only through collective, transformative praxis.

Marx develops this idea while criticizing Bauer's contention that the political abolition of religion is the abolition of all religion. The political abolition of religion means the repudiation on the part of the state of all privileges based on religion. But the state cannot do that unless it has already been emancipated from religion, unless it is capable of viewing all subjects solely from the standpoint of reason. In such a secular state, Bauer argued, religion will, if at all, continue only in the private life of citizens. Though advocating the secularization of the state, Marx did not believe that secularisation alone would make religion wither away. He cited the example of the United States, where religion continued to flourish despite the state not recognizing any religious privileges. He further maintained that where religion is forced to withdraw from public life into the privacy of individual existence there is every likelihood it would breed many more illusions than ever before. Here he draws a parallel between the abolition of religion and that of private property. The state does away with private property by not making it a prerequisite for the right to vote. But this does not prevent private property from continuing to exist in society. In the same way, the state's refusal to recognize religious privileges would make no difference as far as the existence of religion in civil society is concerned.[4]

The emancipation of man from religion requires something more than the mere secularization of the state. That something more consists in removing the roots of religion in practical life. But where in practical life do we find the roots of religion? In the state. For, the existence of religion results from a privation and the source of this privation can be none other than the nature of the state itself.

> "Religion no longer appears as the basis, but as the manifestation of secular narrowness."[5]

It must be noted here that, for Marx, the state whose nature reveals best the roots of religious alienation is the secular state ; for in its case there is no confusion between the sacred and the profane.

In a brilliant piece of analysis he shows how the relation between man and the secular state foreshadows the relation between man and God. To follow his reasoning it is necessary to know his distinction between civil society and the state. In the early stages of capitalism there was little state intervention in economic affairs. With laissez-faire in full swing everyday life was governed by the interplay of competing private interests. Individuals did not concern themselves with the common good, which it was considered the business of the state to look after. It is to refer to social relations of this kind that Marx employs the term, civil or bourgeois society. Under competitive capitalism there is a clear demarcation between civil society in which individuals pursue exclusively their private ends and the state which is supposed to seek the common good. What is more, each individual is split into two: into a bourgeois and a citizen. As a bourgeois he is engaged in the war of all against all; as a citizen he is member of the political community of the state.

But does the state promote the common good? By no means. It functions, in fact, as the guardian of private property, as an instrument of the privileged classes. This is not due to any evil design on the part of the state personnel but due to the very nature of the state. To promote communal interests the state will have to abolish private property. But how could it do that when private property is the very presupposition of its existence? For the state, to abolish private property is to abolish itself. The belief, therefore, that men realize their social essence in and through the state is itself an illusion.

Now to return to the point at issue, where the secular, political state has attained to its full development, man leads, in consciousness as well as in reality, a double existence - one celestial and the other terrestrial. As a citizen, he enjoys a celestial existence in the political community where he regards himself as a communal being. In civil society, on the other hand, he carries on a mundane existence, acting simply as a private individual, treating himself and other men as mere means. About civil society, the state constitutes a spiritual realm just as heaven does about earth. The state overcomes the war of all against all, characteristic of civil society, in the same manner in which religion overcomes the narrowness of the profane world i. e. by acknowledging and re-establishing it and allowing itself to be dominated by it. In his day to day bourgeois life man is a profane being. In the state, on the contrary, where he is regarded as a social, universal being, he is the imaginary member of an imaginary sovereignty invested with an unreal universality.[6]

Marx further argued that the alienation of human sociality in the state is the reason for the alienation of the same sociality in the heaven of religious belief. It is because man is not able to realize his social essence in everyday life that he fashions a surrogate in the form of a heavenly community. Religion is "an expression of the fact that man is separated from the community, from himself and other men."[7] His relation to God is the ideal form taken by his relation to the state. So that the illusion that he is realizing his social being through the state is compounded with the greater illusion that he can realize it in the community of heaven. It follows then that religion is not merely a protest against but also a reflection of the political estrangement of human essence. There is thus a close analogy between religious and political alienations in respect of structure and movement, with this capital difference, however, that the former emerges in consciousness, while the latter takes place in the realm of practical life.

This analogy shows a certain identity in difference, unity in tension, between the two alienations. So much so that man's relation to the state has itself something of a religious character. That is why Marx can use religious terms like spiritual and celestial to describe the state. He also qualifies man's relationship with the state as 'the human core of religion.'[8] More explicitly,

> "The members of the political state are religious because of the dualism between individual life and generic life. They are religious in the sense that man treats political life, which is remote from his existence, as if it were his true life."[9]

Heaven expresses in a religious form what the state expresses in a secular fashion - the alienated essence of man. What Marx is driving at will become clear to anyone who stops to consider how even today the masses look to the state for their 'salvation' and tend to worship institutions and persons embodying political power.

In sum, political alienation is not only the cause but also the secular anticipation of religion. If so, to free humanity from religion it is not enough to destroy the religious character of the state; it is necessary to destroy the state itself. Human beings must recapture their social being which they had projected on the state. When they realize their sociality in day-to-day life, the state will become superfluous:

"Human emancipation will only be complete when the real, individual man has absorbed into himself the abstract citizen; when as an individual man, in his everyday life, in his work, and his relationships, he has become a social, universal being; and when he has recognized and organized his powers (*forces propres*) as social powers so that he no longer separates this social power from himself as political power."[10]

3

Material Production and God

Base and Superstructure

We have seen how Marx traces the origin of religion to the process whereby man's social essence becomes estranged and assumes the form of political power. He proceeds to show that politics itself is no autonomous sphere but is determined by the economy - by the structures of production, distribution, and consumption. It is here that the deepest roots of religion are to be sought. The following passage gives us a synthetic view of the relation between economic structure and other sectors of societal life:

> "This material, directly perceptible private property is the material and sensuous expression of alienated human life. Its movement - production and consumption - is the sensuous manifestation of the movement of all previous production, i. e. the realization of the reality of man. Religion, the family, the state, law, morality, science, art, etc. are only particular forms of production and come under its general law. The positive supersession of private property, as the appropriation of human life, is, therefore, the positive supersession of all alienation, and the return of man from religion, the family, the state, etc. to his human, i.e. social life. religious alienation as such occurs only in the sphere of consciousness, in the inner life of man, but economic alienation is that of real life and its supersession, therefore, affects both aspects."[1]

Here Marx is viewing society from the standpoint of alienation and its supersession. He shows how the different structures of alienation (economic, political, ideological) are interrelated. All of them have one thing in common - they are products of man. He who produces material goods also produces law, state morality, religion, and philosophy. But beneath this fundamental similarity, there is an essential difference. The laws of material production shape every other manner of production. Hence economic alienation is original and primordial, while the others are only derivative. Religion, politics, law, and the like depend on the economy not only for their origin but also for their continued existence.

> "For all human servitude is involved in the relation of the worker to production, and all types of servitude are only modifications or consequences of this relation."[3]

What is the basis for the assertion that the economy determines every other dimension of human existence? No clear-cut, unambiguous answer is forthcoming. Marx seems to ground his claim on the dialectic of consciousness and being. In contrast to Hegel who affirmed the primacy of consciousness over being, Marx held that it is being that determines consciousness, not the other way round:

> "Morality, religion, metaphysics, and all the rest of ideology as well as the forms of consciousness corresponding to these, thus no longer retain the semblance of independence. They have no history, no development; but men developing their material production and their material intercourse, alter, along with this their actual world, also their thinking and the products of their thinking... It is not consciousness that determines life, but life that determines consciousness."[3]

By 'being' Marx means man's social existence. But all social life is practice, especially the practice of material production. Being thus tends to be equated with praxis. Likewise, he seems to consider the different elements of the superstructure as but so many forms of consciousness. Hence the reduction of realities of the superstructure to their economic base is at the same time the reduction of consciousness to being. If economy determines every other level of society, it is because being determines consciousness. This interpretation is reinforced by Marx's comment,

"Religious alienation as such occurs only in the sphere of consciousness, in the inner life of man, but economic alienation is that of real life and its supersession, therefore, affects both aspects."[4]

Marx never went back on this view of the relation between, base, and superstructure, between being and consciousness. He reaffirmed it in the famous Preface of 1859:

"The mode of production of material life determines the general character of the social, political, and spiritual processes of life. It is not the consciousness of men that determines their being, but, on the contrary, their social being determines their consciousness... With the change of the economic foundation the entire immense superstructure is more or less transformed."[5]

Marx applied the same principle to the historical stage of transition from one mode of production to another. It is the transformations taking place on the level of economic practice that explains the collapse of societies. In his view, all earlier forms of society foundered on the development of wealth, in other words, on the development of social productive forces. The feudal institutions broke down under the impact of urban industry, trade, modern agriculture, and even under individual discoveries such as gunpowder and the printing press. With the emergence of new productive forces and the expansion of individual trade, the economic conditions upon which the community rested were dissolved. The same fate befell political relationships corresponding to different constituents of community. Similarly, the new attitude to nature resulting from the growth of productive forces cut the ground from under religion - the idealized form of community life - and undermined the character and points of view of individual people.[6]

Marx, however, did not think of the relation between base and superstructure in terms of one-way causality. He admitted that once religion, state, etc. have come into being they can react on the base. In *Wage-labour and Capital* he wrote:

"Man himself is the basis of his material production, as of all production which he accomplishes. All circumstances, therefore, which affect man, the subject of production, have a greater or lesser influence upon all his functions and activities including his functions and activities as the creator of material wealth, of commodities. In this sense, it can truly be asserted that all human relations and functions, however, and wherever they manifest themselves, influence material production and have a more or less determining effect upon it."[7]

More importantly, besides the architectural model (base-superstructure) he also employs the model of organic totality. In any organic whole every element at the same time the cause and effect of every other element; no part is intelligible outside of its relationship with the whole. Marx saw this verified in developed capitalism. In the completed bourgeois system, he contends, "every economic relation presupposes every other in its bourgeois economic form, and every result is thus also a presupposition, as is the case with every organic system."[8] And an organic system is a totality. It becomes a totality by subordinating all elements of society to itself, thus transforming them into the organs it needs. Here no particular element can claim precedence over the others. The organic model, though, is never employed by Marx at the expense of the architectural. He sees the social whole as a unity in tension between dialectically opposing poles: between the mode of production and the superstructure and, within the mode of production itself, between productive forces and relations of production. But the *ultimate* determining principle always remains the production of material life.

As an element of the superstructure, religion arises from economic alienation. But Marx was not content with enunciating general principles. He also undertook an analysis of the capitalist mode of production, in the course of which he tried to lay bare the genetic link between economic estrangement and religious consciousness. To understand this link we must first consider the main dimensions of economic alienation: the alienation of the product, of the activity of production, and of the essential being of the producer.

Alienation of the Product

The worker enfleshes his creative powers in external objects; he impregnates them with his spirit and intelligence. Work, therefore, is a process of self-objectification; and the product, the extended being of the producer.[9] But under the regime of capitalist private property, where a privileged class controls the means of production, the process of self-objectification becomes one of self-estrangement, since the producer is deprived of his product. The greater the world of products he brings into being the greater is the alienation of both what he is and what he has. As the young Marx wrote,

> "... the more the worker expends himself in work the more powerful becomes the world of objects which he creates in face of himself, the poorer he becomes in his inner life, and the less he belongs to himself ... The worker puts his life into the object, and his life then belongs no longer to himself but to the object. The greater his activity, therefore, the less he possesses. What is embodied in the product of his labour is no longer his own. The greater this product is, therefore, the more he is diminished. The alienation of the worker in his product means not only that his labour becomes an object, assumes an external existence, but that it exists independently, outside himself, and alien to him, and that it stands opposed to him as an autonomous power. The life which he has given to the object sets itself against him as an alien and hostile force."[10]

This much must be obvious even to a superficial observed considering the vast difference in the level of consumption of capitalists and workers. For a more scientific understanding of the mechanism whereby the labourer is robbed of his product, we must turn to the theory of surplus value. Briefly, the argument runs as follows. Production under capitalism presupposes an exchange between the employer and the worker, the latter receiving from the former a sum of money in return for his work. On the surface, what transpires between them is an equal exchange; but in reality, it is an unequal one. For what the worker gives in exchange for wages cannot be labour. How could he give labour when he has already been deprived of the means of production? He can work only after the exchange with the employer, who alone owns the means of production. The sole commodity he owns and can give in exchange is labour power i.e. his capacity to apply mind and body for the production of goods. Therefore, the wages he receives must be equal to the value of his labour power as a commodity. Now, as in the case of any other commodity, the value of labour power is measured in terms of the socially necessary labour required to produce it, which, in turn, amounts to the labour expended in producing the means of subsistence (food, clothing, housing, medicines, etc.). Let us suppose that the value of the commodities the worker has to consume in order to build up the labour power spent in a day's work is six Rupees. Six Rupees, then, will be his daily wage.

But labour power is not just one commodity among many. It has this unique property that its use value consists in creating - given the objective conditions of production - other use values and thereby also fresh exchange value. In other words, it not only has a value but also produces new values. Let us again suppose that the total value created in one day equals ten Rupees. The worker then has not only reproduced the equivalent of his wages but also produced an additional value of four Rupees. This is surplus value, which the capitalist pockets without giving anything in exchange.[11]

The capitalist, however, does not appropriate surplus value merely for spending it on consumption. He reinvests part or whole of it in further production. Thus surplus value becomes surplus capital, which goes on expanding in successive cycles of production. So much so that, over time, the entire capital is nothing but accumulated surplus value.

> "In surplus capital, all the elements are the products of alien labour - alien surplus labour which has been changed into capital."[12]

But capitalism involves not only exploitation but also domination of labour. Capital, as objectified, alienated labour, " assumes mastery and command over living labour." What is worse, the mastery exercised by capital is itself the product of living labour. It is living labour that confers on the product an independent mode of existence opposed to itself, and an autonomous value. As though the product of labour has acquired its soul from living labour and has established itself opposite the latter as an alien force.[13] For the worker this means a twofold servitude, affecting his existence both as a worker and a physical subject.

The worker can create nothing without nature. Nature provides the material in which his labour is realized, out of which he produces things. Nature affords the means of existence for his labour. It provides the means of existence not only for labour but also for the labourer as a physical subject. He must eat in order to be able to live and work. Under the regime of private property, however, the more the worker transforms the external world of sensuous nature by his labour the more he is deprived of the means of existence in the two senses just explained. First, the external world becomes less and less a means of existence of his labour; second, it becomes progressively less a means for the physical subsistence of the worker.

> "The culmination of this enslavement is that he can only maintain himself as a physical subject so far as he is a worker and that it is only as a physical subject that he is a worker."[14]

The result is that the worker and his product (capital) move in opposite directions and that both in terms of quantity and quality. Quantitatively, the greater the volume of capital, the more the direct producers are deprived of the product; qualitatively, the more power, and glory accrue to capital and the capitalist class, the greater is the degradation and powerlessness of the workers.

> "Labour certainly produces marvels for the rich but privation for the worker. It produces palaces, but hovels for the worker. It replaces labour by machinery, but it casts some of the workers back into a barbarous kind of work and turns others into machines. It produces intelligence, but stupidity and cretinism for the workers."[15]

Alienation of Productive Action

The product is but congealed human labour. Where it is alienated, the act of production too is alienated. "How could the worker stand in an alien relationship to the product of his activity", asks Marx, "if he did not alienate himself in the act of production itself?"

> "The product is only the resume of the activity of production. So if the product is alienated, the act of production too will be alienated. Labour becomes *the alienation of activity and the activity of alienation.*"[16]

The alienation of the act of production is caused by the nature of productive forces and production relations. Productive forces comprise all the forces set in motion when labour power (including science, technical know-how, and organization) is applied to raw materials with the help of instruments of production. In class societies, the relations of production consist of the relation between those who own the means of production, control the production process and appropriate the product, and those others who are directly involved in the production. Productive forces concern man's relation to nature, while relations of production refer to the relation between human beings in the process of production. The two together constitute the economic structure of society.

Where the direct producers are deprived of the means of production, work loses all human quality. It is external to the worker, not a spontaneous expression of his nature. Consequently, instead of finding fulfillment in work; he denies himself, has a feeling of misery rather than of well-being. He does not develop freely his mental and physical energies but is physically exhausted and mentally debased. The worker, therefore, feels at home only during leisure time, whereas at work he feels homeless. His work is not voluntary but imposed, is not a means to satisfy his own needs but a means for satisfying other people's needs. The alienating character of work may be seen from the fact that as soon as there is no physical or other compulsions the worker avoids it like a plague. In short, work becomes self-sacrifice, a form of mortification.[17]

Within the system of private property especially in its capitalist form productive forces have a dehumanizing impact on work. Later in this study, we shall discuss how the technical division of labour deprives work of all wholeness. For the present, we confine ourselves to focussing the negative influence of machinery on the act of production. Marx discerns three stages in the development of the technical forces of production represented respectively by tools, machinery, and automation. In the first stage, the worker is master over his instruments of production. He animates the tools with his own skill, which only transmits the activity of the worker to the object. Tools are truly means of labour, subject to the will of the labourer. Not so where machine is used. Here the workers' skill counts for little. It is the machine that possesses skill, as though it were endowed with a spirit of its own in the form of the mechanical laws operating in it. The activity of the worker is reduced to a mere abstraction determined and regulated by the movement of the machinery. Science no longer exists in the consciousness of the worker as it did in earlier days; rather it resides in the machinery and that, too, in the manner of an alien force. Thus domination by capital assumes the form of domination by machinery:

> "The production process has ceased to be a labour process in the sense that labour is no longer the unity dominating and transcending it. Rather labour appears merely to be a conscious organ, composed of individual living workers at several points in the mechanical system; dispersed, subjected to the general process of the machinery itself, it is itself only a limb of the system, whose unity exists not in the living workers but in the living (active) machinery, which seems to be a powerful organism when compared to their individual, insignificant activities. With the advent of machinery, objectified labour appears in the labour process itself as the dominating force opposed to living labour, a force represented by capital in so far as it appropriates living labour."[18]

What is true of the impact of the machine on work activity is also true of the automaton, since it is only "the most perfected and most fitting form of the machine." But as automation develops intensively and extensively, a new form of alienation emerges consisting of the marginalization of labour: Labour ceases to be an essential part of the process of production. What appears as the mainstay of production is neither the immediate labour performed by the worker nor the time that he works "but the appropriation by man of his general productive force, his understanding of nature, and the mastery of it."[19] In other words, the most important factor of production is the general productive force of the community as a whole, represented by highly developed science and technology. With the spread of automation, conditions will ripen for people's effective control over the economy. Marx thus ends with the claim that the marginalization of labour - the last form of work alienation caused by the development of productive forces - will signal the dissolution of capitalism and the birth of a new social order.

Alienation of the Producer

The alienation of work involves alienation of the worker. For work is not something added to him, as though he did not need to work to be a complete being. Man *is* his work. "What is life but activity?"[20] As constitutive of human essence, work is always social, never merely individual. Man works in association with, and for, others ; he produces not only things but also human beings. Similarly-through work he relates himself to the whole of nature, unlike animals It is work that enables him to transcend his limits and become what he is: a universal essence encompassing the world of objects and the community of men. It is this universal essence Marx has in mind when he speaks of man's generic being (Gattungswesen):

> "Man is a generic being not only in the sense that he makes the community (his own as well as those of other things) his object both practically and theoretically, but also (and this is simply another expression for the same thing) in the sense that he treats himself as a universal and consequently free being."[21]

But, under capitalism, man's universal essence cannot come to its own. Where the product is expropriated, part of his own being is wrenched away from the producer, leaving him diminished, mutilated. He also suffers a diminution of being in the very act of production, which, instead of being the spontaneous unfolding of his universal being, is degraded to a mere means to individual subsistence.[22] Further, as a result of the estrangement of the product and the act of production, he is also estranged from his fellowmen, from their products, and their work.[23] Marx sees in this social fragmentation the supreme expression of alienated humanity:

> "In general, the statement that man is alienated from his generic being means that each man is alienated from others, and that, teach of the others is alienated from human life."[24]

Man's alienation from his social, universal essence takes different forms, of which we shall now discuss three - commodity, money, capital.

The production of commodities presupposes the labour of individuals or groups working independently of one another. Where it is the dominant mode of production as in capitalism, the labour of independent, private producers is social in a two-fold sense. In the first place, each product must satisfy a definite social demand; it must be not only a use value but a use value for others. Secondly, in order that the various products may satisfy society's needs, they must be exchangeable for one another. For products of utterly different kinds of labour to be exchangeable, they must all have something in common, which can only be abstract human labour. And the amount of abstract human labour embodied in any product is what constitutes its value as distinct from its use value.

Since, however, producers do not come into social contact either before or during production, the specifically social character of their individual labour does not manifest itself until exchange takes place. In other words, the labour of individuals serves social needs solely in virtue of the relations which exchange establishes between the labour products.

> "That is why the social relations connecting the labour of one private individual (or group) with the labour of another seem to the producers, not direct social relations between individuals at work, but what they really are: material relations between persons and social relations between things."[25]

Instead of finding natural expression in direct relations between producers (through common ownership, co-operation, planning), human sociality becomes an objective attribute attaching to things or to the relation between things. Thus what is profoundly human is reified. Worse, the commodity as estranged human social essence dominates man. Marx says,

> "The magnitudes of the value of commodities, are perpetually changing, independently of the will, foreknowledge, and activity of those who make

the exchanges, whose own social movement seems to them a movement of things, of things which control them, instead of being controlled by them."[26]

Money is a particular commodity set apart to serve as the universal equivalent of all commodities. It is exchange value in so far it detaches from commodities and becomes itself a commodity. No wonder that the estrangement of the human, which commodities represent, reappears in the money form, but pushed to a higher degree. The young Marx had already seen this in the course of his early economic studies and had spoken of money as "the alienated and self-alienating generic being of man."[27] He also showed how money becomes the repository of qualities and powers which really should belong to man.[28] Later he would explain how with the expansion of commodity production money becomes master over men.

The need for exchange and the transformation of the product into a pure exchange value arises with division of labour where the production of goods the community needs devolves upon different individuals. Which, in turn, is a manifestation of the social character of production. But as the division of labour and the social character of labour grows, the power of money also grows. So much so that "the exchange relation establishes itself as a power external to and independent of the producers." From being a means to promote production exchange becomes a relation alien to the producers. The more producers become dependent on exchange, the more exchange - therefore also money - becomes independent of them. The gap between the product as use value and the product as exchange value appears to widen. Thus arises the seemingly transcendental power of money.[29]

The alienation of human sociality reaches its peak in money as capital. Capital is money pregnant with money. As capital, money assumes the form of machinery, raw materials, and labour power. Machinery and. raw materials, when animated by living labour, bring into existence products that realize a value greater than that of their constituents. This creates the illusion that capital is endowed with a power of its own, whereby, in changing form, it increases in magnitude. In reality, however, surplus value is created not by capital but by labour. Further, as capitalism develops and moves securely on its own foundations, it follows its own internal laws over which neither workers nor consumers nor even individual capitalists exercise any control.[30] With this, the domination of society by capital is complete.

The Production of God

Significantly, the formal features of religious alienation noted earlier are also verified in economic alienation. First, capitalism tends to create false consciousness in people (mystification): The product of man appears as his producer; the producer, in turn, appears as the product of his product. Second, the worker suffers universal deprivation. He is robbed of his product, of his creativity, and of his social being; his life is impoverished; his freedom curtailed; his humanity diminished. Third, his universal essence is subjected to fragmentation and division, society breaking up into conflicting individuals, groups, and classes. Capitalism also creates a rupture in man's *being-with-nature*. To crown it all, human beings are reduced to slavery - slavery to commodity, money, capital. These dimensions of economic alienation are also present in pre-capitalist class societies, though they reach their fullest development only in capitalism.

The resemblance between religious and economic alienations has deeper implications, which need to be further explored. It is revealing that Marx invariably appeals to the phenomenon of religion when he wants to shed light on economic alienation. After stating that the more the worker produces the less he has for himself, he adds,

> "It is just the same as in religion. The more of himself man attributes to God the less he belongs to himself."[31]

A similar comparison is found in *Capital*:

> "Just as in the sphere of religion, man is dominated by the creature of his own brain (God); so, in the sphere of capitalist production, he is dominated by the creature of his own hand."[32]

Again, in discussing commodity fetishism:

> "To find an analogy, we must enter the nebulous world of religion. In that world, the products of the human mind assume independent shapes, endowed with lives of their own, and able to enter into relations with men and women. The products of the human hand do the same thing in the world of commodities."[33]

Religion also comes in handy as an illustration of the alienation of human activity in the process of production:

> "Just as in religion, the spontaneous activity of human fantasy, of the human brain and heart, reacts independently as an alien activity of gods or devils upon the individual, so the activity of the worker is not his own spontaneous activity. It is another's activity and the loss of his own spontaneity."[34]

Finally, Marx draws a parallel between the reification of human essence into money and the projection of the same essence in the notion of God:

> "Just as man, so long as he is engrossed in religion, can only objectify his essence by making it into an alien, fantastic being, so under the sway of egoistic need, he can only affirm himself and produce objects in practice by subordinating his products and his own activity to the domination of an alien entity, and by attributing to them the significance of an alien entity, money."[35]

These texts may seem to mean nothing more than an extrinsic similarity between the structures of economic and religious alienation. In reality, much more is at stake, as may be seen from his statement that the emancipation of the working class includes the emancipation of humanity as a whole, since "all human servitude is involved in the relation of the worker to production, and all the types of servitude are only modifications or consequences of this relation."[36] The claim that economic servitude contains all other forms of servitude must be understood in the full dialectical sense. In dialectical causation the effect is but a becoming-explicit of what is already implicitly present in the cause; the consequent is already in germ in the antecedent. If so, religion is inchoately present in the heart of the economic process.

This interpretation is reinforced by the fact that Marx frequently applies religious terms to economic realities. Speaking of the profane core of Jewish religion, he refers to money as the jealous god of Israel beside which no other god can exist, as the universal and self-sufficient value of all things which deprives the whole world of their proper value, and as the alienated essence of man's work which he worships.[37] Elsewhere Marx speaks of the omnipotence of money, of money as the highest good, and the visible deity.[38] It follows, then, that the sacred deity of the temple is the ideal reflection of the profane deity of the market; that economic alienation is not merely the source but also the this-worldly anticipation of religion.

Here one might object that Marx's analysis is valid only for societies based on commodity production, that he fails to explain how religion existed in earlier societies. True, his writings do not contain any systematic treatment of the history of religion from the standpoint of the dialectic of base and super-structure or of being and consciousness. But he did give some thought to the matter. He recognized variations in the content of religious consciousness corresponding to differences in the mode of production. According to him, what gave rise to religious beliefs in primitive societies was the limited development of productive forces and the immaturity of social relations.

The productive organisms of ancient days were far simpler and easier to understand than those of bourgeois society. They were based either on the immaturity of the individual who had not yet severed the umbilical cord which bound him to the community or upon direct relations of dominion and subjugation. They were the outcome of a low level of the evolution of the productive forces when the relations of human beings to one another and to nature were relatively immature.

> "This restrictedness in the world of concrete fact was reflected in the ideal world, in the world of the old natural folk religion."[39]

Here, one perceives a certain shift in Marx's line of reasoning. He first sought to trace the origin of religious consciousness to the relations of production based on private property, in other words, to the exploitation of man by man. How then to account for the existence of religion already in tribal societies founded on common property? This problem must, it seems to me, have led Marx to seek the source of religion not only in private property but also in the immaturity of productive relations which characterized social formations before the emergence of private property. In the bargain, however, he falls into another inconsistency. If religious alienation existed even before the division of society into classes, his thesis that private property is the resume and matrix of all human alienation cannot stand. All this shows that Marx did not succeed in developing his thinking into a consistent materialist theory of religion.

Be that as it may, he attempted to explain the variations in religious consciousness in terms of changes in the mode of production. Yet another example of this concern is his statement in Capital that for a society in which the relations of production are such that products are related to one another as repositories of abstract, undifferentiated labour,

> "Christianity, with its cult of the abstract human being, is the most suitable religion, above all, Christianity in its bourgeois phases of development such as Protestantism, Deism and the like."[40]

Observations like this have profound implications for any sociology of religion. They tell us that the specificity of religion in different historical epochs must be studied in relation to the specificity of the economic conditions prevailing in each period.

Since the religious illusion has its source as well as profane anticipation in practical life, the abolition of that illusion calls for a complete restructuring of man's practical relationship with nature and his fellowmen:

> "Such religious reflections of the real world will not disappear until the relations between human beings in their practical everyday life have assumed the aspect of perfectly intelligible and reasonable relations as between man and man, and as between man and nature. The life process of society, this meaning the material process of production, will not

lose its veil of mystery until it becomes a process carried on by a free association of producers, under their conscious and purposive control. For this, however, an indispensable requisite is that there should exist a specific material groundwork (or a series of material conditions of existence) which can only come into being as the spontaneous outcome of a long and painful process of evolution."[41]

4

Praxis for Integral Freedom

The criticism of heaven led Marx to a criticism of the earth. It enabled him to lay bare the dynamic structures of alienation embedded in political relations and the capitalist mode of production. But he was convinced that criticism, by itself, does not take one beyond a mere interpretation of the world. His concern was to criticize the world in view of changing it. And he saw clearly that only by praxis can man free himself from economic and political alienations and thereby also from all forms of false consciousness.

The Concept of Praxis

Praxis is generally contrasted with theory. Both terms have a long history. For the early Greek thinkers, theory meant the spiritual vision of abstract qualities. It was called philosophy when it sought to know the ultimate, divine ground of all reality. Praxis, on the other hand, comprised all actions ensouled by theoretical knowledge. Aristotle distinguished between theory, praxis, and poiesis. By theory he understood mere contemplative knowledge, knowledge for its own sake; by praxis, moral behaviour illumined by thought; by poiesis, technical manual labour having thought for its handmaid. Subsequent philosophy ruptured the close link between theory and praxis until they were brought together once again by Hegel. For Hegel, praxis is history itself since it is the visible, concrete manifestation of absolute Reason (Spirit). The theory of the world, therefore, can appear only when the world itself has unfolded all its possibilities. Philosophy is "its own time grasped in thought." In this perspective, theory and praxis are dialectically mediated moments in the progressive self-revelation of the Spirit.

Here is the point of departure for the Marxian philosophy of praxis. Marx would, of course, reject the conception of praxis as the manifestation of Reason, conceived as prior, though but logically, to the world. In the place of Reason, he would place the concrete man who creates himself in creating history. In fact, Hegel had already shown - and Marx was generous in acknowledging it - that man's self-creation is a process, that he is the result of his own labour. He had also shown the driving force of this process to be the dialectic of negativity, according to which reality unfolds all its possibilities by first developing internal contradictions and then overcoming them in ever-higher syntheses This holds true of man as well, who can grow into his full stature only by alienating his powers in the objective world and by transcending the same alienation.[1] Marx endorsed this view and made it the cornerstone of his own philosophy.

In the dialectical perspective of Marx, one may distinguish two conceptions of praxis: one neutral, the other value-laden. In the neutral sense, praxis means the totality of sense experience.[2] Sense experience or sensuousness includes both action and passion, perception, and need, in a word, the whole of man's relationship with his environment through seeing, touching, hearing, feeling, loving, willing, acting, and suffering. The second conception of praxis derives from the historical dialectic of alienation and its supersession and entails three successive phases: the praxis of alienation ("the alienation of activity and the activity of alienation"), the praxis of disalienation (revolution), and the praxis of the liberated man in socialism. In the previous chapters, we have delineated the salient features of alienated and alienating praxis. We shall now focus the praxis of revolution. But it must be kept in mind that revolutionary praxis, being but a phase in the dialectical movement of history, can be understood only in the context of the past it seeks to supersede and the future it wants to create.

The Praxis of Revolution

The third thesis on Feuerbach reads:

> "The coincidence of the changing of circumstances and of human activity or self-changing can only be grasped and rationally understood as revolutionary practice."[3]

Revolutionary praxis, then, consists of the process whereby human beings change themselves in changing their environment. Taken in isolation, this definition would seem to cover even factory labour, in so far as workers develop their skills in producing commodities. Evidently, this is not what Marx meant to convey. The transformation of man and the world he envisaged goes much deeper and calls for the overthrow of dehumanizing and oppressive social structures.

In an article written in 1844, he defined revolution as "the overthrow of the existing ruling power and the dissolution of existing social relationships."[4] By social relationships he meant the relations of production, which, in class societies, are founded on the exploitation of labour. Hence the coming revolution will consist of the abolition of the kind of labour that produces surplus for the owning classes.

> "In all former revolutions the form of activity was always left unaltered and it was only a question of redistributing this activity among different people, of introducing a new division of labour. The communist revolution, however, is directed against the former mode of activity, does away with labour and abolishes all class rule along with the classes themselves."[5]

What is aimed at is an economic transformation that requires not only a change of distribution but a new organization of production.[6]

But organizing production on a new basis entails a complete remoulding of man and society. The revolution ahead will not consist of substituting the rule of one class for that of another or in a merely political revolution "which will leave the pillars of the building standing."[7]

By abolishing private property, it will render impossible the continuance of class, state, and ideologies. More, it will bring about the emancipation not only of the working class but of humanity as a whole. The goal, then, is nothing less than a new creation peopled with new men and new women.

But who will be the historic agent of revolution? A class must be formed, argues Marx, which has radical chains, a class which is the dissolution of all classes, a class that has a universal character because its sufferings are universal, which does not seek a particular redress because the wrong done to it is not a particular wrong but wrong in general, a class which has no traditional privileges to maintain but only seeks to attain to the privilege of being human, a class which cannot emancipate itself without emancipating all the other spheres of society, a class, which, suffering under the total loss of humanity, can redeem itself only by the total redemption of humanity. Such a class is the proletariat.[8]

But the proletariat cannot demolish the prevailing system so long as objective conditions have not matured. For they can create the future only out of the possibilities inherent in the present. And the main objective prerequisite for revolution is the sharpening of the contradictions latent in capitalism, especially the contradiction between productive forces and relations of production.

> "For an oppressed class to emancipate itself it is essential that the existing forces of production and the existing social relations should be incapable of continuing to exist side by side."[9]

Such a situation will be created by capitalism itself. Its own immanent laws will lead to the ever-greater centralization of capital. As a result of competition, the smaller capitalist will be eliminated by the bigger ones, thus furthering the concentration of the means of production in fewer and fewer hands. On the other hand, labour will become more and more co-operative and socialized. Likewise, science and technology will develop to a point where their use will increasingly require the combined efforts of many The contradiction between the centralization of the means of production and the socialization of labour will cause recurring crises in the shape of over-production, inflation or unemployment, all leading up to a major crisis that will shake capitalism to its very foundations.[10]

However, objective contradictions and crises will result in a revolution only if, concomitantly, there is a subjective crisis, a crisis of consciousness on the part of the working class. The proletariat as the agent of revolution must be the unity of the objective and the subjective, of praxis and theory. From being only a *class-in-itself* they must become a *class-for-itself*. For Marx, a group of people forms a *class-in-itself* in so far as they occupy the same position in any given mode of production and, objectively, share the same culture and interests. Factory workers form a class in this sense because it is their common lot to have to sell their labor-power to make a living. But they become a *class-for-itself* only when they acquire a consciousness of their common interests as opposed to the interests of the other classes. Speaking of the French peasantry he says:

> "In so far as millions of families live under economic conditions of existence that separate their mode of life, their interests, and their culture from those of other classes, and put them in hostile opposition to the latter, they form a class."[11]

Where, on the contrary, there is only a local interconnection among individuals and no sense of community born of the identity of interests, no national bond, and no political organization among them, there is not yet a class.

How does the proletariat arrive at correct consciousness? Marx and Engels believed that for the creation of communist consciousness on a mass scale "it is necessary for men themselves to be changed on a large scale, and this change can only occur in a practical movement, in a revolution."[12] This would mean revolutionary consciousness is a result of working-class struggles. But do not struggles presuppose consciousness as their motive power? In keeping with his economic interpretation of history, Marx would argue that the required critical awareness will itself be the product of the capitalist mode of production:

> "When the worker recognizes the products as being his own and condemns the separation of the conditions of his realization as an intolerable imposition, it will be enormous progress in consciousness, itself the product of the method of production based on capital, and a death-knell of capital in the same way that once the slaves became aware that they were persons, that they did not need to be the property of others, the continued existence of slavery could only vegetate on as an artificial thing, and could not continue to be the basis of production.[13]

Working-class consciousness is revolutionary only if it is critical, only if it is "poverty conscious of its moral and physical poverty, degradation conscious of its degradation, and for this reason trying to abolish itself."[14] This calls for something more than a mere emotional revulsion against capitalism. Workers must have a theoretical grasp of its exploitative and alienating character. To arrive at it, all they have to do is to know themselves; in knowing themselves they will know the social system as a whole. They do not need to "seek science in their own minds; they have only to take note of what is happening before their eyes and to become its mouthpiece."[15] They will then see in poverty its "subversive, revolutionary side, which will overthrow the old society."[16] Out of their self-understanding will be born not only a science of revolution but also a revolution of science, a truly revolutionary science.

Critical consciousness at once presupposes and generates new needs in the proletariat; without the mediation of needs, consciousness cannot become praxis.

> "Theory is only realized in a people so far as it fulfills the needs of the people."[17]

But it is not any need Marx has in mind but radical needs.[18] Only those needs are radical which arise from the root of man; and "for man the root is man himself."[19] Hence for the proletariat to experience radical needs is to effectively desire a new, fuller, and richer humanity; it involves at the same time the determination to do away with all conditions that debase and dehumanize them.

Revolutionary consciousness must find concrete expression in the organization. The many minds and wills must fuse into one corporate force. Only through the conscious organization will the exploited be able to create conditions where they can be human "not only in thinking, in consciousness, but in massy being, in life."[20] The massy being inchoately present in their organized existence is more than a mere means for transforming society. It is rather an end in itself, being an anticipation of the reintegrated humanity of the future. Marx seems to have seen such anticipation in the life of contemporary French workers:

> "When communist artisans form associations, teaching and propaganda are their first aims. But their association itself creates a new need - the need for society - and what appeared to be a means has become an end. The most striking results of this practical development are to be seen when French socialist workers meet together. Smoking, eating, and drinking are no longer simply means of bringing people together. Society, association, entertainment which also has society as its aim, is sufficient for them; the brotherhood of man is no empty phrase but a reality, and the nobility of man shines forth upon us from their toil-worn bodies."[21]

This hymn to the working class has also a prescriptive meaning. It tells us what every working-class organization ought to be. In its life, organization, and struggle, the proletariat must strive to embody the values of the new social order they want to create. This is an essential prerequisite for the success of the revolution itself - a prerequisite not in the moral but in the dialectical sense. For, a fundamental principle of Marxian dialectic, or of any dialectic for that matter, is:

> " Nothing can emerge at the end of the process which did not appear as a presupposition and precondition at the beginning."[22]

Socialism is not created out of nothing; nor does it descend from on high. It can only be the outcome of the forces already at work in capitalism and, above all, in the revolutionary movement. If this movement were inspired by private interest, competition, and consumerism, it would prove incapable of fashioning a future founded on community interest, co-operation, and creative freedom.

Here one might ask, what should be the attitude of workers to their own exploiters? Marx never advocated class hatred. On the contrary, he explicitly stated that the revolution must emancipate the whole of society including the bourgeoisie. Understandably, because the proletariat is not just one class among many but "a class in civil society which is not a class of civil society, a class which is the dissolution of all classes". Proletarian consciousness, therefore, is a class-consciousness that is at the same time the dissolution of all class consciousness; that is, it must have the character of universal consciousness.

The scope of this study does not permit us to go into the concrete manner in which revolutionary consciousness must translate itself into historical praxis. At the initial stages, struggles will aim at securing higher wages and better working conditions. Marx saw in trade-unionism a means for organizing workers and educating them in socialism. He hoped that the separate economic struggles of the working class would grow into a political movement with the object of achieving their interests in a general form possessing a socially coercive force.[23] The goal of this political movement will be nothing short of conquering political power.[24] Once in power, the victorious class will substitute for the old class-ridden society an association which will exclude classes and their antagonism, a society in which people's power will not have to assume the form of state power.[25]

Revolution as Dialectical Supersession

It is often said that the aim of revolutionary action is the destruction, pure and simple, of capitalism so that on its ruins a socialist society can be built. This is far from what Marx intended. His conception of transition to socialism is essentially dialectical. To grasp this we must return to his criticism of the Hegelian dialectic. For Hegel, alienation consisted in the very fact of the existence of objects confronting man, the subject. How could one feel at home in a world where objects impinge on one's life from every side? The only way to overcome alienation is to eliminate objectivity. This precisely is what Hegel attempted to do when he reduced the world of objects to a projection of the Spirit. Objects, for him, are nothing but Consciousness become visible and tangible. If so, man is not living in a strange world but in a world born of the very stuff of his own authentic selfhood.

The idealistic view of alienation and its abolition was totally unacceptable to Marx. Alienation, he argued, cannot consist in man's being confronted with objects. Rather, it is of man's very essence to relate to objects, whether given or produced by him. When through work he objectifies himself in products, he is but acting according to his true being. What constitutes alienation is something else - the circumstance that the products of labour set themselves up as alien and hostile to him.[26] Therefore, superseding alienation means not suppressing the objective world but divesting it of its hostile character. In other words, the objects of human creation will have to be preserved and abolished at the same time. (However, in fairness to Hegel it must be stated that he, too, conceived the supersession of alienation as entailing both abolition and preservation, a fact Marx himself refers to. If the former erred it was in equating alienation with the existence of objects independent of the mind.

The distinction between objectification and alienation plays a crucial role in the Marxian dialectic of history. In capitalism, objectification and alienation combine to form a single process. In producing goods (objectification), workers fashion their own fetters (alienation). But this was not the case in all periods of history. In the patriarchal mode of production, for example, members of the family produced use-values which never became exchange values or capital. So too, in socialist society men will go on producing objects without their ever becoming private property. Work as objectification, therefore, is constitutive of the essence of man; not alienation. But in so far as mankind can develop its potentialities only by alienating itself and transcending the same alienation, one could maintain that even alienation pertains to man's social-historical essence.

Now, there is no doubt that the conception of revolution as involving both abolition and preservation - a conception which logically follows from the distinction between objectification and alienation - shaped Marx's understanding of the transition from capitalism to socialism. Take, for instance, his view of private property. Mere than anyone else, he showed how private property dehumanizes man and disrupts human community. Yet he also stressed the contribution it has made to the expansion of mankind's productive forces and to the creation of wealth. He wrote:

"The meaning of private property, released from its alienation, is the existence of essential objects for man, as objects of enjoyment and action."[27]

Again,

"Everyday, material industry...shows us, in the form of sensuous useful objects, in an alienated form, the essential human faculties transformed into objects."[28]

Hence the aim of revolution is the abolition not of property but of the private character of property.

The same holds true of the division of labour in capitalism. It, too, is a cause of human alienation in so far as it hampers the free development of human powers. It arises not from the free decision of all but from man's aggression against man or from the working out of the impersonal laws of the market.[29] But there is also a positive side to division of labour. Besides enhancing the productivity of labour, it expresses the social character of labour within alienation.[30] Put differently, it is the form taken by man's universal essence within the framework of universal social fragmentation. Hence the goal of revolutionary action is not so much the abolition of the division of labour as the abolition of the conditions under which individuals are not free to choose what to do and how.

It is in the same dialectical sense that we should understand the supersession of the state. What is to be done away with is the state as an institution set up above and in opposition to society, not state as an organizing principle of community life. Therefore, to abolish the state is not to opt for anarchy but to recapture the social essence of man alienated in it, so that the relations between members of society will once more be directly social, no longer mediated by an external, oppressive institution.

In this perspective, even feudal relations are both abolished and preserved in socialism For, if capitalism is the negation of feudalism, socialism as the negation of the negation cannot but be a reaffirmation of feudalism. True, under feudalism man was alienated. But, due to the subordinate role played by commodity production, the relationship between persons had not then taken on the character of the relation between things. This transparence of human relations is a positive value and should be carried over into socialism, but released from the limits imposed by feudalism.

Since socialism is the complete and conscious return of man to his social being, a return "which assimilates all the wealth of previous development", it will restore whatever was good even in pre-capitalist social formations. To cite but one instance, of ancient Greek society Marx, observes how its conception of man was nobler than that of capitalism. In those days nobody raised the question, which form of landed property is best suited to the production of wealth? The question, rather, was, which mode of property creates the best citizen?

> "Thus the old view, in which the human being appears as the aim of production, regardless of his limited national, religious, political character, seems to be very lofty when contrasted to the modern world, where production appears as the aim of mankind, and wealth as the aim of production."[31]

Marx goes on to say that the conception of man as the supreme goal of production will become fully effective only with the abolition-preservation of capitalism. Once freed from its limiting conditions under capitalism, wealth will become an expression of the universality of individual needs, capacities, pleasures, productive forces. It will witness to the development of human mastery over the forces of nature, of external nature as well as of humanity's own nature. In the new society, wealth will result from the working out of man's creative potentialities, "with no presupposition other than the previous historic development, which makes this totality of development of all human powers as such the end itself."[32]

It follows from Marx's comments on the loftier conception of man in ancient society that his understanding of revolution as abolition and preservation applies equally to the realm of ideas. In the realm of ideas as well, one has to distinguish between objectification and alienation. It is in the nature of man not only to fashion material objects as embodiments of his creative powers but also to form ideas for either explaining the world or projecting models for subsequent praxis. This essential function of consciousness is alienated when the same ideas distort reality or assume the character of autonomous entities. Thus come into being forms of false consciousness or ideologies. However, ideologies are not just unmixed error. They are distortions of truths about man. It is the function of dialectical criticism to recognize the element of truth contained in them. Such criticism is necessary, though not sufficient, prerequisite for socialist revolution.

The understanding of revolution as dialectical supersession cannot be reconciled with any one-sided, negative attitude to the past. While it is true that the proletariat, the agent of revolution, must "rid itself of the accumulated rubbish of the past", it is no less true that it can construct socialism only out of the wealth of historical tradition:

> "Men make their own history, but they do not make it just as they please; they do not make it under circumstances chosen by themselves, but under circumstances directly encountered, given and transmitted from the past."[33]

The Total Man and the Eclipse of God

Revolution is the decisive historical event out of which is born the Total Man, man in creative communion with nature and his fellowmen. His birth is at the same time the eclipse of the divine. In a celebrated passage containing the quintessence of his thought, Marx says:

> "Communism is the positive abolition of property, of human self-alienation, and thus the real appropriation of human nature through and for man. It is, therefore, the return of man himself as a social, i.e. really human being, a complete and conscious return that assimilates all the wealth of previous development. Communism as a fully developed naturalism is humanism and as a fully developed humanism is naturalism. It is the definitive resolution of the antagonism between man and nature, and between man and man. It is the true solution of the conflict between existence and essence, between objectification and self-affirmation, between freedom and necessity, between individual and the species. It is the solution to the riddle of history and knows itself to be the solution."[1]

Communism is here described both negatively and positively; negatively, as the supersession of private property, the root of all human alienation; positively, as the re-appropriation by man of his true, social nature. The negative and the positive are but two sides of the same coin. The solution of the conflicts created by private property is the self-revelation of man as he ought to be. We shall now examine how communism resolves the conflict between man and nature, between man and man, and between freedom and necessity, and in that context delineate the features of the Total Man envisioned by Marx. (Here a word of caution is called for. In all dialectical thinking, clearcut definitions are not possible. Concepts flow into one another, everything being related to everything else. They also have a concrete, temporal dimension involving the reciprocal immanence of past, present, and future. Every reality is seen in relation to what it has evolved from and what it evolves into. The student of Marx, therefore, must learn to let his mind shuttle constantly between concepts, and between past, present, and future.

The Cosmic Man

The abolition of private property will release all the potentialities latent in man. He is first a natural being, essentially related to nature both in terms of action and passion. On the one hand, he is endowed with natural powers and faculties which need nature for their self-actuation. Only by acting on nature can he develop his drives and abilities. On the other hand, he is also "a suffering being, and since he feels his suffering, a passional being. Passion is man's faculties striving to attain their object."[2] Like plants and animals, he too is a conditioned and limited being. The objects of his drives exist outside himself as objects independent of him; yet they are objects of his needs, indispensable to the exercise and development of his faculties:

> "The fact that man is an embodied, living, real, sentient, objective being with natural powers, means that he has real, sensuous objects as objects of his being, or that he can only express his being in real, sensuous objects."[3]

Therefore, to be related to nature is integral to man's being, not something added on to it from outside.

But man is not merely a natural being, but a human natural being. He is potentially a universal being, and, as such, has to express and vindicate himself in thought as well as in action. In their immediate givenness, neither man as subject nor nature as object is human. Their progressive humanization is the work of history:

> "And as everything natural must have its origin, so man has his process
> of genesis, history, which is for him, however, a conscious process and
> thus one which is consciously self-transcending."[4]

Man becomes a universal essence by integrating nature into the centre
of his existence. He appropriates more and more of nature, making it the
object of his knowing, feeling, and acting. Through artistic creation and
the natural sciences, he draws nature into the orbit of his consciousness,
moulding it into his spiritual inorganic body. Likewise, by adapting
objects of nature to satisfy his varying needs, he transforms it into his
material inorganic body:

> "Nature is the inorganic body of man; that is to say, nature excluding the
> human body itself. To say that man lives from nature means that nature
> is his body with which he must remain in a continuous interchange in
> order not to die."[5]

> This interdependence of man and nature means, in the end, that "nature
> is interdependent with itself, for man is part of nature."

But man cannot make nature his inorganic body without at the same
time incorporating himself in it. When he works, he infuses reality
with his spirit and shapes it in his own image so that the resulting
product mirrors his universal being.[6] By thus humanizing nature he
humanizes himself. The process of the progressive humanization of man
and nature, however, is frustrated by the institution of private property
which deprives the worker of the fruit of his labour.

> "While, therefore, alienated labour takes away the object of production
> from man, it also takes away his generic life, his real objectivity as a generic
> being, and changes his advantage over animals into a disadvantage in so
> far as his inorganic body, nature, is taken from him."[7]

Not until private property is abolished will the labourer rejoin his
inorganic body and recover his cosmic existence.

In the new social order based on the common ownership of all
property, a radical change will take place in man's experience of the
world. Under the regime of private property, the products of labour
appear hostile and alien. Everything around - houses, gardens,

automobiles and what not - seems to menace one with 'No admission' or 'Trespassers will be prosecuted'. In such a world, one feels rejected and unwanted. In communist society, on the contrary, objects, instead of repelling man, will welcome him, providing the vital milieu for him to commune with nature and fellow humans. They will appear what they really are - the objectification of human powers.[8] Become human, they will help each man realize to the full his unique individuality. Work as self-objectification will become self-affirmation; and man will feel truly at home in the world:

> "It is only when the object becomes a human object, or objective humanity, that man does not become lost in it."[9]

The abolition of private property will also witness an explosion of human sensuousness. The presence of objects as bearers of beauty and meaning will react on the producers, refining, and perfecting their sensibility. The beautiful and the sense of beauty presuppose and fashion each other. Only music, for instance, can awaken the sense of music. Conversely, even the most melodious music will have no meaning for the unmusical ear. This is because objects can exist for man only if he has a corresponding faculty for it. They can convey a meaning only if his senses are attuned to them. Now, with the wealth of human creation available to him, the sensuousness of the communist man will be of a higher order. His senses will prove capable of true human enjoyment; turning to objects, he will be affirming and realizing his own selfhood:

> "For it is not only the five senses, but also the socalled spiritual senses, the practical senses (desiring, loving etc.), in brief, human sensuousness and the human character of the senses, which can only come into being through the existence of its object, through humanized nature. The cultivation of the five senses is the work of all previous history."[10]

The more the senses and their objects become humanized, the more diversified will be man's appropriation of nature. True, capitalism too creates a variety of needs in people. (How else could it sell its wares?) But they are mostly artificial engineered needs. Directed at the consumption of commodities, they can all be finally reduced to the need for money:

> "The need for money is, therefore, the real need created by the modern economic system, and the only need it creates."[11]

The need for money and for the commodities money can buy, impoverishes man's relationship with the world:

> "Private property has made us so stupid and partial that an object is only ours when we have it, when it is directly eaten, drunk, worn, inhabited, etc, in short, utilized in some way."[12]

With the socialization of property, however, a new and richer mode of appropriating objects is made possible for man. Each individual will then appropriate the world in an all-inclusive manner as becomes the Total Man. All the ways in which he relates to the world - seeing, hearing, smelling, tasting, touching, feeling, thinking, willing, loving - will become so many modes of appropriating reality, of attaining fuller humanity. Not only action but also passion, suffering, will assume the character of joyous self-expansion towards the world.[13] Thus human sensuousness, which under relations of private property had atrophied, will rise up to new life.

Marx concludes,

> "The supersession of private property, will bring about the complete emancipation of all human qualities and senses, because these qualities and senses have become human, from the subjective as well as objective point of view. The eye has become a human eye when its object has become human, social object, created by man and destined for him."[14]

If communism humanizes subject and object, man and nature, it is by socializing them. In the new society "man becomes a social object... and society becomes a being for him in this object."[15] This brings us to the notion of communism as the resolution of the conflict between man and man.

The Social Individual

When Marx discusses the relation between man and nature, he is speaking not of the isolated individual but of man in community. The isolated individual is, for him, a mere abstraction and, as such, has no real existence. Man always works in association with, and for, other men. Even the lone peasant ploughing his field works as a social individual. He works for the maintenance of his family. He also uses tools handed down by previous generations and avails himself of the store of science and technology accumulated by society:

> "Even when I carry out scientific work etc. which I can seldom conduct in direct association with other men, I perform a social, because human, act. It is not only the material of my activity - such as language itself which the thinker uses - which is given to me as a social product. My own existence is a social activity. For this reason, what I myself produce, I produce for society with the consciousness of acting as a social being."[16]

Under capitalism, however, human sociality can find only a distorted expression. No doubt the division of labour, the co-operative character of production, the growth of productive forces, and the complexity of market relations knit individuals into a network of local, national, and even international relationships. Capitalism pulls down the walls between castes, sexes, religions, cultures, and races to usher in a regime of universal interdependence. But this is a process at the objective level, taking place, as it were, behind the back of social actors. At the level of conscious decision, individuals are indifferent, if not hostile, to one another, perpetually engaged in the war of mutual elimination. The combination of material, objective interdependence and personal indifference is the specifically capitalist expression of human sociality. Nevertheless, it is precisely this alienation that creates the conditions for the birth of the socialist man. The universal character of capitalist production alienates the individual from himself and others, but at the same time, it universalizes the nature of his relationships and capacities.[17]

The reason for the conflict between the objective interdependence and subjective independence of persons lies in private property and the relations of commodity exchange resulting from it. It is because there are independent producers in competition with one another that social relations become reified into objective processes over which men have no control. It also explains why products of labour divide rather than unite human beings Therefore, only in a society founded on common property will nature and labour products form the basis for human solidarity. Marx explains:

> "We have seen how, on the assumption that private property has been positively superseded, man produces man, himself and then other men; how the object which is the direct activity of his personality is at the same time his existence for other men and their existence for him. Similarly, the material of labour and man himself as a subject are the starting-point as well as the result of this movement (and because there must be this starting point private property is a historical necessity). Therefore, the social character is the universal character of the whole movement; as society itself produces man as man, so it is produced by him. Activity and enjoyment are social in their content as well as in their origin. They are social activity and social enjoyment. The human significance for nature only exists for the social man, because only in this case is nature a bond with other men, the basis of his existence for others and of their existence for him. Only then is nature the basis of his own human experience and a vital element of human reality. The natural existence of man has become his human existence and nature itself has become human for him. Thus, society is the accomplished union of man with nature, the veritable resurrection of nature, the realized naturalism of man and the realized humanism of nature."[18]

Three moments can be discerned in the socialization of man and nature as described here. The first is the socialization of the product. The product becomes man's *being-for-others*, his existence at the service of the community, and the existence of the community for him. The second is the socialization of human activity and enjoyment. All activity becomes co-operative, not in the sense of material dependence as in capitalism, but subjectively, in so far as production proceeds from communal decision. The same applies to the enjoyment of goods, since distribution and consumption will be determined by social needs. Finally, socialization will affect the very being of man. Just as products will lose their abstract existence as commodities, so too men and women will be freed from their abstract existence as 'capitalists' 'labourers' etc. They will regain their concrete being as persons in all their spiritual wealth and grandeur. In rejoining nature, they will rejoin their fellowmen. Nature will rise from the ruins of capitalism as the social inorganic body of man, revealing its human face; and man will see the unfolding of all his possibilities as a natural essence.

Because in the new society nature assumes the character of the common vital element uniting each man with the rest of society, in reshaping nature through work, he will be directly transforming himself and other men. Work will render the bond between human beings ever stronger, ever more human. The goal of production, therefore, will no more be commodities but the human community. Production for profit will give way to man's self-creation. Marx sees an evolution in this direction already in the advanced stages of capitalism. As little by little the system of bourgeois economy develops, he argues, there develops also its negation. If originally society - human beings in their relation to one another - was but a means to production, now it tends to progressively become "the final result of the social process of production." Everything (the product, machinery, raw materials, science etc.) which has a fixed form reveals itself to be a vanishing element, continually superseded in the movement of production. Even the immediate production process appears as one such element. The same applies to the conditions of production. What abides as subjects of this entire movement are "only the individuals, but individuals who are related to one another in relations which are both reproduced and created anew. It is their own constant process of movement in which they renew both themselves and the world of wealth which they create."[19]

It is the triune, dynamic relation between man, nature, and society which Marx has in mind when he says, "Society is the accomplished union of man with nature." He finds a paradigm of this in authentic man-woman relationship. "The immediate, natural and necessary relation of human being to human being is also the relation of man to woman." The relation of man to woman is a natural one. As embodied beings, both form part of nature and are attuned to each other through essential tendencies and drives. For man to be thus dynamically relatedto woman is to have the latter as his external nature; conversely, woman has her external nature in man. Each tends to the other as the object of action and need. But man and woman are not only natural beings but also human natural beings, who, as conscious individuals, can stand apart and confront each other. Their mutual relationship is not only natural but also human. By relating oneself to the other as nature, as is the case with the sexual act, one meets also the human in the other. The communion of bodies born of natural, biological drives is at the same time a communion of mind and heart. So, too, every human relation between them assumes the character of a natural relation. Consequently, woman as a human being becomes man's external nature; and man as a human being becomes woman's external nature. Here "man's relation to nature is directly his relation to the human and his relation to the human is directly his relation to nature." More, where man and woman look upon each other not merely as sexual objects but as persons, their needs become humanized. The relationship between man and woman, says Marx, "shows how far man's needs have become human needs, and consequently how far the other person as a person has become one of his needs and to what extent he is in his individual essence at the same time a social being."[20]

Just as man and woman relate to each other as human beings through the mediation of the body, so in the new society each individual will join all others through the mediation of the social inorganic body, i.e. nature and the product of labour. Just as man and woman include each other as the object of action and need, so will the social individual comprise the whole of mankind as the object of his sensuousness and action. He is the Total Man, the living synthesis of the particular and the universal:

> "Though man is a unique individual - and it is just his particularity which makes him an individual, a really individual, communal being - he is equally the whole, the ideal whole, the subjective existence of society as thought and experienced, just as in reality he exists both as the contemplation and real enjoyment of social existence and as the totality of human life expression."[21]

The Total Man is the focal point of Marx's vision of the future. In his later writings, he generally employs the term social individual to convey the same idea, though the more Feuerbachian generic being is never entirely discarded. In his mature economic works, the stress is not so much on describing the features of the Total Man as on showing how the further development of capitalism - the growth of productive forces and the diversification of social relations - will create the conditions for his emergence. Himself a productive force, each man will tend to reflect the level of science and technology achieved by society as a whole. With the reduction of necessary labour (labour needed to produce the means of subsistence), made possible by increase in productivity, he will have ample leisure for the pursuit of higher activities like education, artistic creation, and ever new forms of social intercourse.[22] More, his relationship with other men will become multi-faceted, corresponding to the universality of relations of production, circulation, and consumption.[23] However, these tendencies immanent in advanced capitalism will come to fruition only under socialist relations of production.

Since under socialism, men will relate to one another in ways freely chosen by themselves, the well-being of each will have for its condition the well-being of all. Each individual will then experience the appropriation of nature on the part of others as his own: "the senses and enjoyment of other men have become my own appropriation."[24] An analogy might help clarify Marx's thinking here. In family parents do not consider it a loss when children eat well and are happy; rather, it is a matter of personal satisfaction to them. This is because members of the family form but one 'We' as regards ownership, work, and sentiment. Similarly, in socialist society each individual will find his fulfillment in that of the community. For the first time in history the need for one's fellowmen will be the primary human need:

> "History is a preparation and a development which has for its goal that man becomes an object of sensuous perception and that the need for man as man makes its appearance."[25]

It is in terms of this need that Marx defines the wealth and poverty specific to socialism.

> "The rich man is one who at the same time experiences the need for the total expression of human life."[26]

The need for others, considered as passion, is poverty in socialist fashion:

> "Poverty is the passive bond which leads man to experience a need for the greatest wealth, the other person."[27]

The birth of the Total Man will mark the definitive supersession of both collectivism and individualism. In ancient societies, the individual was subordinated to the collectivity. He did not enjoy the status of an autonomous centre of decision. Marx traces this state of affairs to the low development of productive forces. In contrast to ancient societies, bourgeois society is characterized by individualism. Here society is reduced to a means to individual ends - to private interest and profit-seeking. Negated in the everyday life of buying, selling, producing, and consuming, human sociality detaches from individuals and installs itself in opposition to them in the form of commodity and the state. Only in socialism will man's true personal-social essence be reaffirmed. His being and consciousness will then be directly social, rendering superfluous the mediation of either commodity exchange or dehumanizing social institutions. For, all means of production will be commonly owned and exploited in view of satisfying genuinely social needs.

The Realm of Freedom

The emergence of the social man and of nature as his *being-for-others* will at the same time be the dawn of the age of freedom. To understand how, we must first reflect on Marx's conception of freedom in general. It is in terms of self-transcendence that he generally defines freedom. Man is free because he is capable of crossing all limits, subjective as well as objective, whereas animals are confined within bounds set by nature:

> "Of course, animals also produce. They construct nests, dwellings, as in the case of bees, beavers, ants etc. But they only produce what is strictly necessary for themselves or their young. They produce only in a single direction, while man produces universally. They produce only under the compulsion of direct physical needs, while man produces when he is free from physical need and only truly produces in freedom from such need.

Animals produce only themselves, while man reproduces the whole of nature. The products of animal production belong directly to their physical bodies, while man is free in face of his product. Animals construct only in accordance with the standards and needs of the species to which they belong, while man knows how to produce in accordance with the standards of every species and knows how to apply the appropriate standard to the object. Thus man constructs also in accordance with the laws of beauty."[28]

Freedom as self-transcendence is here viewed in relation to the object of production, to productive activity, and to man himself as the producer. The production of animals is tied to a limited range of objects. Man, on the contrary, can reproduce the whole of nature. His productive activity is universal; not repetitive, as with animals, but inventive. That is why he can stand outside his product and confront it as an 'other'. Similarly, unlike animals, he can face his own activity as an object, maintaining a certain otherness in regard to it. At no time is he fully identified with what he does or how he does it. He can always leave behind one kind of work and take to another. Further, whereas animals produce under the constraint of physical needs, that is, under the law of necessity, man produces even when there is no physical constraint. In no way is he bound by the measure to which reality has to conform. He is the source of ever new norms, ever new meanings, which he confers on the world around. He alone is the creator of beauty.

But what is it that makes him free in relation to the product, to the act of production, and to himself as its subject? The answer is,

"Conscious life activity distinguishes man from the life activity of animals. Only for this reason is he a generic being...Only for this reason is his activity free activity."[29]

Clearly, the root of freedom lies in consciousness whereby man is enabled to confront the environment as well as himself as objects and thus to transcend them. But transcending means leaving behind the given in order to march forward to new modes of being, acting, and having. If man never fully coincides with what he actually produces or what he experiences as a need, it is because he can, as a conscious being, project ever new models to be created through subsequent practice.

The prospective, creative nature of freedom comes out clearly in the following passage from Capital:

> "A spider carries on operations resembling those of the weaver; and many a human architect is put to shame by the skill with which a bee constructs her cell. But what from the very first distinguishes the most incompetent architect from the best of bees, is that the architect has built a cell in his head before he constructs it in wax. The labour process ends in the creation of something which, when the process began, already existed in the worker's imagination, already existed in an ideal form. What happens is not merely that the worker brings about a change of form in natural objects; at the same time, in the nature that exists apart from himself, he realizes his own purpose, the purpose which gives the law to his activities, the purpose to which he has to subordinate his own will."[30]

The Marxian conception of freedom, therefore, is dialectical, consisting as it does in negating and affirming - in negating the limits imposed by objective and subjective conditions and affirming the new yet to be created. The limiting conditions represent the element of necessity inherent in every act of freedom. It is in overcoming necessity that freedom is achieved. In this sense freedom and necessity are opposed to each other. On the other hand, there will be no free act if there is no necessity, no limiting conditions to be overcome. An illustration might clarify the point: To remain rooted in one place and to leap forward are diametrically opposed actions. Yet the first is an essential condition for the second; one cannot leap without having one's feet firmly on the ground. Both actions form a unity in tension. Likewise, freedom entails both victory over necessity and creation of the new.

For Marx, freedom, and necessity are not merely abstract but also historical concepts. History is the story of man's struggle against necessity, of his progressive conquest of freedom. At the dawn of history, his struggle was directed mainly against the inexorable forces of nature - decay and death, heat and cold, rain, and storm - which not only curtailed freedom but also threatened life itself. Slavery to nature found its ideological reflection in bondage to gods, spirits, and demons. With the birth of science and technology and with the growth of productive forces, man began slowly to free himself from nature's dominion, a process which yet remains to be completed. In the meanwhile, he became slave to human masters and to the institutions, customs, and laws the latter framed to serve their own nefarious ends. Thus arose relations of servitude such as between master and slave, lord and serf, capitalist and labourer. The capital-labour relation, however, is essentially different from all earlier forms of social servitude. Slave and feudal societies were characterized by relations of personal dependence. The slave was the property of the master; the serf was tied to the land. With the decay of feudalism, the reign of personal dependence came to an end. But capitalism, which grew out of feudalism, brought its own form of human servitude marked by personal independence on the one hand and objective dependence on the other.[31] It is often claimed that capitalism is best suited to the freedom of the individual since he can pursue unhindered his private interest and thereby serve the common interest. Free competition is seen as "the collision of unfettered individuals who are determined only by their own interests, as the mutual repulsion and attraction of free individuals, and hence as the absolute mode of existence of free individuality in the sphere of consumption and exchange."[32]

Marx rejects this view as absurd. The independence of the individual in bourgeois society is only apparent. For, instead of private interest promoting common interest, in capitalism "each individual reciprocally blocks the assertion of the other's interests, so that, instead of a general affirmation, this war of all against all produces a general negation."[33]

Moreover, and this is the crucial point, private interest is itself a socially determined interest; its content, form, and means of realization are given by social conditions independent of individuals.[34] These conditions are the conditions of exchange. Since each works for himself, he must exchange his product for that of others in order to have a share in the social produce. He, therefore, is subject to the laws of the market, themselves determined by the needs of capital. What is called free competition is, in reality, the free development of capital:

"It is not individuals who are set free by free competition; it is rather capital which is set free. As long as production resting on capital is necessary, hence the fittest form for the development of the forces of social production, the movement of individuals within the pure conditions of capital appears as their freedom."[35]

The freedom of capital appears as the freedom of capitalists and workers. As for the reality behind the appearance, Marx says:

"This kind of individual freedom is therefore at the same time the most complete suspension of all individual freedom, and the most complete subjugation of individuality under social conditions which assume the form of objective powers, even of overpowering objects - of things independent of the relations among individuals themselves."[36]

After describing the two historical stages in the development of social relations, Marx continues:

"Free individuality, based on the universal development of individuals and on their subordinating their communal, social productivity as their social wealth, is the third stage."[37]

Free individuals are persons who are dominated neither by oppressor classes nor by necessary laws of economy. Positively, they are persons who have brought under their control both productive forces and social relations. But will man ever be able totally to overcome economic necessity? No. A residue of necessity will always remain so long as he must work in order to satisfy his needs. There is, however, a privileged area of human activity that is not under the constraint of material needs - that of aesthetic creation.

"The realm of freedom only begins, in fact, where that labour which is determined by need and external purposes ceases; it is, therefore, by its very nature, outside the sphere of material production proper. Just as the savage must wrestle with nature in order to satisfy his wants, to maintain and reproduce his life, so also must civilized man, and he must do it in all forms of society and under any possible mode of production. With his development the realm of natural necessity expands because his wants increase; but at the same time the forces of production, by which these wants are satisfied, also increase. Freedom in this field cannot consist of anything else but the fact that socialized mankind, the associated producers, regulate their interchange with nature rationally, bring it under their common control, instead of being ruled by it as by some blind power, and accomplish their task with the least expenditure of energy and under such conditions as are proper and worthy of human beings. Nevertheless, this always remains a realm of necessity. Beyond it begins that development of human potentiality for its own sake, the true realm of freedom, which, however, can only flourish upon that realm of necessity as its basis. The shortening of the working day is its fundamental requisite."[38]

The development of human potentiality for its own sake clearly refers to the cultivation of spiritual and aesthetic faculties. The production of the beautiful is essentially free because it is not determined either by physical needs or social necessity. It is not a means to material life but an end in itself, a spontaneous overflow of man's being. That is why any work of art has the nature of a gift. It is preeminently a form of man's *being-for-others*. Significantly, Marx qualifies artistic creation along with the pursuit of knowledge, science, etc. as higher modes of human activity.[39] Here is proof that he did not consider material affluence ('to each according to his need') the end-all of human life, The satisfaction not of material needs but of the need for joyous self-creation is the goal of life.

The statement that the true realm of freedom lies beyond the economic, does not imply any dichotomy between the production of the useful and the creation of the beautiful. Whether labour approximates to artistic creation or not depends on the level of productive forces and on the nature of the relations of production. The limited character of productive forces that marked earlier social formations in a way favoured aesthetic creation. Greek art and epic, for instance, still constitute for us a source of aesthetic enjoyment and in certain respects prevail as the standard and model beyond attainment. Their charm, says Marx, "does not conflict with the primitive character of the social order from which it had sprung. It is rather the product of the latter, and is due rather to the fact that the immature social conditions under which the art arose and under which alone it could appear can never return."[40]

But how is it that primitiveness fostered artistic creation? Because, not yet subjected to technical division, labour in those days was eminently concrete and particular. Its product always turned out to be something whole and complete, as is the case even today with handicraft production. More importantly, the act of production called for the involvement of the whole person, not merely of any one of his faculties. Such concreteness and wholeness of labour suited aesthetic creation. For only the whole is beautiful. And the praxis that creates things of beauty has its source in that subterranean centre of each person where the whole range of his faculties and impulses forms but a single primordial focus of creative energy. That is why spontaneous creation is a casualty in any society which reduces persons to abstractions. And this is just what capitalism does. It splits society into two poles - capitalists as personified exchange value, and labourers as owners only of labor-power. As a result, the worker "is absolutely indifferent to the specificity of his labour; it has no interest for him as such, but only inasmuch as it is...a use-value for capital."[41] Further, the ever more complex division of labour renders all work mechanical, fragmentary, incapable of effecting a whole product. Art and capitalism are, therefore, irreconcilable. The more purely and adequately the polar relation between capitalists and workers develops the more 'labour loses all characteristics of art'. The particular skill of the worker becomes ever more abstract and irrelevant. It is reduced to mere abstract labour "indifferent to its particular form."[42]

With the abolition of capitalism, man will recover the wholeness of being and acting. Material production will tend to coincide with aesthetic creation. Because production will spring from communal decision and will be carried out in co-operation, each individual will be able to claim the whole product as the fruit of his labour. Products, instead of becoming commodities, will serve as social use-values, each in the fullness of its concrete determinations. As productivity increases and the instruments of labour become automated, it will be possible for producers to gain mastery over the process of production as a whole. Human beings will slough off their class character and emerge as concrete persons. In short, socialism will bring about the tantalization of the human, thus facilitating the creation of beauty.[43] The beautiful proceeds from the wholeness of man and results in the wholeness of life.

Atheism and Beyond

The new man born of the proletarian revolution will not have exhausted all human possibilities. He will still be a subject of praxis aimed at the further humanization of himself and the world. But his practice will no more be alienated, no more a mere means to subsistence, but an end in itself. Since consciousness is nothing but praxis rendered transparent to itself, the socialist man will be the bearer of a new consciousness, reflecting all the wealth of his *being-with-nature-and-society*. Rooted in correct practice, the new consciousness will necessarily have the quality of truth.[44] In its sweep it will be truly cosmic; for man will relate to nature not as to something he *has* but as to what he *is*.[45]

Encompassing the whole of mankind, socialist consciousness will reveal itself as universal:

> "My universal consciousness is only the theoretical form of that whose living form is the real community."[46]

In sum, the whole universe will become transparent, filled with a meaning and purpose radiating from within man himself. Understandably, such a transfiguration of consciousness rules out the continuance of any form of false consciousness including belief in God. The definitive supersession of religion finds its most succinct formulation in the following passage:

> "Since, however, for socialist man, the whole of what is called world history is nothing but the creation of man by human labour, and the emergence of nature for man, he, therefore has the evident and irrefutable proof of his self-creation, of his own origins. Once the essential being of man and of nature, man as a natural being and nature as a human reality, has become evident in practical life, in sense experience, the quest for an alien being, a being above man and nature (a quest which is an avowal of the unreality of man and nature) becomes impossible in practice. Atheism, as a denial of this unreality, is no more meaningful, for atheism is a negation of God and seeks to assert by this negation the existence of man. Socialism no longer requires such a roundabout method; it begins from the theoretical and practical sense perception of man and nature

as essential beings. It is positive human self -consciousness, no longer a self-consciousness attained through the negation of religion; just as the real life of man is positive and no longer attained through the negation of private property, through communism."[47]

Marx's reasoning here follows a twofold dialectical movement. First, from praxis to theory. The loss of humanity at the practical level was what gave rise to the theoretical quest for God. Once man recovers his true essence in practical life he will have the theoretical certainty of his own self-creation. For in socialism theory and praxis will converge and find their unity in sense experience.[48] And the sense experience of the socialist man will include the awareness of his rootedness in himself, of the coincidence of his existence with his essence, of what he is with what he ought to be.

The second movement follows the dialectic of alienation and its supersession. This process reveals three phases in the development of human consciousness: atheism, practical humanism, and positive humanism. Atheism is the negation of God. Since God is the mystified expression of human essence, to deny him is to affirm the greatness of man. But atheism is only theoretical humanism, as it leaves the secular roots of God intact.

Communism

Marx understands communism here as the historic act that overthrows capitalism, 'the vindication of real human life as man's property."[49] But even the humanism represented by communism is an imperfect one; for it is still affected by the negation of private property. It is only a humanism in becoming, not yet become, not yet moving on its own foundations. Not until the affirmation of man ceases to be mediated by the negation of private property will mankind arrive at the third and final stage of positive humanism or socialism. Positive humanism will consist of 'the theoretical and practical sense-perception of man and nature as essential beings." The term essential being must be understood in the Hegelian sense to mean the ultimate substratum and centre of unity underlying the world of appearances. To qualify man and nature as essential is to declare them to be the ground of all being and meaning. Once man realizes that he is the Ultimate, "the quest for an alien being, a being above man and nature... .becomes impossible in practice." Positive humanism, therefore, represents that stage in the development of human consciousness where not only religion but also atheism will have become irrelevant.

The impossibility of the quest for God is not purely conceptual, based on any logical contradiction inherent in religion, but practical, derived from entirely new conditions of life and work. Practical life will be such as to exclude the need for God, whether as a source of meaning or legitimation or consolation.

Under socialism, man will not need God to explain reality. To the primitives nature was a riddle. Unable to understand its working, they sought an explanation in invisible powers lurking behind these visible phenomena. Though the progress of science and technology has dissipated primitive consciousness, nature continues to hold depths man has not fathomed. Capitalism, in its turn, has created new riddles inasmuch as social relations now assume the character of relations between things and appear independent of human beings. No wonder, religious beliefs persist. With the advent of socialism, man's relationship with nature and society will become transparent, 'perfectly intelligible.'[50] He will see in nature society's existence for him, and in society his own universal nature. History, too, will shed its veil of mystery and manifest itself as the long process of his self-creation through labour, of his emergence in time. He will know himself to be the light that illumines all stages of human development; he will see that he is the key to the solution of all problems regarding human destiny.

Nor will there be in socialist society any room for God as a provider of legitimation. For there will be neither exploitation nor domination to be legitimized. Besides, with no division of labour into mental and manual, there will cease to exist, ideological classes, whose role it was to fabricate myths and illusions for the benefit of the ruling classes. Only such theories will hold sway as are born of the life of the masses engaged in the creation of the useful and the beautiful. There will be no political basis for religion, either. Since the production of goods will be directly social, man's social essence will no more be alienated into the profane heaven of the state, whose reflexion was the heaven of religious hope.

The socialist man will be the bearer not only of the entire wealth of past historical development but also of humanity's hopes for the future. As such, his presence in the midst of the world he has fashioned will be one of creative exuberance. The challenge of never-ending self-creation will render obsolete the search for consolation in a Creator; communion with the family of man will replace communion with the divine. This is what Marx wants to convey when, commenting on the ancient practice of offering all surplus produce to the gods, he exclaims:

> "What a paradox it would be if the more man subjugates nature through his labour and the more divine miracles are made superfluous by the miracles of industry, the more he is forced to forgo the joy of production and the enjoyment of the product out of deference to these powers."[51]

An Atheism of Ambivalence

In this chapter, my task is to make a critical evaluation of the Marxian theory of religion. Here one is confronted with an initial problem. To evaluate any theory one needs a criterion. If the criterion adopted is external to the theory i.e. smuggled in from some other philosophy, the assessment will not find favour with the proponents of the theory. If, on the other hand, it is integral to the theory under consideration, the evaluation will be vitiated as it presupposes the truth of what is to be proved. Nor may we find a way out by appealing to the criterion of internal coherence. A theory may be internally coherent, yet false. The only valid approach, therefore, is to look for a criterion that is at once internal to the theory and likely to be accepted by persons of other philosophical persuasions. In my view, such a standard of evaluation is provided by the concept of praxis as enunciated by the young Marx.

The second thesis on Feuerbach reads:

> "The question whether human thinking can pretend to objective truth is not a theoretical but practical question. Man must prove the truth, i.e. the effectiveness and power, the 'this-sidedness' of his thinking in practice."[1]

Now, what is that praxis which is to serve as the yardstick of truth? Evidently, not praxis in the narrower sense of revolutionary action. It can neither prove nor disprove the truth, say, of the aesthetic experience of a work of art. The criterion of truth, in general, can only be praxis in the broader Marxian sense of human sensuousness (Sinnlichkeit), meaning our global, active-passive encounter with reality. Here is the point of departure for all theoretical reflection.

> "Sense experience must be the basis of all science. Science is only genuine science when it proceeds from sense experience, in the two forms of sense perception and sensuousness, that is, only when it proceeds from nature."[2]

This view is basically in keeping with the Aristotelian tradition which also holds that we have no conceptual knowledge that does not ultimately derive from the senses. Only that knowledge is true which is an articulation of what is implicit in the domain of sensuousness.

Hence the verification of any theory consists of ascertaining whether it corresponds to our total experience or, more precisely, to the unity of the world experienced and the human subjects experiencing it. What is thus ascertained, however, is only logical truth, the conformity of thought with what exists. But the truth about humans is not only logical but also dialectical. For the human reality which experience reveals is both being and becoming. It manifests itself as tending to be what it is not and not to be what it is, as existence straining toward its true essence. Hence a theory is fully true when it expresses not only what is but also what ought to be. Moreover, it must itself become a factor in the transition from the is to the ought. Authentic thinking is but an element of that human reality which is in creative tension towards its own future. This means that only such conceptions and beliefs are dialectically true as have the power to humanize the world. Understood thus, dialectical truth does not exclude the logical but presupposes, subsumes, and transcends it, at the same time. It integrates within itself the beautiful and the good.

Postulatory Atheism

For Marx, atheism was initially an ethical postulate. Human beings are called to absolute freedom, to have no supreme divinity other than their own self-consciousness. But so long as they believe in God, they view him as their master and themselves as slaves. Belief and the realization of freedom are incompatible. Hence the moral imperative to deny the existence of God. God does not exist because he ought not to exist. Is Marx justified in asserting that belief in any form essentially contradicts human freedom? In support of his view, he might have drawn attention to the innumerable mental shackles which contemporary Judaism and Christianity imposed on their respective followers. But such facts do not warrant the conclusion that the quest for freedom cannot be reconciled with religious belief as such. For it is no less a historical fact that religion has also contributed to the humanization of social relations. Besides, pursuing a line of reasoning suggested by Marx and Engels themselves, it could be argued that relatedness to an absolute Other, far, from hampering the realization of freedom, is its essential prerequisite. Of crucial importance is the following statement found in *The German Ideology*:

> "Only in association with others has each individual the means of cultivating his talents in all directions. Only in a community, therefore, is personal freedom possible."[3]

There is a deeper reason why the individual can achieve freedom only in a community. To be free, it is not enough for a person to be a self-determining agent; it is equally necessary that he is recognized as such by other individuals. Alone and isolated, no human being can be free. If recognition on the part of others is a condition for the possibility of freedom in ordinary social life, does not absolute freedom presuppose recognition by an absolute Other? Where the absolute Other is eliminated, is there not the danger that in his quest for freedom the individual may set himself up as the Absolute, reducing everybody else to the condition of slaves? Will not rejection of the Absolute lead to political absolutism and totalitarianism?

Let us now return to the more basic assumption of Marx that the human being is called to absolute freedom. I call it an assumption because it is not derived from any scientific analysis of mankind's collective historical experience. That man is called to be his own creator is, with Marx, an axiom. At the very heart of his philosophy of history, one finds an act of faith in the total perfectibility of the human, in its capacity to transcend all limitations. This act of faith forms the background of his subsequent investigations into the dynamics of historical change leading up to the classless society. But in declaring man to be his own maker, Marx reinstates, unwittingly, the same Absolute which his atheism sought to demolish. His atheism, therefore, is riddled with its own opposite. Later in this chapter, we shall discuss the deeper implications of this fundamental ambiguity. In the meanwhile let us address ourselves to the question whether the Marxian project of the Total Man is realizable. A positive answer is implicit in the materialist conception of history. According to it, if man projects his true essence outside himself in the person of an imagined God, it is because in practical life he is estranged from the product of his labour. Once economic alienation is eliminated, it would be possible for him to realize in practice the true human essence which he till then attributed to God. But is the claim that religious belief is born of economic alienation sustainable in the light of our global historical experience?

The Materialist Interpretation of Religion

Marx has tried to show that the idea of God arises from man's need to explain, legitimate, and compensate for his fractured existence in the sphere of material production.

He is right in rejecting that God who is brought in from outside to bridge the gulf between the known and the unknown, the chasm between expectation and fulfillment. Believers, no doubt, have used the notion of a Creator to explain or explain away what they could not fathom. The attempt, however, has proved self-defeating. For, as soon as the socalled mysteries are cleared up with the advance of science and technology, the believer is forced to make a shameful retreat and look for another lacuna in human knowledge to buttress his already shaken faith. Moreover, in all such attempts at explanation one starts with the world as the premise and tries to derive from it the conclusion that God exists. What one thereby arrives at is a spurious Absolute, external to the world. The true Absolute is not an explanatory principle situated outside the world, but the depth-dimension of human existence, individual and collective. It is the ultimate meaning of history encountered in the realm of practice. Of this true Absolute, the God of explanation is but a caricature.

Paradoxically, despite his avowed atheism, Marx's philosophical concern has much in common with the religious quest after the ultimate meaning of human existence. What is his theory of alienation and its supersession but an attempt to unravel the hidden meaning and ultimate goal of history? This is not to ignore the crucial difference between the believer and Marx. For the former, ultimate meaning reveals itself in history while at the same time transcending it. He stands in a dialogical relationship with the Ultimate without ever coinciding with it. Marx, on the contrary, sees in man himself the final source of all meaning. The classless society he envisages is "the solution of the riddle of history and knows itself to be this solution."[4]

Believers will have little difficulty in concurring with Marx's violent attack on the God of ideological legitimation. It is his abiding contribution to have unmasked the class character of God in much of popular worship. The same God is very much alive even today where religious leaders are in league with the powers that be. Eliminating him is a prerequisite for complete human emancipation. Having said this, one must hasten to add that the search for unconditional legitimation has also a positive meaning. Generally, a theory or belief is deemed to have legitimating power when it helps the ruling classes to force the rest of the population to conform to norms of conduct conducive to their own interests. The ought implicit in every theory of legitimation is reinforced with theological rationalizations and religious sanctions to make it all the easier for the masses to internalize it. But there is also another ought, unconditional in its own right, which calls upon human beings to fight injustice and to promote life and freedom. If one were to ignore it, it would amount to denying one's own humanity. Nor can it be explained away as a mere projection of the mind. Rather it is the very source and motive force of the human project. Where this ought does not hold sway, no genuine humanizing revolution is possible. For, revolution too has its ultimate legitimation deriving from the unconditional demand to break loose from all fetters and march forward to the realm of freedom. The unconditionally of this demand is, in truth, the annunciation of the Divine.

There is also much truth in Marx's criticism of religion as the provider of illusory compensation for the miseries of life. By promising compensation in the life beyond, religion has more often than not dampened people's spontaneous urge to revolt against injustice. It has made cult a substitute for socially relevant practice. But this is only one side of the picture, the only side Marx cared to see. On the more positive side, there have been many religions which, at least initially, represented the protest of the masses against the prevailing inhuman conditions of life. In fact, protest is at the root of the dynamism that leads human beings to project a world of love, peace, and harmony unbounded. Historically, such protest has spawned not merely symbolic but also socio-political models to be realized through collective practice. In such cases, the protesters have invariably come into conflict with the guardians of the status quo. A telling instance of this is the Hebrew prophecy with its violent anti-cultism and fierce denunciation of social injustice and political oppression. The same is true of Jesus of Nazareth whose protest against the oppressive religious and political structures, of his day had to be paid for in blood. Similarly in India, the rise of Buddhism signaled the revolt of the masses against caste inequality, priestly domination, and the despotism of rulers. As far as Christianity is concerned, the original protest against exploitation and domination reasserted itself time and again through dissenting Christian movements and sects (Albigenses, Waldenses, Anabaptists). One such initiative was the League of the Just founded by Weitling, which sought to restore the early Christian communism as recorded in the Acts of the Apostles. Significantly, it is the League of the Just that gave birth to the First Communist International!

The close affinity between prophetic Christianity and Marxism has been recognized by Marxists themselves. In 1971 Fidel Castro told a group of Latin American priests, "Religion is for man; its purpose is man. Therefore, gentlemen, I insist that Christianity is ten times, ten thousand times more similar to Communism than it could ever be to capitalism." Again, in an address to Chilean Christians he said:

> "We have often spoken of the history of Christianity, the Christianity that brought forth martyrs, so many who died for their faith... Christianity was the religion of the poor, of the Roman slaves, of those who died by the tens of thousands, devoured by lions . in the circus; it is the religion that spoke forthrightly of human solidarity and of love of neighbour, and that condemned avarice, gluttony and all forms of selfishness. It is the religion that two thousand years ago called money-changers money-changers and Pharisees ph arises and that condemned the rich...If we look for parallels between the goals of Marxism and the loftiest precepts of Christianity, we see how many times they coincide...Looking at all we have in common, we begin to see the real possibility of a strategic alliance between revolutionary Marxists and revolutionary Christians."[5]

Expressions of sentiments like these are nothing new. Much before Fidel Castro, Engels had spoken in a similar vein:

> "The history of early Christianity has notable points in common with the modern working-class movement. Like the latter, Christianity was originally a movement of the oppressed people; it first appeared as the religion of slaves and freed men, of poor people deprived of all rights, of peoples subjugated or dispersed by Rome."[6]

Where prophetic protest is smothered or is prevented from translating itself into relevant practice, the spiritual forces it releases tend to find alienated expression in the search for mere other-worldly compensation. That is why in periods of collective frustration and revolutionary impotence there is a proliferation of religious illusions, dreams, phantasies, devotions, and rituals. Even these are not aberrations pure and simple but distortions of something fundamental to being human: the urge for absolute transcendence over all the limitations of the Here and Now. Man cannot do without Utopia in one form or another, whether it is called *nirvana*, *Mukti*, heaven, or classless society. And the longing for the Utopia necessarily bodies forth in myths and symbols. For the ultimate horizon of human existence defies all conceptualization. Not reason but imagination is the faculty that can give it a concrete shape. Believing and hoping are kin to aesthetic creation which too fashions a world beyond the everyday world. Only the vision, however dim, of absolute transcendence, can release man's creative powers for remoulding society. Nothing less can elicit unreserved and unconditional heroism and commitment. However, the symbolic project must be linked to socially transformative practice. Where the link is broken, the heaven of religious imagination becomes a mere illusion, an opiate of the masses.

The Secular Anticipation of Religion

By highlighting the role of religion as the provider of explanation, legitimation, and compensation, Marx has already shown the close bond between religion and economy. But this does not satisfy him. He goes further and tries to prove that there exists within economic life itself a secular anticipation of religion. Man relates to the product of labour (commodity, money, capital) much the same way as he relates to the God of religion. That there is much truth in this assertion none will contest The religion of everyday life often boils down to the cult of money. The tendency is not confined to capitalist society either. From the earliest days, human beings have tended to worship not only the products of labour and the instruments of production - of which the clearest instance is provided by *Ayudhapuja* - but also the various elements of nature such as trees, rivers, mountains, and animals. But this in no way proves the economic origin of religion. The question remains unanswered why the human mind goes off in a tangent in the direction of the absolute and the unconditional when confronted with the limited, the conditional, and the transient. Marx seems to see in this leap from the relative to the absolute nothing but an aberration of human consciousness provoked by the perverted nature of the world we live in. But is it really the case? Is not the leap inherent in the very essence of the human being as the only being capable of negating all limits and having the Absolute as the essential pole of his selfhood?

A positive answer would be consonant with Marx's own reasoning. Against Hegel he argues:

> "An objective being acts objectively, and it would not act objectively if objectivity were not an inherent part of its essential nature. It creates and establishes only objects because it is only established by objects because it is fundamentally nature."[7]

In like manner, one could argue that if human beings invariably tend to project the Absolute and the Unconditional even when they relate to things that are relative and conditioned, it is because they have already been projected by it. If the conclusion is legitimate, being related to the Absolute is as much part of man's essential being as is being related to nature. So much that even the denial of the Absolute becomes invested with the character of absoluteness. And atheism passes over into its opposite.

In fact, even a cursory analysis of our global experience of reality will' show that the religious dimension is not a derivative of the economic. A purely economic activity is but a product of abstraction. In real life, even a simple activity like sowing has many dimensions of meaning. It has obviously an economic meaning since its purpose is producing something meant to satisfy a material need. It has also an aesthetic meaning. The sower, unlettered though he might be, scatters the seed not in a haphazard manner but according to a rhythm and pattern. In sowing, he also creates the beautiful. Again, the same work has an ethical content. For it is motivated by a sense of duty, be it towards his kin or his employer. Finally, one can discern a religious meaning as well, in so far as the sower relates his work to the ultimate meaning of life. The aesthetic, the moral, and the religious dimensions of meaning are implicit in all economic activity as its fundamental presuppositions. And what is presupposed by economic activity cannot at the same time be its derivative. From this, the conclusion should not be drawn that religious consciousness enjoys absolute autonomy vis a vis economic life. All the levels of meaning we have discerned are closely intertwined, each conditioning and conditioned by the others. Hence the possibility is not precluded that certain specific modalities of religious consciousness and practice can be traced to economic causes. How far this is possible is a matter not of speculation but empirical investigation.

At this juncture in our investigation, it is worthwhile enquiring into the reason why Marx failed to give due weight to the non-economic aspects of human existence. 1 think it is because he did not consistently apply the principle he himself had formulated that only such knowledge is valid as is derived from praxis in the sense of our global human experience. For him, praxis meant a unity in tension of different polarities: the material and the spiritual, the objective, and the subjective, the structural and the personal, the actional and the passional. But in his actual philosophical investigations, he tended to stress the first term in each of the polarities mentioned above to the neglect of the second. The reason for this distortion of perspective lies in the fact that he developed his ideas in reaction against the philosophers of his day, particularly Hegel and Feuerbach. Hegel had reduced all human activity to the activity of thinking and interpreted the world of objects as but a product of the thinking subject. Marx, in his turn, went to the other extreme and affirmed the primacy of material (economic) activity over the spiritual and overstressed objective structures and processes to the neglect of human subjectivity. Similarly, as against Feuerbachian materialism which viewed man's sensuous relation to nature as one of passive contemplation, he laid undue emphasis on action to the detriment of the passional and the contemplative. I shall now point out some implications of this shift in emphasis concerning two of the aforementioned polarities: actional-passional and structural-personal.

The Neglect of Subjectivity

Man's sensuous presence in the world involves both action and passion. He is a passional being, first of all, in the sense that he experiences passion for (intense longing for) things, persons, and values. He is passional also in the sense of suffering from the world that impinges on him. (Passion is derived from the Latin root 'patior' meaning to suffer.) Action and passion (passion in the twofold sense just explained) form a dialectical unity, the one implying and presupposing the other. There is no action without passion for the product and for the work that brings it into being. Action also involves passion in the sense of suffering from, as it means overcoming the resistance of matter and letting oneself be carried away by the project in hand. All action is instinct with passion, and all passion, unless otherwise impeded, issues in action.

In day to day life, man not only moulds reality but also is moulded by it. He not only gives himself to but also receives from, the total milieu of being. He has an essential openness to Being. And Being is both what he fashions and what fashions him. It impinges on him in manifold ways. It reveals itself now as beauty, now as a challenge, now as solace. When, for instance, you enjoy the sunset or contemplate a work of art, your experience is not one of acting but of being under a spell, of being swept off your feet and carried away to unknown realms. Here it is not you who command the situation; it is rather the situation that commands you. You obey, you listen, you let yourself be invaded. Before such self-revelations of being you remain wordless and mute. Yet this passivity of yours is not like that of a ball set in motion by an external agent. It is not a want but a wealth, not an emptying out of your being but its blossoming out into fulness.

That which takes hold of you may be something limited like the beauty of a flower, the smile of a child, the radiance of a human presence, or the fascination of a project to be realized. But a closer look at the same experiences will show that they have also a dimension of absolute transcendence. Of course, the self-revelation of the absolute in the relative, of the unconditioned in the conditioned, will vary in intensity from person to person and from situation to situation. There are privileged moments when the experience of being taken hold of by the numinous and the ineffable radically transforms both the person to whom it is granted and the community to which he belongs. Nevertheless, the encounter with the Absolute is not to be seen as something exceptional, reserved for an elite. In a certain sense, it is the vital milieu in which all human beings live, the horizon in which they produce and consume, buy and sell, love, and hate. If Marx failed to take note of this aspect of human existence, it is in part due to his excessive preoccupation with action. Hence the need for Marxism to rehabilitate the category of sensuousness as the unity of action and passion, creation, and contemplation.

A similar distortion of perspective has vitiated Marx's approach to the polar relation between the personal and the structural. Men and women do not live in isolation but inserted in social structures, meaning stable patterns of behaviour, roles, and responses, handed down from the past. Once such structures have come into being and have started moving around their own axes, they enjoy a certain autonomy and follow their own internal laws of development. They then, shape the lives of individuals, limiting the range of options available to them. The analysis of such structures and the laws of their development formed the central theme of Marx's studies. Not that he reduced persons to structures. Much as he stressed the determining influence of structures, he was clear in his mind that with them individuals maintain a degree of independence. In his general philosophical formulations hs asserted in no uncertain manner that, in the final analysis, it is not structures but men and women who make history. So too, the goal he set for the coming revolution is the liberation of individuals from the determinism of structures. However, in his preoccupation with the analysis of the capitalist system, he failed to do justice to the sphere of the personal and the subjective, the sphere where the human drama of hope and despair, love and hate, death, and survival is enacted. No wonder he has provided no analysis of man's existential alienations: sin, guilt, anxiety, despair, the vulnerability of freedom, and death. An example is the casual way he deals with the problems of death, regarding which he has only the following to say:

> "Death seems to be a harsh victory of the species over the individual and to contradict their unity but the particular individual is only a determinate generic being and as such he is mortal."[8]

Here the individual is left to seek compensation for mortality in the immortality of the human species!

Had Marx paid sufficient attention to these existential problems, he might have been led to a more critical assessment of his atheist stance. For it is in the limit-situations of despair and death that human existence hovers in the border-land between the conditioned and the unconditioned, between being and non-being.

I have tried to argue that religiosity is an original, primordial dimension of human existence and not a by-product of economic alienation. If my reasoning is correct, the Marxian claim that religion will disappear with the socialist restructuring of the economy falls to the ground. Let us now admit, for argument's sake, the truth of the economic interpretation of religion. Even then the disappearance, once and for all, of belief remains doubtful. For the definitive abolition of private property, which, for Marx, is the concrete embodiment of economic alienation and the birth-place of all other alienations, can in no way be guaranteed. It is more a matter of hope than a matter of scientific prognosis. Of course, Marx does claim that capitalism will pass over into socialism with the inexorability of a law of nature. But the inexorability is itself conditional upon the level of consciousness of the working class. That is, capitalism will surely collapse when the objective conditions for it will have matured and the working class chooses to revolt against it. But historical experience since Marx provides no guarantee that the consciousness of workers is inevitably moving in that direction. Rather, what one sees is the opposite trend - its progressive integration within the capitalist system of values. If Marx failed to foresee these developments, it is mainly because an excessive concern with objective structural processes prevented him from exploring the subjective conditions of revolution.

Even assuming that working-class consciousness will become radicalized and capitalism will be overthrown, there is no reason to think that economic alienation, in one form or another, will not reappear

The elimination not merely of exploitation but also its very possibility is conceivable only if the new relations of production under socialism will have brought about a radically new consciousness among men and women, a consciousness irrevocably and inexorably anchored in the pursuit of the common good. But that would mean that human beings as conscious subjects are but products of objective circumstances, which would contradict Marx's own assertion that they are also makers of circumstances. If the human subject is not reducible to the object it is possible that even after the revolution there might persist the subjective, psychostructural roots of alienation like self-interest and the will to power.

The Absolute Negated and Reaffirmed

My attempt thus far has been to show that the Marxian thesis regarding the origin and abolition of religion does not stand the test of practical verification. I shall now try to draw out some of the deeper implications of the supersession of religion, again supposing history, follows the path Marx has chalked out.

As has already been shown, supersession in the dialectical sense means both abolition and preservation. It involves preservation because every alienation is alienation of something essential to man. This applies to religion as well. The significance of religion consists in its being an expression, though clothed in the language of illusion, of man's true being as his own creator. In any supersession, this positive content will have to be carried over into the future. What does carrying over in our context mean? The answer is contained in Marx's famous comment on the abolition of German philosophy:

"You cannot transcend philosophy without realizing it."[9]

The target of attack here is not any philosophy but German idealism 'which abstracts from real man' and flourishes only inside the cranium. For such a philosophy to cease to be a sum of mere abstractions, it must become reality through historical practice. Applied to religion, this means that the idea of God can be abolished only by realizing it in practice. And to realize it in practice means to be in real life what God means in the realm of phantasy: to be one's own creator, to be one's own ultimate source of being, to be the fulness of being, knowing, and loving. Paradoxically, then, the point of arrival of Marxian atheism is the practical realization of the Divine. In other words, "the criticism of religion ends with the doctrine that man is the supreme being for man."[10]

What is that practice which is equated with the realization of the Divine? At first blush, it would appear that what is envisaged is life in the post-revolutionary classless society. But that would mean that, with the advent of socialism, humanity will have reached the plenitude of being and therefore also the end of history. True, there are assertions in Marx's writings that are open to such an interpretation. For instance, he speaks of Communism as perfect humanism and perfect naturalism and as the true resolution of all conflicts. But when he qualifies his philosophy as perfect humanism and naturalism he is only dissociating himself from the imperfect one of Feuerbach. So too, what he announces is not the neutralization of the polar tensions constitutive of human existence but the resolution of the antagonism between man and nature, between man and man.

This interpretation dovetails with the distinction Marx makes between objectification and alienation. Objectification is the process whereby human beings develop their essential powers by externalizing them in products, Alienation, on the contrary, is objectification turned inhuman and enslaving. Hence what will be superseded in the classless society is alienation, not objectification, not the dialectical tension inherent in all work. In the new society, work will continue, and with it the never-ending adventure of human self-creation. Marx explicitly states that the true history of man will begin only with communism, the epochs that lead up to it being nothing but his pre-history. The classless society, therefore, cannot be equated with the practical realization of the idea of God. Moreover, since at no stage of its further development can it claim to have exhausted all human possibilities, the God-project will always remain a receding horizon. Thus out of the supersession of religion is born a new Absolute. An Absolute, because as the ultimate goal of all human striving, it relativizes every stage in the history of the classless society; a new Absolute, because, unlike the God of traditional religion (as Marx understood him) it is not outside the historical process but its immanent, though unattainable, end.

Admittedly this interpretation is valid only if the supersession of religion is understood dialectically as abolition-preservation. However, in support of the non-dialectical understanding of supersession as destruction pure and simple, one might adduce the text in the Manuscripts of 1844 where Marx argues against Hegel that what religion represents is not man's self-consciousness but his alienated self-consciousness, thereby implying that there is nothing in religious consciousness that is worth carrying over into the future. If this is what Marx meant, he would be doing justice neither to Hegel nor to himself. For, Hegel too saw in religion an alienation of human self-consciousness. Nor did Marx deny that it is human self-consciousness that becomes estranged into religious faith. The difference between them is one of emphasis. Whereas the former stressed the self-consciousness that becomes estranged in religion, the latter focussed on the estranged character of the self-consciousness that assumes the illusory form of religion. The supersession of religion, therefore, means, for Marx as well as Hegel, the elimination not of the self-consciousness involved in belief but of its alienated character. More precisely, what is to be done away with is not the notion of God as the ultimate ground of all being but the projection of the same notion outside man as something alien and opposed to him. The re-emerging Absolute, then, is neither alien nor opposed to the human community; In a sense, it is the human community. At the same time, it does not coincide with any stage in the post-revolutionary history of mankind. It will always maintain a certain otherness as the ultimate horizon of human possibility. Humanity can at best approximate to it without ever being able to realize it. It will always be on the march in search of its own true visage, engaged in a perpetual quest after its own fulness, without that visage and that fulness ever becoming a reality. Nor can it give up the quest as it would amount to denying its own true essence. Thus, it would seem, Marx condemns the men and women of classless society to the same "unhappy consciousness" which Hegel attributed to the believer.

Relapse Into Apocalypticism

Are we then to understand that the essential thrust of Marx's philosophy of history is religious? In a certain sense, yes. For in his overall perspective, human beings stand in a relationship of creative tension towards the horizon of their own Absolute Future. Nonetheless the attitude this relationship engenders radically differs from every other type of religiosity. To understand how, it is necessary to consider, however briefly, the main forms of religious consciousness assumes.

1. *Cosmic religiosity:* Here the Absolute is seen as mediated through the phenomena of nature: through the sun, the moon, rain, thunder, lightning, vegetation, birth, and death. To the believer, the Divine appears either as the primal force (*Sakti*) or the law (*Rita*) underlying the smooth running of the material universe of which he knows himself to be but a part. The cosmic Absolute is both transcendent and immanent. Immanent, because it is the same force that makes the sun shine and the human eye see. the same power that controls vegetative, animal as well as human reproduction; transcendent, because that force, that power, is never adequately present in the human microcosm. The mystery of the universe overflows the limits of the immediately given and experienced. Cosmic religion, therefore, is characterized by a sense of wonder in the face of the unknown and the numinous. It has its own sense of time which is cyclic, reflecting the cycle of the seasons, of sunrise and sunset, night and day, birth and death, rain, and drought. Germane to this sort of belief is an ethical stance that is basically conservative, consisting as it does in conformity to the laws of nature Cosmic religiosity becomes magic when the believer tries to control the Divine through the symbolic, microcosmic presentation of the macrocosm.

2. *Gnostic religiosity:* It conceives the Absolute as lying beyond the world of everyday experience, as the ultimate spiritual ground of all that is visible and tangible. In the Indian tradition, it is called the *Brahman.* It

transcends the empirical individual but at the same time is identical with his deepest self, the *Atman*. This identity is but a spiritualized version of the magical identity between the microcosm and the macrocosm. All gnosis is genetically linked to cosmic religiosity. In seeking to go beyond the visible world of multiplicity, it also reinstates the same world as the play (*Leela*) or the manifestation of the power (*Maya*) of the *Atman-Brahman*. That is why the gnostic lives in two worlds . in the world of transcendental truth (*Paramarthika-satya*) and of empirical truth (*Vyavaharika-satya*), shuttling between the two as it suits his whim. As far as ethics is concerned, his attitude is essentially a-moral. In his view, good and evil belong to the world of Maya and have to be superseded in the quest for true knowledge (*jnana*). But, in practice, he will conform to all rules of customary morality. Words like revolution make no sense to him as he has resolved all contradictions - including the contradiction between the rich and the poor, the exploiter and the exploited - in the all-encompassing unity of the *Atman-Brahman*.

3. *Personalist religiosity*: Here the believer sees the Ultimate and the Unconditioned neither as a cosmic force nor as the impersonal *Brahman* but as a person who loves and hates, punishes and rewards, creates and redeems. He relates to the Absolute as the totally Other. He can become that Other only through love. For only through love can two become one without either losing his identity. The awareness of time proper to personalist religiosity is neither cosmic nor meta-historical (as is the case with the gnostic) but ecstatic. It collapses the past, the present, and the future into a sort of timelessness. But this is true, only of the peak moments of devotional ecstasies. In everyday life, the devotee falls back upon cyclic time as expressed in the cycle of devotions - daily, monthly, yearly. In matters of morality, he tends to conform to the status quo, however inhuman it might be. Nevertheless, the experience of emotive union with the Absolute undergirding this kind of religiosity may infuse some gentleness, benevolence, and compassion into the existing social relations.

4. *Prophetic religiosity*: Prophetic faith encounters the Divine as the totally Other who is at the same time involved in history. What marks it off from every other religiosity is the fact that it experiences the Absolute as a challenge, as an ethical imperative to shake off all shackles and create a future of love, freedom, and community. This involves a new sense of time where the focus is the future yet to be created. For the same reason, the present is surcharged with meaning as the meeting point of divine challenge and human response. Prophetic religiosity is essentially subversive, a catalyst of disequilibrium and a sign of contradiction. It is always in creative tension towards mankind's Absolute Future. That future, however, will not mean the end of all human creativity. What it will eliminate, once and for all, is human alienation. Humanity will never coincide with the Absolute.

The types of religiosity I have described are seldom found in their purity, but tend to merge, one with the other: the cosmic with the personalist and the gnostic, the personalist with the prophetic. In any such combination, one will be dominant while the other remains subordinate. However, in many respects, prophetic religiosity signals the birth of something radically new in so far as it entails a new sense of time and an ethics of subversion.

The four types by no means exhaust the religious phenomenon. They have this in common that they presuppose the existence of an Absolute as the beginning and end of all that exists. Quite otherwise is it with the attitude generated by the Marxian outlook. Here the Absolute is presupposed not as already existing but as yet to be fashioned through human praxis, revolutionary and post-revolutionary. Since in this perspective too man stands in a certain relationship with an Absolute, his attitude may rightly be qualified religious, for lack of a better term. To distinguish it from prophetic religiosity to which it is most akin, let us call it projective religiosity.

5. *Projective religiosity*: The Absolute, which humanity is called to create, is nothing but its own plenitude. History is in travail to bring forth the Divine. Inherent in this hope is an awareness of time closely

resembling the prophetic. There is, however, a significant difference. With prophecy, history is man's dialogue with God. Since the God who addresses him is not only the *Not-yet* but also the *Already*, he can be encountered in the Here and Now of history, though the individual's total fulfillment will have to await the coming of the humanity of the end-time. Hence the human being can live out his short span of life in the hope that on death he will be gathered up into that Divine which had already come into his life. In the Marxian perspective, on the contrary, man lives in monologue with his own Ultimate Future which, however, will never come into being. For, were it to become a reality, it would be the end of history. But, according to Marx, history will never come to an end. Man, therefore, is confronted with a tragic either-or. If he chooses to be God, he ceases to be a historical being; if, on the other hand, he chooses to continue to be a historical being, he has to give up any hope of becoming God. This ambivalence also vitiates Marx's ethics of human self-creation. He bases his ethics on the hope of realizing mankind's Absolute Future. At the same time, he frustrates that hope by refusing to put an end to history. Man is thus left with a hope that annuls itself, with an ethics that calls in question its own premises. Hence the likelihood of his falling from the sublime ethics of self-creation to the mundane ethics of self-preservation.

The possibility of falling from authenticity is something which projective religiosity shares with the prophetic, though not necessarily for the same reasons. Both have shown a tendency to pass over into their opposite. They can survive in their purity only so long as they are able to maintain their ethical end-oriented tension. Once hope in the future dies, they recoil on themselves in narcissistic introversion. Loss of hope means loss of the Absolute. But no human being can live without an Absolute. Hence he will inevitably absolutize the relative and invest it with divinity. This has happened to the prophetic religion par excellence which is Christianity. With the non-advent of the Reign of God that Jesus had preached, the community of believers took the place of the promised future. The result was the church. A similar trend may be noticed in the development of Marxism as a historical movement.

The non-event of the proletarian international revolution, the failure of national revolutions (where they occurred) to carry through the project of eliminating classes, the world-conquering advance of the demon of capitalism, the inability to formulate relevant strategies under changed circumstances, the afore-mentioned theoretical ambiguities: all resulted in a loss of hope within Marxism It, therefore, fell back on itself, congealed into secular churches or sects, each with its dogmas, its priestly caste, its infallible magisterium, its sacrament of initiation, and system of ex-communication.

Institutionalized into secular churches, Marxism can only follow the way of social conformism. But it cannot entirely discard its revolutionary heritage. Else it would be accused of betraying the working class. A way out is provided by the ritualization of revolution. Revolution is symbolically re-enacted in an ever-recurring cycle of strikes, demonstrations and slogan chanting. In this manner, the radical rhetoric of yore is maintained, if not further sharpened. In the process theory too changes. What was a theory of revolution becomes a science of the necessary laws of motion of society. The responsibility for the abolition of classes is transferred from the proletariat to the inexorable working out of the dialectic. Rid of the burden of the revolution, Marxists can from now on settle down to enjoy the flesh-pots of capitalism and bourgeois politics.

Thus Marxism which began as a critique of religion has itself become something of a religion. So true is this that the criticism Marx leveled against the religions of his day can with justice be applied to the sectarian communist parties of today. The notion of the classless society has become the new opiate of the masses lulling them into acquiescence in capitalist social relations. And the dialectic is to Marxists what divine Providence has been to many Christians - a theoretical tool that explains everything, legitimizes everything.

For Marxism to become a creative force in history, it must recognize the hidden Absolute of its theory. Likewise, religion must recognize the atheism lurking beneath its practice, if not also its theory. Just as

Marxism must go beyond itself by incorporating the kernel of truth in religious belief, so must religion supersede itself by assimilating the truth of Marxism. In the proportion in which Marxism and religion undertake in all seriousness the quest after authenticity and relevance, they will converge and become a single force for the progressive humanization of society.

Part - 2
ESSAYS

The Dialectical Method I

Why study Marxism at all, one might ask. For two reasons:

1. To bring about radical changes in Indian society, we need first to understand the existing social relations. Marx can help us fashion the tools required for analyzing society. Not that he has the solution to every problem we pose or has said the last word on society and history of all times. In many respects, his thinking needs to be completed, if not corrected. Nevertheless, to think that one can fashion a theoretical weapon for change without taking into account the contribution of Marxism is an illusion.

2. There is a tendency among the Indian intelligentsia to reject or accept Marxism uncritically, which is understandable where Marxism parades itself as a set of eternal, immutable dogmas. Such uncritical response can harm rather than further the cause of socialism.

Hence, here I shall be subjecting Marx to a critical evaluation. I am putting forward no claim to be an authority on Marx. The reflections offered are to be taken as part of an on-going quest which I am sharing with readers who may be engaged in a similar quest.

In considering any thinker one must ask three questions:

1. What does he say?

2. How did he arrive at what he says?

3. How does he set forth what he has to say?

The first question deals with the content of his thought; the second and the third with the method of inquiry and exposition, respectively.

The method Marx employs both in his investigation and exposition is dialectical. Dialectical too is the content of his philosophy. With him, method and content form a unity. The dialectic governs both thought and reality. Hence to have a complete view of Marxian dialectic it is necessary to have gone through his philosophy as a whole. It is, however, legitimate and necessary to discuss the dialectic first. Legitimate, because Marx himself does so in several places, though not systematically; necessary because without at least a provisional understanding of his method, it is not possible to grasp what he says.

Marx was by no means the first to use the dialectical method. The method has a long history going back to the early Greek philosophers like Parmenides, Zeno, and Socrates. The term itself originally meant the art of conversation. Suppose I come out with the statement, "There is democracy in India". You who listen to me may counter, "There is no democracy in India". Thus arises a conflict of views between us. I adduce arguments to prove you false. You do the same to prove me wrong. In this war of words, I realize that there is some truth in what you say, and you realize that there is some truth in what I say. Each realizes his/her position is only partially true. This impels us to arrive at a new formulation which eliminates the error of our earlier statements while preserving the elements of truth. The new formulation could be: "There is only formal democracy in India." Thus the whole conversation tends to develop contradictions and by resolving them arrives at fuller truth.

The basic moments or stages of the dialectical process are already here: *thesis, antithesis,* and *synthesis.* The same movement may be discerned also in all genuine thoughts. The thinker who formulates an assertion must go on to negate it himself so that by setting one view against another he may arrive at a truer grasp of reality. Hence the pregnant words of Plato:

> "Thought and speech are the same thing, but the silently occurring internal dialogue of the soul with itself has been specially given the name of thought."[1]

It was Hegel who for the first time made this three-fold rhythm of conversation into the moving principle of all thought and reality. A grasp of the dialectic as employed by him is necessary for understanding Marx, who was in his youth an ardent disciple of Hegel.

The Dialectic According to Hegel

It is not possible to give a comprehensive view of the dialectical method of Hegel. For our purpose, it is enough to concentrate on the dialectic of knowing as found in his *Encyclopedia* and on the dialectic of the subject and the object, elaborated in his *Phenomenology of the Mind*.

The Dialectic of Knowing

Hegel distinguishes three stages in the process of knowing: *understanding*, *negative reason*, and *speculative reason*. Understanding sees the world as a sum of fixed, stable objects. To it, each reality appears as having definite proportions, as complete in itself, and fully at repose, and, for that reason, also different from, and opposed to, every other thing.

Thus the table I write on has definite properties, fixed contours, and occupies a specific place. It marks itself off from other objects. This mode of knowing is governed by the principle of identity which says, "A thing is what it is and nothing else." The book in my hand is a book. It cannot be a book and a pen at the same time. If the book were also a pen, there would be a contradiction. And understanding abhors all contradiction and strives to eliminate it. The principle of identity, therefore, includes the principle of non-contradiction. Understanding is the basis of the common-sense view of the world. On it is founded ordinary social life. When I give a loan to someone, I presume he will remain identical to himself and will not claim to be someone else when it comes to repaying it. So too, no science is possible if the object of investigation does not remain what it is. It is because things remain what they are that scientists can describe their properties and formulate laws. Hegel viewed all philosophy before him as but the product of understanding. What the philosophers did was to define the immutable, eternal essences of things. They could not have done so if they did not believe that things remained identical to themselves.

The knowledge gained through understanding is not false. But it is incomplete. If one believes understanding reveals the whole truth, one is wrong. To gain fuller knowledge, one must go beyond understanding and attain to negative reason. To negative reason, things appear other than what they did to naive understanding. What earlier appeared complete now shows itself in need of completion; the closed discloses itself as open to other things; the immutable shows itself to be mutable; the eternal to be transient. Consider the book in my hand. In a few years, it will turn into mere dust. It will become the opposite of what it is, a non-book. The seed buried in the soil is tending to become a tree, to become non-seed. Thus everything tends to become what it is not, and not to be what it is. All fixed determinations collapse and pass over into their opposites. Concepts lose their stable boundaries and start flowing into one another. In short, thought is here governed by the principle of negativity, meaning, "Everything is what it is not".

Without negativity, there is no time. Time presupposes change. Were the sun to remain identical to itself (at least on the level of appearance), if it did not go through the process of rising and setting, there would be neither morning, noon, evening nor night. Further, no negativity means no action. And action involves the negation of a given condition. When I start writing, I am negating what I was doing before. When I walk to the wall over there, I am negating my position here at my table. On negativity too is founded freedom and history. Freedom involves negating what one is at any given time to become what one is not yet. And what is history but freedom writ large?

Negative reason takes us beyond the one-sidedness of understanding. But it too is one-sided. It sees in things only the urge to negate themselves. To attain to complete truth we must push forward to the still higher standpoint of speculative reason. The principle governing it is neither identity nor negativity but totality. It means: "Everything is what it is and what it is not". To return to the example of the seed, understanding sees it as identical to itself (The seed is the seed); negative reason sees it as negating itself (The seed is non-seed); speculative reason sees it as both identical and opposed to itself (The seed is both seed and non-seed).

Speculative or positive reason thus leaves behind the one-sidedness of understanding and negative reason, while at the same time preserving the truth contained in them. Only totality reveals complete truth. On the level of understanding, there is only bare unity. On the level of negative reason, there is opposition (as between the seed and the non-seed). On the level of positive reason, there is the unity of opposites. Put differently, the first stage represents affirmation; the second, negation; and the third, negation of the negation.

The Dialectic of Subject and Object

What I have explained so far is the bare outline of the dialectic as enunciated by Hegel without any explicit reference to the content of his philosophy. In his case too, the method is not external to the content. Hence it will be useful to consider the dialectical process as found in Hegel's *Phenomenology of the Mind* (which is the work that influenced Marx most), where method and content fuse into one. This work traces the path the individual has to follow in arriving at absolute knowledge. It consists of three stages: *consciousness*, *self-consciousness*, and *reason*.

Consciousness includes both sense-knowledge and understanding in the sense explained earlier. In sense-knowledge, the object is seen as existing out there, independent of the subject. But the independence of the object is only apparent. The tree in my garden appears in no way to depend on me. It is there, will be there, whether I think it or not. But when I try to describe it every word I utter (this, hard, green, shady, tall, etc.) turns out to be a universal concept, applicable to other trees and other objects as well. And universal concepts exist only in the mind of the thinking subject. The concept, *man*, does not exist; what exists is this particular man, Peter. Thus sense-perception proves self-contradictory.

The subject, therefore, moves on to the phase of understanding. Understanding divides the world into two tiers:

1. The realm of appearance accessible to the senses, and

2. The realm of stable essences hidden behind appearances.

Even this approach proves invalid. The subject realizes that what it called essence is nothing but its own product, that what lies behind the curtain of appearances is nothing but its own self, and that to be conscious of the object is to be self-conscious. Put differently, the object negates itself and becomes its opposite, the subject. Here consciousness passes over to its antithesis, self-consciousness.

Self-consciousness is a higher level of knowledge, compared with the earlier stage when the object was thought of as totally independent of the subject. Still, it too is partial knowledge and must be superseded. The complete truth is attained only when the individual reaches the stage of reason. Reason synthesizes the partial truths represented by consciousness and self-consciousness. It sees the object as both other than and identical with itself. An example might help here. The spider spins a web, from out of its own stuff. The web is outside, other than, the spider; yet, in a sense, it is one with the spider. If the spider were conscious, it would see itself in the web. Similarly, he who has arrived at reason sees the external world as both identical with and different from his own self. Initially, as the subject of mere consciousness, he felt threatened, insecure, and alien in an alien world. Arrived at self-consciousness, his feeling was one of loneliness and boredom. It is only with the dawn of reason that he feels at home in the world. Here he sees himself in the object and the object in himself. This whole process follows the structure and movement of the dialectic as explained in the beginning. Consciousness is marked by *identity*. The object is perceived as identical to itself and opposed to the subject. With self-consciousness, the object passes over into its opposite, the subject. Hence *negativity*. Reason represents the moment of *totality*, the unity in opposition of subject and object.

The dialectic of subject and object just explained must be seen in the broader context of Hegel's philosophical system as a whole. Its starting point is what he calls the *Idea*. The Idea is the last term in a series of concepts, beginning with the most abstract one of 'being'. Being unfolds dialectically into ever more concrete, ever more complex concepts until the movement comes to rest in the Idea, the most comprehensive, inclusive concept. Hegel employs the term Idea, to refer now to the last term in the series, now to the series as a whole.

The Idea represents the ultimate reason of the universe. Though the primal source of everything, it (unlike the God of theism) does not exist before the world. Nonetheless, it is real and constitutes the thesis of the entire movement. It then negates itself and becomes other than what it is. From being immaterial it becomes the material *Nature*. Nature is the Idea in its otherness, the Idea becomes incarnate. The Idea as Nature dialectically evolves from lower to ever higher forms until it becomes conscious of itself. This signals the birth of the *Spirit*. The Spirit is the synthesizing unity of Idea and Nature. But the Spirit itself has to go through a long process before it can realize all its possibilities. First, it manifests itself as *the subjective spirit* in individuals; then as *the objective spirit* in the family, morality and the state; and finally, as *the absolute spirit* in and through art, religion, and philosophy. The transition from the subjective to the absolute spirit provides the context for the dialectic of subject and object explained earlier. (The perceptive reader will have noted the close resemblance between the Hegelian triunity of

Idea, Nature, and Spirit, on the one hand, and the Christian belief in the Trinity of Father, Son, and Holy Spirit, on the other. Hegelianism is, in fact, a rational, conceptual re-interpretation of Christian dogma.)

Marx's Critique of Hegelian Dialectic

Early in life, Marx felt the need to come to terms with the Hegelian dialectic. The main conclusions he arrived at may be found in the last section of his *Economic and Philosophical Manuscripts* written in 1844. This section bears the title, "Critique of Hegel's Dialectic and General Philosophy." Here we find the following significant statement:

> "What is great about Hegel's Phenomenology and its final result – about the dialectic of negativity as the moving and creative principle – is first that Hegel conceives the self-creation of man as a process, as the process whereby he objectifies himself in products that set themselves up in opposition to him, as the process whereby he alienates himself and overcomes the alienation. Hegel, therefore, grasps the nature of labour and conceives the objective man true, real man as the result of his own labour. The real, active relation of man to himself as a universal being or the realization of himself as a real universal, that is, a human being, is possible only if he gives outward expression to his universal powers and relates to them as objects. This, to begin with, is not possible without alienation. Man's universal being can come about only through the collective labour of mankind, and as a result of history."[2] (Free translation)

Marx agrees with Hegel that:

1. man is not a static being but a process, a becoming, of which he is both the initiator and the result,

2. that the dynamic principle of this process is the dialectic of negativity which impels man to march forward to the full development of his powers by first alienating them in objects and then overcoming that alienation, and

3. that the process of alienation is a necessary one.

Here, we have the central axis of Marx's philosophy of man and history.

Marx, however, disagreed with Hegel on many fundamental points. An examination of these differences will bring to relief some of the salient features of Marxian dialectic. The first difference concerns the subject of dialectic. We have already seen that the starting point of the Hegelian system is the Idea. It is the Idea that dialectically passes over into its opposite which is Nature and finally manifests itself as absolute Spirit in Philosophy. The Idea is the hidden subject of the evolution of nature and history. Of this subject "real man and real nature become mere predicates."[3] Men and things are agents only on the level of appearance. In the last analysis, it is the Idea or Spirit that acts through them. Besides, even when Hegel speaks of individuals as acting, he takes them not as concrete men and women "with eyes, ears, etc. living in society, in the world, and nature"[4] but as mere bearers of abstract self-consciousness. Instead of viewing consciousness as an attribute of human beings, he sees human beings as attributes of consciousness. This was unacceptable to Marx. For him, the subject of the dialectical movement of history is the concrete human being. But the concrete human being is such just because he is essentially related to nature. He relates to nature through perception, needs, and action. Similarly, he also relates to other human beings, who too form the object of his perception, need, and action. It is this man, inserted in nature and society, who externalizes and alienates his powers in objects outside and then overcomes the same alienation.[5]

Second, since Hegel conceives the subject of the dialectical movement to be the Idea or man as mere consciousness, the process of alienation and disalienation is only abstract and conceptual. If your true self is consciousness, your activity will be mental. So also the product of that activity. That is why "when Hegel conceives wealth, the power of the state, etc. as entities alienated from the essence of man, he conceives them only in their thought form."[6] Hence alienation is overcome only conceptually, leaving things as they are in reality.

> "The whole history of alienation and retraction of alienation is, therefore, only the history of the production of abstract, absolute thought."[7]

Take religion, for instance. You overcome it when you realize that the truth of the belief in God is found in philosophy which teaches you that the absolute is not outside you but your own true inner being. Thus conceptually you have left religion behind. But this does not prevent religion from persisting in real life. The whole attempt, therefore, is a vain exercise proper to intellectuals who are themselves estranged from real life.

For Marx, on the contrary, alienation and the overcoming of alienation take place not in the mind but on the level of practical activity, the activity of concrete persons, who, in transforming the environment, transform themselves. Of course, Hegel too speaks of man fashioning himself through labour. But by labour he understood mental labour, the act of thinking.[8] Marx sees labour as proceeding from man's embodied, sensuous existence.[9] Admittedly, such labour is conscious. But it is more than mere consciousness. More, consciousness cannot change the world; labour does. Hence the process of overcoming alienation means not merely interpreting but also changing the world.

Third, there is a crucial difference between the Hegelian and the Marxian concept of alienation. For Hegel, the very existence of objects outside the thinking subject is an alienation. The subject cannot but feel alienated when he is confronted with objects that are opaque and opposed to it. As Marx points out, with Hegel,

> "Objectivity as such is regarded as an alienated human relationship which does not correspond to the essence of man which is self-consciousness."[10]

Hence the need to surmount the object of consciousness. This is done by showing that the object is nothing but congealed consciousness, nothing but the subject in its otherness.

Thus to recover his true essence man must eliminate not only alienation but also objectivity.[11] Here Marx parts company with Hegel. For him, that human beings are confronted with objects is in no way an alienation. Rather, it is what constitutes human existence. Man is a natural being, both because he emerged from nature and because he relates to it through his powers and faculties, through action and passion. If man acts on objects in nature, it is because he is essentially an objective being. The subject who fashions objects is at the same time fashioned by objects. [12]

If the mere existence of objects does not constitute alienation, in what does it consist? Marx says that the objects man creates set themselves up in *opposition to him* and *dominate* him from outside. Implied here is a distinction between objectification and alienation. Objectification is a process whereby human beings produce objects which reflect their creative powers. Objectification becomes alienation only when the objects created enslave the producers and stifle their humanity. Hence to overcome alienation, it is not necessary to destroy the world of objects. It is enough to destroy their alien, dehumanizing character. The supersession of alienation on the part of man, says Marx, is "the real appropriation of his objective being by the destruction of the alienated character of the objective world."[13] The task is at once less and more demanding than in Hegel. Less demanding, because what is required is the elimination not of the object but its alienated nature; more, because it is not possible to think alienation away; one has to abolish it through action.

Fourth, with Hegel, "because the conception is formal and abstract, the overcoming of alienation becomes a confirmation of alienation."[14] To understand the force of this argument we must consider Hegel's view of the course of the dialectical movement as a whole. We have seen that its point of arrival is the Absolute Spirit. In a certain sense, it is also the point of departure. Just as in a syllogism the conclusion is already in the premises, so too the Absolute Spirit is already in the Idea and its progressive manifestation in nature and history. In other words, it is not only the final result of the dialectical movement but also the movement as a whole. Hence every alienation that occurs in the course of the movement is an essential moment or element of the Absolute Spirit. Which means, the dialectic, while claiming to overcome alienations, in reality, legitimates them.

Finally, Hegel begins with the Idea and arrives at nature and history. He starts with the world of abstractions in order subsequently to descend to the real earth. When he does, he naturally tends to translate the concrete universe into so many abstractions. Thus the real concrete escapes him. Instead of seeing the real tree, he sees only the idea of the tree. His main error, argues Marx, consists of inverting the relation between ideas and the world. For, ideas are ideas of living men and women in vital exchange with nature and one another. The right approach, therefore, is, to begin with, the dialectical relation between man and nature and, from that point of view, explain ideas. Genuine materialism and positive science must make the social relationship of man to man the basic principle of theory.[15] Here is the core of the dialectical method as employed by Marx. In the preface to the second edition of *Capital*, he writes,

> "My own dialectical method is not only fundamentally different from the Hegelian dialectical method but is its direct opposite. For Hegel, the thought process (which he transforms into an independent subject, giving to it the name of 'idea') is the creator of the real; and for him, the real is only the outward manifestation of the Idea. In my view, on the other hand, the idea is nothing other than the material when it has been transposed and translated in the human head."

The word, material, in this context, does not mean 'pertaining to brute matter' but the reality of man's social, historical existence. (This will be substantiated in subsequent chapters). Significantly, what is proposed here as the method is closely linked to the 'materialist' conception of history. To say that in our thinking and research we *should* start with the concrete to arrive at ideas is to propound a method; to say that our ideas and conceptions are *determined* by our concrete social existence is to propound the materialist conception of history. Here too content and method form a unity.

Some Conclusions

Marx's critique of Idealism throws light on the kind of materialism he advocated. The materialism and idealism of his day differed fundamentally in the way they understood the relation between subject and object. Materialism held the primacy of the object, understood as comprising all extended realities, subject to chemical, physical, and mechanical laws. The subject, consciousness, was seen as derivative of the object. The Idealists on the other hand chief among whom was Hegel went to the other extreme and affirmed the primacy of the subject. They reduced the object to the subject, the material to consciousness. We have already seen how Hegel views the object as but another mode of being of the subject. Marx would consider both approaches one-sided and false. He sought to redeem the element of truth in materialism and spiritualism. In his view, the relation, subject-object, is primordial. Man cannot be defined except in relation to nature. Nor can nature be defined outside its relation to man. Marx says,

> "But nature taken abstractly, for itself, and rigidly separated from man, is nothing for man."[17]

Neither the subject nor the object can be reduced to each other. Each finds its external nature in the other. This does not mean that Marx gives equal weightage to man and nature, to subject and object. Against materialism, he affirmed the active, dynamic character of man's relation to the world.[18] Man is not just one among the objects of nature. He can engage in purposive action by changing objects around him according to his ideas, thus progressively humanizing them. In the process, he becomes ever more deeply anchored in nature, ever more natural. That is why Marx can call his philosophy naturalism or humanism.

> "We see how consistent naturalism or humanism is distinguished from both idealism and materialism, and at the same time constitutes their unifying truth. We see also that only naturalism can comprehend the process of world history."[19]

If my interpretation is correct, dialectical materialism as formulated by Engels and later made into a dogma by orthodox Marxism stands in opposition to the thought of Marx. Engels ignores the major dialectic of subject and object, of man and nature, which was central to Marx. He makes the object (matter) into an autonomous sphere governed by its own dialectical laws of motion. These laws are then reflected in the subject, in consciousness, which, in turn, is viewed as an autonomous sphere. He wrote,

> "Thus dialectics, reduced itself to the science of the general laws of motion both of the external world and of human thought two sets of laws which are identical in substance."[20]

Whereas for Marx, thought is a function of man's practical relationship to the world (nature and other men), here it is but a mere reflection of the laws of development of matter. Thus Engels falls into that crass materialism which Marx tried to dialectically overcome. Seen from another angle, dialectical materialism turns out to be idealism. For, the dialectical laws of motion supposed to govern matter take on the status of a metaphysical principle, analogous to the Hegelian Idea underlying the evolution of nature into Spirit.

These preliminary reflections serve a double purpose. On the one hand, they warn the reader against approaching Marx with the mental categories derived from 'dialectical materialism'; on the other, they prepare the ground for the study of Marxian dialectic both as a method and as a principle governing the historical process. In the coming issue, I shall deal with the Marxian dialectic as a method both of knowing and of relating what is known.

(Negations No. 2, April-June 1982; *Marx Beyond Marxism*, Chapter 1)

8

The Dialectical Method II

In the previous chapter, we discussed the salient points of the Hegelian dialectic and noted Marx's critical stance regarding it. It remains to see how the latter made use of the same method both in investigating reality and in setting forth his conclusions. With Hegel, Marx shared the view that thought can arrive at truth only by developing contradictions and resolving them. The same law he saw at work in reality. By reality, however, he understood the historical process of human beings transforming nature and society. So far so good. But when it comes to defining the Marxian dialectic further, difficulties crop up. Marx has nowhere systematically dealt with the matter. He chose to practice the dialectic rather than theorize on it. The few reflections he has made on the subject are scattered throughout his works.[1] And the reader is left to piece them together and form his own opinion. This is what I have done.

One can discern three dialectical approaches in Marx:

1. the dialectic of appearance and essence,

2. the dialectic of the abstract and the concrete, and

3. the dialectic of theory and praxis.

They don't run on parallel lines but are closely linked and mutually complementary. If we treat them separately, it is only for the sake of clarity of exposition.

The Dialectic of Appearance and Essence

All philosophers begin with the world as it appears. But soon they find they cannot go by appearances, that truth lies behind or beyond what appears. Thus the *Advaitins* hold that the world, as it manifests itself, has only practical truth (*vyavaarika-satya*). Ultimate truth (*paramarthika-satya*) is to be sought beyond appearances. Hegel too takes us beyond the realm of appearance to that of absolute truth, which he calls the Idea or the Spirit. This urge to penetrate beneath appearances is legitimate. If appearances were the whole truth and nothing but the truth, philosophy would be superfluous, and common sense would be all that is needed. However, what is beyond appearances can be reached only through appearances. This insight formed the starting point also of Marx's theory of knowledge. He writes,

> "Sense perception... must be the basis of all science. Only when science starts from sense perception in the dual form of sensuous consciousness and sensuous need, i.e. only when science starts from nature, is it real science."[2]

One should not, however, get stuck at sense experience but probe deeper to discover the essence of things. The essence is the underlying structure and movement of reality. As a structure, it is a whole, formed by interrelated parts or elements; as movement, it is caught up in a process of birth, growth, and disintegration. Since essence is also a process, Marx often reduces it to the fundamental laws of the development of reality. His philosophical, as well as sociological investigations, were attempts to penetrate below appearances and reveal the underlying essence.

Let me cite a few examples. In analyzing Jewish religion as it appears in everyday life, he says that its 'empirical essence' is to be found in the market relations of buying and selling.[3] Similarly, he saw that commodity relations are nothing but the distorted expression of the social essence of man.[4] To the superficial observer, private property appears as something objective, as having nothing to do with the subjective labour of the working class. On closer analysis, however, it becomes clear that "the subjective essence of private property is labour."[5] The same approach underlies Marx's later investigations into capitalism. The exchange between the capitalist and the labourer appears to be an equal exchange (so much wages for so much work). But in reality, it is an unequal one, the labourer giving more than he receives.[6] So too, against the bourgeois economists, who stressed what goes on, on the surface of capitalism such as competition and the market, Marx argues,

> "But it is clear from the outset that, just as the apparent motions of the heavenly bodies only become comprehensible to one who knows their real movements, which are not directly appreciable by our senses; so a scientific analysis of competition is only possible to one who has grasped the inner nature of capital."[7]

And the inner nature of capital is to be sought in the production process itself.

All true investigation must proceed from appearance to arrive at the essence. Having arrived at the essence, one should not set it up as an absolute and abide by it forever. Else one would only end up with mere abstractions without content. One must retrace one's steps from the essence back to the order of appearance whence the journey began. All dialectical thinking is circular or, better, spiral. The goal is to show concretely how the essence appears, how the deeper reality manifests itself in everyday life. This third phase represents the synthesis of appearance and essence. Here appearance is grasped in its inner structure and movement. The dialectic of appearance and essence throws light on the structure of Capital. The first volume deals with the essence of capitalism consisting of the production of surplus-value. Subsequent volumes show how the essence manifests itself on the surface – in circulation, in market relations, and above all, in periodic crises. (It will be shown below why Marx does not begin describing capitalism as it appears and then proceeds to the unveiling of its essence.)

The Dialectic of the Abstract and the Concrete

This is not so much a new dialectical procedure as a variation of the one just discussed. For Marx, as for Hegel, only that knowledge is concrete which is 'rich in determinations', that is, rich in the dimensions, attributes and elements of reality it reveals. The abstract, on the contrary, is poor in content, consisting as it does of one or other dimension only.

Investigation begins with the concrete as immediately given, as presented to the senses. But the concrete, as it initially presents itself, is concrete only in a limited sense. When I want to study a village, I first visit the place, take note of the people, things, events, and institutions there. The knowledge thus gained is concrete. But it is still vague, being no more than a sum of impressions. It tells me nothing about the laws underlying the lives of the people, about the way the different sectors of life are interrelated or about the deeper trends and forces at work. Thus the knowledge of the concrete as immediately given proves inadequate. I must go beyond it if I want to attain comprehensive knowledge.

But how? By a detour of abstraction. From the concrete as immediately given, I must separate out – this is what abstraction means – the diverse elements. Each of them must then be studied separately, and the elements that go to form it must be ascertained. From among the elements laid bare I must identify the one that is most fundamental i.e. presupposed by all others. But were the inquiry to end with analysis, one would be left with a fragmented view of the village. Hence it must move on to the next phase.

Here, analysis gives way to synthesis. What was earlier separated must be put together. This involves discovering how the different elements hang together, forming a closely-knit network of relations. The related whole or structure must, in turn, be seen as a moment in a continuing process, as related to the past and the future. It is this dynamic structure that explains what happens on the surface of everyday life in the village. In this way, we return to the concrete we started from. But it is no longer the concrete as immediately given but as mediated by the twofold movement of analysis and synthesis, hence rich in content, a "concentration of many determinations, hence unity of the diverse." It is the true concrete which "appears in the process of thinking,... as a result, not as a point of departure, even though it is the point of departure for observation and conception."[8]

The same method is to be followed in the study of the capitalist economy. The starting point will be the concrete as immediately given, namely, population. For people are the subject and foundation of the social act of production. But the term, people, is an abstraction if we leave out the classes out of which it is composed. Even class is an empty phrase if we do not consider the elements on which it rests, such as wage-labour and capital. These, in turn, become fully intelligible only when we know what they presuppose – exchange, division of labour, prices, commodity. Thus from the immediately concrete, from the population, we arrive at ever thinner abstractions by way of analysis. Now the process must be reversed and through ever higher synthesis regain the concrete,[9] the concrete as a product of thought.

If the right approach is from the immediate, concrete to the mediated concrete by way of analysis and synthesis, how is it that in *Capital* Marx begins with the most abstract notion of commodity and thence proceeds to ever more concrete concepts? The answer is to be sought in the distinction Marx makes between the method of investigation and the method of exposition. The method of presentation, he says, "must differ from that of enquiry. The latter has to appropriate the material in detail, to analyze its different forms of development, to trace out their inner connections. Only after this work is done, can the actual movement be adequately described."[10]

Enquiry must cover the entire movement from the concrete to the abstract and back to the concrete. In the exposition, on the contrary, it is enough to follow the movement of thought from the most abstract to the concrete as a product of thought.

The Dialectic of Theory and Practice

The dialectical method of investigation is meant to help us know the world. But we need not only to know the world but also to shape it through action. We act on objects, thereby transforming them to meet our needs. In the process, we bring about changes in ourselves. Now the question naturally arises, How does knowing stand in relation to acting, theory in relation to practice? Are they just two modes of relating to the world, which run parallel without ever meeting? In the case of many philosophers, the answer would seem to be yes. Take *Advaita*, for instance. You can learn and expound it without any serious, consideration of the concrete world of human action and human suffering. The same is true of all thinkers like Aristotle who hold that science is possible only about universal essences. What living persons and social classes did was of no concern to them. In contrast to them, Marx held, correctly that all genuine thought must proceed from, and issue in, action or practice.

Before we proceed further, it is necessary to define the meaning of the term, praxis. Marx uses the term in more than one sense. In the broader sense, praxis is human sensuousness or sense-experience. Sensuousness includes not merely the activity of the five senses but also "thinking, contemplating, wanting, acting, and loving."[11] It comprises all the ways in which human beings relate to the world whether actively or passively.[12] Hence, it may be taken to mean our global encounter with reality – with the reality of objects experienced and of subjects experiencing them. That Marx identified sensuousness with practice is clear from his criticism of Feuerbach for understanding sensuousness only as passive contemplation and not as practical activity.[13] If praxis is the same as sensuousness, it is clear it cannot be the privilege of any one class but the life situation of all men and women, whether rich or poor, rulers or ruled. All human existence is practice.

Praxis is never neutral. It is right or wrong; humanizing or alienating. It is alienating when it debases the human, cripples freedom, and creativity. This is the case in all societies founded on exploitation and domination. Marx saw in wrong economic relations the primary source of alienating praxis. He spent a considerable part of his life exposing the dehumanizing character of capitalism. The labourer who works for wages without any share in ownership or management, is carrying on, day in and day out, the practice of draining out his humanity. Work is for him "an alienation of activity and an activity of alienation."[14] Not only workers but also the consuming and governing classes engage in wrong praxis. Dehumanizing is all activity in blind conformity with the prevailing social system. So also an activity that is mechanical, repetitive, and routinized, where the agent raises no questions, entertains no doubts. Such is the case of the bureaucrat who goes through his bundle of files in routine fashion; of the teacher who performs the daily ritual of doling out ready-made answers for ready-made questions, and the pupils who learn them by rote; of the policeman who shoots at people at the sound of his superior's whistle, as though by mere reflex; of the salesgirl who greets every prospective buyer with the same synthetic smile and mouths the same stereotype formulae in praise of her wares.

Is all praxis then dehumanizing? By no means. Marx also speaks of genuine praxis which he calls, 'practical-critical activity'. He takes Feuerbach to task for conceiving praxis 'only in its dirty Judaical manifestation', i.e. only in its manifestation as buying and selling.[15] What distinguishes genuine from alienating praxis is criticism aimed at the object, subject, and the mode of action. Criticism raises questions like, Does this mode of acting rest on a correct understanding of reality? Will it contribute to the free and full development of the community of persons? In raising such questions, one is also questioning one's own prejudices and preconceptions. All criticism is, in the end, self-criticism. Critical action brings about change not only in the environment but also in the agent. Hence it is revolutionary. Marx says,

> "The coincidence of the changing of circumstances and human activity or self-changing", "can be conceived and rationally understood only as a revolutionary activity."[16]

If even in class societies human beings can engage in critical action, it means that they are not totally determined by circumstances but are capable of determining circumstances. Marx unequivocally rejects that kind of materialism which "forgets that circumstances are changed by men."[17]

Having defined the meaning of the term, praxis, we are in a position to pose the further question, What has praxis to do with the acquisition of true knowledge and the formulation of correct theories? Marx answers,

"The question whether objective truth can be attributed to human thinking is not a question of theory but is a *practical* question. Man must prove the truth, i.e. the reality and power, the this-sidedness of his thinking in practice. The dispute over the reality or non- reality of thinking that is isolated from practice is a purely scholastic question."[18]

In this assertion is contained the quintessence of Marx's theory of knowledge. It can be interpreted in terms either of common sense or of dialectical thinking. According to common sense, a statement is true if it conforms to reality. The conformity of thought with reality is what philosophers call logical truth. It formed the cornerstone of all traditional theories of knowledge. From the commonsense point of view, Marx's statement would mean that our thinking is objectively true only if it mirrors adequately what is going on in the realm of practice. And if praxis is understood as sensuousness in the broad sense of the term, he is saying nothing new. Long before him, Aristotle had said all conceptual thinking must originate in sense perception. But, even a first look at the passage cited above will show that the author is trying to convey something more than the platitude that our statements are true only if they conform to reality.

To understand that 'more', it is necessary to shift our perspective from logical to dialectical thinking. Logical truth presupposes reality to be static, given once and for all, to which our statements are to conform. If reality is static, our pronouncements upon it will have the character of eternal and immutable truth. Quite different is the perspective of dialectical thinking. It sees reality not as a state of affairs but as a process, as the process of man's continuous, vital, sensuous exchange with nature and society. In short, reality is history. History is the striving of the human community to realize its hidden possibilities, its real essence. What is here referred to as the essence of man is not anything pre-given or pre-determined but something he has to create. But, in class societies concrete existence thwarts the realization of humanity's essential possibilities. Seen from this angle, truth assumes a new meaning. It consists not in the conformity of assertions with reality but in the conformity of reality itself with what it *essentially* is. Put differently, it is the conformity of existence with essence, of what *is* with what *ought to be*. Hence, not only statements but also things, persons, events, and institutions can be true or untrue. They are true if they exist in a manner suited to the unfolding of genuine human potentialities. If I am a slave condemned to take orders from my master, my existence is untrue, because it hampers the realization of my freedom and creative powers. So also life under capitalism, resting as it does on the exploitation of man by man.

From this, it follows that for the full revelation of truth one must wait for the end of the history of human alienation. Just as the truth of the bud is the flower, of the child the adult, so, for Marx, the truth of the present history is the classless society. The idea that truth is a future to be fashioned is something Marx takes over, via Hegel, from the Judaeo-Christian tradition.

Seen in the light of dialectical truth, Marx's statement, cited earlier, takes on a new and profound meaning. To prove the truth of one's thinking in practice means, in the first place, to trace the origin of thought in genuine practice. For "true practice is the condition of a real and positive theory."[19] And practice is true only if it is not alienating; positively, only if it helps the human community realize its possibilities of freedom, sociality, and creativeness. Only that thinking which arises from the matrix of humanity's practical striving for fuller being can be credited with truth. This implies, further, that the thinker himself must be involved in praxis, in creating a better world. Genuine thought can only be born of commitment. However, to prove the truth of our thinking it is not enough to establish its origin in critical praxis. Ideas arising from true praxis may still be hypothetical. To prove their validity they must, in turn, become practice. If thereby society becomes more humanized, then one has the certainty that they were the right ideas. In short, thinking is true when it not only arises from but also leads to critical, humanizing praxis.

For a theory to be true, it is not enough that it conforms to reality; it must also be able to *transform* it. Truth, therefore, is no abstraction; but is itself 'reality and power'. To grasp the force of this last phrase, it must be recalled that the German word for 'reality' is wirklichkeit, from the verb, wirken, meaning to work, to effect. Only such theories as having the power to effect positive changes in the world are true in the dialectical sense.

Clearly, then, at no time in the present pre-history of human alienation can theory or practice claim to be wholly true. Theory needs to be constantly revised in the light of practice and practice re-oriented in the light of theory. In this spiral movement, complete truth will ever remain a receding horizon. To refuse to revise theory in the light of praxis is dogmatism. To refuse to revise practice in the light of theory is to condemn oneself to historical irrelevance and revolutionary impotence.

But are we not caught up in a vicious circle? Are we not judging the truth of theory by the standard of praxis, and the truth of praxis by the standard of theory? The objection would be valid if theory and praxis formed two water-tight compartments. But not in the Marxian perspective where the two form a unity in tension.

Praxis already includes consciousness. It is shaped by theoretical presuppositions. At the same time, consciousness, in so far as it has been elaborated into a system of concepts, maintains its own otherness in relation to praxis. In day to day life men and women can make their doing and thinking the object of criticism. And where the subject critically reflects on himself – on his activity and consciousness – there is already a circular movement. But it is not a vicious but a vital circle, one deriving from man's capacity to transcend himself, to be what he is not and not to be what he is. This circularity is constitutive of all genuine thought.

Dialectical truth, however, does not cancel out logical truth. The latter is not sheer falsehood but a necessary phase all thought has to go through. It is both negated and preserved in the higher conception of truth as a humanizing creative force. Where logical truth does not subserve this higher truth, it becomes a disvalue. For instance, the science that has gone into the making of the atom bomb is logically true but dialectically false.

Admittedly, at more than one point in this short exposition of the dialectical method of enquiry, I have tried, at the risk of being subjective, to make explicit what is implicit in Marx. In justification I might add that the truth of a text is not something ready-made, lying enclosed between the covers of a book. It has, rather, to come to life in the dialogue between the author and the reader. The reader is not a mere passive recipient but a co-creator of truth.

Evaluation

None will deny that thought can make progress only by resolving the contradictions it meets on the way. In this general sense, dialectic is germane to the human mind, anywhere at any time. It is not the invention, much less the monopoly, of any one thinker or school of thought. The Buddha's thinking is eminently dialectical, as may, be seen from his dialogues. So also the language and thinking of the Bible. One should not, however, make a fetish out of the triad of thesis, antithesis, and synthesis, as though it were the essence of the dialectic. Neither Hegel nor Marx attached any importance to the number three. The emergence of contradiction and its resolution can take place in four, five, or even more stages. The essential thing is that genuine thought does not rest content with the initially given, whether you call it appearance, the immediate or the concrete. From the given, it must move on to the hidden structure or essence. In a yet final movement, it must overcome the one-sidedness of the previous stages and attain a total view of reality.

The dialectic of appearance and essence provides an indispensable tool for the analysis of any reality. It helps us steer clear of the aberrations of both essentialism and existentialism while preserving the elements of truth in them. Essentialist philosophers tended to abstract the essences of things, and make them the privileged object of reflection. Their concern was not the concrete man who has his birth and death, joys and sorrows, but the essence of man, whichever way one chose to define it. And the essence of man is not born, does not suffer or work or end his life in despair. No wonder, essentialism ended up with irrelevant and inane abstractions. It was in reaction to this kind of philosophy that existentialism came into being, led by thinkers like Kierkegaard, Heidegger, Sartre, and Gabriel Marcel. These went in the opposite direction and affirmed the primacy of concrete existence over essence. Their concern was the unique, unrepeatable individual with his guilt, sin, boredom, anguish, and despair. But the unique is incommunicable without universals, concepts, essences. Hence in practice, they had to bring in essences, through the backdoor, as it were.

Marx avoids these pitfalls. He insists that the point of departure and arrival of all enquiry must be the apparent, the concrete, and the practical – that is, the existent. In this sense, he is an existentialist. Also because he too, in a real sense, affirms the priority of existence over essence. At the same time, he redeems what is positive in essentialism by making the investigation of essence an indispensable moment in the search for knowledge. The aim is to know the existent as revealing an essence, the concrete as a dynamic unity of elements, the practical as illumined by theory.

The distinction between logical and dialectical truth, implicit in Marxian thinking, has far-reaching consequences. Logical truth is in itself a-moral. It only tells what reality is. It is merely descriptive, not prescriptive. When I say that under capitalism the worker is exploited, I am uttering a logical truth. It makes no moral demands on me. Having made the statement, I can safely withdraw into my own private world of grabbing and consuming. Not so, if I am dealing with dialectical truth. For, it reveals not only how and what things are but also what they *ought to be*. What ought to be is a call to decision, a challenge to act. Not to respond to it would amount to contradicting the truth of my own being. For I form a continuum with the reality I am criticizing. In this perspective, the true and the good fuse into one; the theorist and the prophet merge to form but one creative subject. Unfortunately, the followers of Marx set asunder what he had put together. The 'ought' was severed from the 'is' and thrown overboard; the ethical was repudiated as bourgeois. This done, Marxists could busy themselves with what was, is and will be; and conveniently forget about what reality ought to be. The result was. Marxism ceased to be what it originally was – an ethical philosophy, a secular movement of man's continuous self-creation.

The conception of truth as power can be a potent weapon for Cultural Revolution. Where alienating practice –economic, political, and cultural – holds sway, there is not the right soil for truth to germinate and blossom. Instead, a vast universe of canonized lies and syphilitic thoughts comes into being. Truth goes a whoring with mammon. Writers, novelists, poets, artists, teachers, priests, yogis – all gleefully prostitute their minds to money and the moneyed. In the process they breed and propagate untruths by the million, poisoning the very air we breathe. Are we then doomed forever to the reign of idiocy? Marx did not think so. He saw clearly that even in alienating social conditions human beings retain some ability to engage in meaningful critical practice. One may or may not agree with his claim that the working class will one day rise up as the herald of saving truth. But one cannot ignore the fact that initiators of genuine theory and practice do arise from different classes and strata in society, since, under capitalism, none is exempt from the experience of alienation.

Let me, in conclusion, note some tensions inherent in the Marxian dialectic of knowledge. In the first place, between realism and idealism. Idealism views the object as totally dependent on the mind; realism, on the contrary, affirms the independence of the object in relation to the knowing subject. Marx claimed his philosophy to be a synthesis of idealism and realism (materialism). But in his writings, one often notices a certain tendency to swing from one extreme to the other. To the realist extreme, when he stresses the independence of social structures and processes from the consciousness of individuals; to the idealist extreme, when, instead of deriving the dialectic from history as he usually does, he makes the historical movement conform to a preconceived dialectical scheme. This is particularly true of his forecast about the polarization of society into the bourgeoisie and the proletariat.

There is also the tension between logical and dialectical truth. Though he affirms the primacy of truth as power, he accords undue importance to logical truth as embodied in the natural sciences. He does not critically evaluate the contributions of natural science in terms of its power to humanize the world. He was probably too much under the spell of the scientism of his day. A related tension in his thinking is the one between science and philosophy. Is Marxism science or philosophy? Those who identify themselves with Marx's stress on dialectical truth will see in his theory a philosophy. Others who focus on logical truth will find enough texts to support their view that, in Marx, philosophy has no higher role than to codify the general conclusions of science. These and other tensions are partly due to his failure to engage in any sustained self-criticism, partly to the nature of his writings as responses to concrete situations and challenges. They may also be seen as proof of his greatness.

> "For all true thought remains open to more than one interpretation – and this because of its nature". (Martin Heidegger).

(Negations No. 3, July-September 1982; *Marx Beyond Marxism*, Chapter 2)

9

Man - A Dialectical Being

In the foregoing chapters, we have dealt with Marxian dialectic as a method of knowing. But, for Marx, the dialectic is not merely a method but also the law of being, being understood as the social-historical existence of humans. To fully grasp his interpretation of the dialectic of being it is necessary to study his philosophy in its entirety. Still a preliminary understanding is possible at this stage of our enquiry. I shall begin with a broad outline of the dialectical structure of human nature as Marx understood it. For this one has to draw heavily upon his early writings, especially the Economic and Philosophical Manuscripts of 1844. In these writings we find many profound insights and suggestions, which, however, Marx was never able to think through or systematize. Their language is markedly Hegelian which make them all the more difficult to read. One is confronted with a welter of ideas, often crisscrossing and seemingly contradictory. Nevertheless, one can discover in them Marx's basic philosophy of man, to which he, by and large, remained true throughout his life, despite certain discontinuities in emphasis and perspectives.

Traditional philosophy defined man as a rational animal, i.e. a member of the animal genus with the specific difference of rationality. For Marx, any attempt to define man is futile. To define something is to mark the bounds that set it off from other things. It means confining.

But man's being defies all limiting and confining. Paradoxically, what distinguishes the human from everything else is that it tends to flow into and merge with the whole of reality. Moreover, the concept of the rational animal is an abstraction. It knows neither birth nor growth nor death. It is eternal and immutable.

Such an abstraction does not interest Marx. His concern is with concrete men and women, who have their birth and death, who eat and mate, love and hate. They cannot be defined; can only be described. But how to describe the concrete human being? Not by enumerating his attributes or properties as one would describe a table in terms of its height, weight, colour, and shape. Properties reveal only the surface not the heart of things. Marx would rather see man as a historical being whose structure reveals a unity-in-tension of polar relations. He is being and knowing, the natural and the human, the individual and the social, the personal and the structural, the particular and the universal, freedom and necessity. Elucidating these polarities will give us an outline of the Marxian conception of man.

A Historical Being

Man is not a ready-made being given once and for all. He is a process, a being that becomes. And history is the story of his becoming, of his growing and maturing.[1] He creates himself in time, fashions his own future. At the heart of this process of self-creation is the power of negativity.[2] As a subject he first negates himself by bodying forth in his products. Products are the objectification of his subjective powers.[3] But in course of time the objects he creates come to dominate him from outside. They stifle his being, preventing the further development of his powers. Objectification thus takes on the character of alienation.[4] To grow to the full measure of his true essence, man must overcome all alienation. He must negate whatever negates - dehumanizes - him. This is the negation of negation. The passage through alienation is a necessary one. Man must first lose himself before he can find himself. First death, then resurrection.[5]

As a historical being, man lives at the point of intersection of the past, the present, and the future. From out of the possibilities offered by the past, he creates the future by acting upon the present. And the future to be created is himself in all his power and glory. For the Marxian man, life is not a luxury but a challenge to launch out into the unknown, a quest for his true visage. He is essentially an ethical being, straining toward what he ought to be. Historicity, understood in this sense, inheres in all the polarities that go to make up man.

Being and Knowing

Abstractly, whatever is, was, or even will be is a being. Of course men and women are beings in this sense. But this is not the sense in which Marx uses the term concerning man. For him man's being is his concrete, social-historical existence. As such, it forms a unity-in-tension with knowing (consciousness). Marx writes,

> "It is true that thought and being are distinct, but at the same time they are in unity with each other."[6]

They are in unity because thought is what makes man's being human. Of all beings he alone has the capacity not merely to know things but to know himself as knowing.

> "The animal is immediately one with its vital activity. It is not distinct from that activity; it is that activity. Man makes his vital activity an object of his will and consciousness. He has conscious vital activity... Conscious vital activity directly distinguishes man from animal vital activity."[7]

The unity of thought and being also flows from the content of thought itself. For what is thought but 'being' become aware of itself?

> "Consciousness (das Bewusstsein) can never be anything else than conscious being (das bewusste Sein), and the being of man is his actual life process."[8]

But thought is also distinct from being. In thought, man can overreach himself; go beyond the narrow bounds of concrete existence by projecting models yet to be realized in action. He can, in other words, envision what ought to be based on what is. In Capital we read,

> "A spider carries on operations resembling those of the weaver; and many a human architect is put to shame by the skill with which a bee constructs her cell. But what from the very first distinguishes the most incompetent architect from the best of bees, is that the architect has built a cell in his head before he constructs it in wax. The labour process ends in the creation of something which, when the process began, already existed in the worker's imagination, already existed in an ideal form."[9]

Thought places man in a situation of tension between the real and the ideal, between the *is* and the *ought*, between existence and essence.

According to Marx, "the being of man is his actual life process." And about this life process he asks further, "what is life but activity?"[10] To be is to act. Man does not first exist and then act. He is what he does and how he does it. His being is praxis. Likewise theory is but another word for knowing, whether elementary or systematized. Hence the polarity of being and knowing can be alternatively expressed as one between theory and praxis. In this sense, the dialectic of theory and practice is more than a method. It forms the dynamic structure of the human being.

Natural and Human

As one who emerged from nature, man is part of nature, a natural being. Everything in nature acts upon and is acted upon by everything else. This is true of man as well. He cannot be defined outside his relation to nature. It is in nature that he finds the objects for the exercise of his essential powers. There is no seeing without colour, no hearing without sound, no smelling without odour, no touch without surface, no hungering which is not for food, no thirsting which is not for drink. This his relation to nature is both actional and passional. As an active natural being, he effects changes in objects around. At the same time as "a natural, corporeal, sensuous, objective being, he is a suffering, conditioned and limited being, like animals and plants."[11]

But man is not only a natural being; he is a human natural being. But the human in him is the result of a process, the product of history. As immediately given, neither external nature nor his internal nature (his embodied sensuous existence) is adequate to his essence. Both have to be progressively humanized through praxis. Through practical activity, man moulds external nature to meet his needs, making its laws subserve his purposes. He gives it a new form and meaning, thus imbuing it with his spirit. Thereby he also develops new perceptions, needs and powers, becomes ever more human. Work is the process whereby man humanizes himself in humanizing the environment. The birth of the new man, therefore, coincides with the rebirth of nature.[12]

Individual and Social

If relatedness to nature is of the essence of man, much more so is relatedness to other human beings. Man's relation to nature includes his relation to other men. For, the other man too is part of nature. Like nature, he too is the object of my perception, need and action. But I relate to him not only as a natural being but also as a natural human being, as a being endowed with consciousness and freedom. The human in me speaks to the human in other persons. Not as though I first exist as a complete human being and then relate to other humans also, complete in themselves. I am, and become, human only through my relatedness to others.

> "The relationship of man to himself becomes objective and real only through his relationship to other men."[13]

What you are before your own eyes depends on the way other people look at you. It is their recognition that makes you aware you are a human being. In its deepest core your individuality is bound up with the society. Marx says,

> "It is above all necessary to avoid once more establishing 'society' as an abstraction over against the individual. The individual *is* the social being."[14]

This does not mean that Marx reduces society to individuals. It was not he but the old materialism of Feuerbach which saw society as a sum of competing individual monads. In his own view "the human essence is no abstraction inherent in each single individual. In its reality it is the *ensemble of social relations.*"[15] Still more unambiguously,

> "Since the essence of man is the true community of man, men, by activating their own essence, produce, create this human community."[16]

Humanness in its fullness resides only in the community; not in any single individual nor in the sum of individuals. Individuals and society form two poles, neither of which can be reduced to the other. The relation between the individual and society becomes estranged when either the individual is sacrificed to the collectivity as in earlier social formations and under totalitarianism or society is sacrificed to the individual as happens under capitalism.

Personal and Structured

Human beings act not only on nature but also on their fellowmen. Such action necessarily assumes clearly defined patterns. Thus come into being various structures. Of these the most basic, according to Marx, is the economic structure, i.e. the relatively stable pattern of production, circulation, and consumption of goods prevailing in any community. It is, in turn, made up of two substructures: productive forces and relations of production. Productive forces have to do with man's relation to nature. They are the forces men bring to bear on nature to produce the goods they need like food, clothing, housing and medicine. Relations of production, on the other hand, mean the relations established between human beings for carrying on material production. From out of the economic structure emerge political structures (i.e. the relations of power and the system of laws) and cultural systems such as science, morality, philosophy and religion. The closely-knit fabric of these structures forms the context into which every individual finds himself inserted from childhood onwards.[17]

As in the case of every other polarity constituting human existence, the relation between persons and structures is one of unity-in-tension: of unity because structures are like secondary organs each community fashions to cope with the challenge of meeting its varied needs, material and spiritual; of tension because, once established, they assume a certain autonomy *vis-a-vis* concrete individuals. Tension reaches the point of alienation when structures rule over men as alien forces or serve as instruments of domination in the hands of a few. Even under such conditions, individuals retain a minimum of resilience to fight the tyranny of the objective conditions that dehumanize them. The pre-history of human alienation will come to an end only with the victory of persons over structures.[18]

The Particular and the Universal

Each man is a *particular* human being chained to the here and the now. He comes of a particular family, born to particular parents. Particular too, is his physical and mental make-up. Each person has his own needs, temperament, abilities, character; is unique, unrepeatable. Particularity is a property of everything in the universe, animate or inanimate. But what distinguishes man from every other species is that he is potentially a *universal being*. Without losing his particularity, he tends to become co-extensive with all that is. First, with all nature. Through praxis and consciousness he incorporates nature in himself, making it his extension in time and space.

> "The universality of man manifests itself in practice, in that universality which makes the whole of nature his inorganic body."[19]

Similarly, he gathers the whole of humanity into himself. Each individual yearns to become all men.

> "Though each man is a particular individual – and it is just his particularity which makes him an individual, social being – he is equally the Totality, the ideal totality, the subjective existence of society as thought and experienced."[20]

Alienation here takes a twofold form. The individual can shrink back into the shell of his particularity, feeling alien in an alien world, incapable of communicating with the world around. Or he sacrifices his uniqueness to the rule of universals, to the stultifying law of the average. Before the State he becomes just a voter, before the law a mere citizen, in bus or train a ticket-holder, in school a number, in the hospital a bed.

Freedom and Necessity

Human beings are subject to a threefold necessity. To the *objective* necessity of the laws of nature which they can ignore only at the risk of their lives. Societal structures too determine their options and decisions. Add to this the *subjective* necessity of needs. People must eat, must sleep, must find shelter if they are to survive and reproduce themselves.[21] Finally, there is the *historical* necessity of alienation. Humanity cannot grow into its full measure without first falling from authentic existence. The road to man's universal essence runs through the wasteland of self-estrangement.[22]

Man, however, is not totally handed over to the rule of necessity. Determined from within and from without, he can also determine himself, to a degree even under conditions of alienation. Necessity and freedom are not absolutely opposed. In a sense, necessity is the condition for the possibility of freedom. Unlike Engels, who, following Hegel, held freedom to consist in the knowledge of necessity, Marx saw in freedom the ability men and women have to overcome necessity. And he roots this ability in consciousness. Man, he says, "is a conscious being, i.e. his own life is an object for him. Only because of this is his activity *free* activity."[23] As a conscious being he can act in freedom from physical needs and from the limits set by his own products.[24] Nor is he doomed to live with alienation. Central to the Marxian perspective is the possibility of creating a new society in which all conflicts will be definitively resolved.[25]

Conclusion

From the foregoing reflections it is clear that Marx's is a philosophy not of *either/or* but of *this and that*. In the polar relations we have highlighted no term will be reduced to, or eliminated by, the other. Even the socialist man will preserve his multi-faceted nature. He will be natural and human, individual and social, personal and structural, particular and universal, determined and free.

For this dialectical conception of man Marx is heavily indebted to Hegel who in turn had sought to incorporate in his system the entire wealth of philosophical reflection from the Greeks onwards. Marx aimed to supersede Hegelian idealism in the threefold sense of the term involving not only negating but also preserving and sublimating. He thus stands in continuity with the intellectual past of the west. This is his strength. Those who, out of misguided loyalty, try to project him as an entirely original thinker neither do him honour nor do justice to history.

With Marx, continuity with Hegelianism is also a source of weakness. As pointed out in a previous article, he considered only that theory to be true which originates and issues in correct praxis. But many of his fundamental insights are not derived from praxis but taken over from Hegel. Particularly so is the idea that history is governed by the dialectic of alienation and disalienation. By its very nature this cannot be verified in praxis. For, the definitive supersession of all alienation depends on the historical praxis of future generations, which is not available to us to be used here and now as a criterion of truth. The Marxian project of the Total Man awaits verification in the future. As such, it remains very much a matter of hope. Paradoxically, this weakness of Marx is at the same time his greatest strength. Men and women may sacrifice their lives to a hope; never to a set of 'clear and distinct ideas'.

The perspectives opened up by Marx provide the framework for a relevant philosophy for contemporary man. But they need to be rethought and completed in the light of the development of science and philosophy over the past hundred years. One area Marx all but ignored is the dialectic of the conscious and the unconscious brought to light by Freud and Jung. Also remains to be asked, Is not the polarity of the finite and the infinite, the relative-absolute, equally constitutive of man? Again, in reaction to Hegelian idealism Marx tended to unduly stress the objective as against the subjective, the structural as against the personal. Which explains the insufficient attention he paid to the problems of subjectivity such as death, despair, anxiety and loss of meaning. The need, therefore for dialogue between Marx and existentialism.

(Negations No. 4, Oct-Dec 1982; *Marx Beyond Marxism*, Chapter 3)

Alienation and the Dialectic of History

In the preceding chapter, I showed how, according to Marx, man is a tensional unity of multiple polarities. Here, I propose to deal with the dialectic as it works itself out in history. In the historical process, one can discern a twofold dialectical movement: One concerns the way men and women relate to the world around. They do so not haphazardly but in accordance with more or less well-defined patterns usually handed down by tradition. In other words, they relate to things and persons through the mediation of structures. Structures may be economic, political, or cultural. These become alienating when they hamper the development of the individual, instead of promoting it. Then comes the challenge to overthrow them and create new structures more conducive to the untrammeled growth of the human. Only through a revolution can disalienation be achieved. This entire process may be called the dialectic of alienation and disalienation. It has to do with the relation between the subject (human beings) and the object (nature, society), between man and structures.

The second dialectical movement concerns the manner in which the different levels of human activity (economic, political, and cultural) relate to one another. Here the focus is not on the relation between man and structures but on the relation between structures themselves. It is this latter dialectic that is meant when we speak of the materialistic conception of history. To use spatial terms, the first dialectical movement may be called horizontal, and the second vertical. The two, of course, are closely interrelated and condition one another, constituting but one dialectical movement of history. In the following pages, I shall confine myself to making some general observations on the dialectic of alienation and disalienation, deferring the materialistic conception of history for treatment in the next chapter.

The concept of alienation constitutes a nodal point in Marx's thinking. Its immediate roots go back to Hegel. In the Hegelian perspective, the ultimate principle and source of all that *is* and *could be* is the Idea. As the object of pure thought, the Idea can neither be seen nor touched. It is beyond all sense perception. But it can unfold its potentialities only by becoming other than what it is; that is, by becoming visible, tangible, audible, etc. And the Idea, become enfleshed and perceivable by the senses, is Nature. Nature is the Idea self-estranged, alienated. An analogy might help here. The concept of the house which the architect forms in his mind has itself neither length nor breadth can be neither seen nor touched. Not so once the house has been actually constructed according to plan. Then it occupies a definite point in space as an object of sense experience. A yet more appropriate illustration is provided by the Christian dogma of the Incarnation. According to it, the Word that was in the beginning with God, ineffable and invisible, becomes flesh in the person of Jesus. Jesus is the Word become other than itself, alienated.

Nature, the Idea made flesh, evolves from inorganic to organic matter, then to sensuous life, and finally emerges as Spirit in human beings. The Spirit too realizes itself by alienating itself in the external world–in the family, the state, organized religion, and art. History, for Hegel, is the onward march of the Spirit, alienating itself and overcoming the alienation. All self-estrangement is definitively left behind when the Spirit realizes that what it looks to be outside itself (family, state, God) is nothing but itself in its otherness, in its estranged existence. For Marx too, history is a process of alienation, but with the capital difference that with him, the subject that alienates itself is not the Idea but concrete human beings. There is yet another difference, equally basic, for an understanding of which we must return to the crucial distinction between objectification and alienation touched upon in an earlier article. The discussion will also throw light on the nature of alienation as an essential moment in the Marxian dialectic of history.

Work as Objectification

Man is endowed with different powers and drives. These he can develop only by working on the environment of things and persons. Through work, he fashions things in his own image. The potter, for instance, takes a lump of clay into his hands and moulds it into the shape he wants. The pot that comes into being under his creative touch reflects the powers that inhere in him as a human subject. Thus in every product of work what was subjective becomes objective. The product is the extension in time and space of the one who made it. In this sense, all work is self-objectification. For the same reason, it is a process of humanization. A park is more human than a jungle; for it embodies the intelligence and the aesthetic sense of those who worked at it. It is by thus objectifying themselves in the world that human beings let their subjective powers blossom out; it is by humanizing the environment that they humanize themselves.

No less than material goods are social structures the objectification of human subjects. The subjective attitudes, values, and beliefs of a community can best be read from the laws, customs, and institutions by means of which they relate to nature and to one another. In a still broader sense, even ordinary sense perception shares the character of objectification. My looking at the tree out there is, from Marx's point of view, an action whereby I constitute it into an object. By the mere fact of my perceiving it, I have conferred on it meaning and value, given it a name and a place in the universe. Looked at from this angle, there are no 'things in themselves', unrelated to man and related only to themselves. Marx says,

"Nature is nothing without man, it exists only as the object of seeing, touching, hearing thinking, willing, and deciding, on the part of human beings."[1]

In a primal sense, therefore, the world we live in is a human world if for no other reason than that we humans live in it. In relation to this primary humanization, activity in the ordinary sense of the term may be called secondary humanization.

From Objectification to Alienation

Objectification in the sense just explained belongs to the very essence of man. But not in all societies has his concrete existence conformed to his true essence. Under primitive communism when private property had not yet come into being, people could develop themselves as subjects by objectifying themselves through labour. But labour then was rudimentary due to the low development of productive forces. With the transition from tribal communism to the regime of private property, work as objectification became a process of alienation. From being a means of self-realization, it became an activity of self-mutilation, of self-castration. But how is it that private property brought in its train human alienation? An adequate discussion of the problem is possible only after we shall have dealt with economic alienation in detail. Provisionally one could say: Once the earth was parceled out as private property, the propertied began to appropriate the produce of the propertyless. The alienation of the product from the producer is the source of every other alienation.

In relation to primitive communism, the regime of private property may be seen as the antithesis. This phase has assumed different forms in the course of history. In Western Europe, it followed the sequence of slavery, feudalism, and capitalism. But Marx did not make the sequence valid for all peoples and nations. He admitted a certain pluralism of historical development. In regard to India, he held that the tribal mode of production was followed not by slavery but by what he called 'the Asiatic mode of production' in which property was held in common by local self-sufficient communities and the surplus was appropriated not by an exploiting class intervening between the people and the state but directly by the state itself. How far what Marx said about pre-capitalist India is true, is a moot question. Be that as it may, he would have argued that even the Asiatic mode had to pass over into some form or other of private property.

But private property is itself destined by its own internal contradictions – the main contradiction consisting in the fact that those who own do not work and those who work do not own – to give way to communism where the property will once again be owned in common. With the once and for all abolition of private property, all other alienations will disappear. As the young Marx wrote,

> "Communism is the positive supersession of private property as human self-estrangement, and hence the true appropriation of the human essence through and for man; it is the complete restoration of man to himself as a social, i.e. human, being, a restoration which has become conscious and which takes place within the entire wealth of previous development."[2]

Once the property is socialized, the product will belong to the producer. As the objectification of human powers, it will contribute to the progressive humanization of man. In the communist society objectification will continue but without ever becoming alienated.

Now, to return to the difference between Hegel and Marx: For the former all objectification is alienation. In other words, what dehumanizes man is the fact that objects exist outside him. For the latter, that man creates objects embodying his powers reveals not his poverty but his wealth and glory. Alienation arises only when the same objects are expropriated by others and, as such, dominate and enslave him. More, alienation is not co-extensive with work as Hegel thought but is found only in modes of production based on private property. It is therefore bound to vanish with the socialization of property.

Alienation is a necessary stage in the development of mankind. Not that it pertains to the essence of the human individual. Else it would be impossible to overcome it. And Marx envisioned communism as the true and definitive supersession of all alienation. The necessity of alienation, therefore, has to be understood in the dialectico-historical sense and applies only to humanity as a whole. Mankind cannot attain to the realm of freedom without passing through a period of universal bondage.

> "The effectual, active relation of man to himself specifically as a human being ... is only possible in so far as he effectively brings forth all his specific powers (which is only possible through the co-operative endeavours of mankind and as an outcome of history) and treats these powers as objects, *which can only be done at first in the form of alienation.*"[3]

Equally necessary is the historical supersession of alienation.

As historical concepts, objectification and alienation must be grasped as dialectically interlinked, forming a unity of opposites. Unity, because it is objectification that becomes alienated, there is no alienation without objectification; opposition because objectification humanizes man while alienation dehumanizes him. In the same way, the history of alienation and the new age of freedom that follows form continuity in discontinuity. There is continuity for the reason that the wealth created through objectification under the regime of private property will be carried over into the future; discontinuity, since the alienating conditions under which wealth was created will no longer exist in a communist society. For Marx, revolution is not annihilation but re-creation. That is why he can speak of the abolition of private property as a process that carries with it the wealth of all previous development.

Dimensions of Alienation

Alienation is embedded in the historical process and, as such, can best be studied in relation to specific modes of production in which property is owned privately. Marx's own analysis centred upon human estrangement under capitalism. It might, however, be useful at this stage of our investigation to indicate, at the risk of schematization, the many dimensions of meaning the term, alienation has.

Originally, the term referred to the act of alienating one's goods in favour of someone else by means of a deed of gift or sale. This meaning too is very much there in the writings of Marx. But for him, alienation means, above all, *the loss of the product* on the part of the producer. This has deeper implications than might appeal to the surface. For, the product, we have seen, is congealed labour and is part of the labourer's total being. Its loss, therefore, entails the mutilation of his essence. For the same reason, it means also *loss of wholeness* or, to use an expression very much in vogue among philosophers today, the demoralization of man. First, the loss of wholeness in relation to nature. The expropriation of the product ruptures the bond between man and nature. Add to this the loss of social wholeness, resulting from the fact that the product ceases to be the bond between human beings. Within the system of private property, whatever man produces becomes an instrument of division and exclusion.

Moreover, the product detaches from the producer, sets itself up in opposition to him; and, finally, dominates him from outside as an alien power. Consider the behaviour of commodities in the market. Whether they sell cheap or dear is no way determined by those who produced them. Alienation, therefore, involves *the loss of freedom.* Inherent in it is also conflict: conflict between the producers and the product, between producers and consumers, between the rulers and the ruled, between the teachers and the taught. These conflicts ultimately boil down to the conflict between man and nature, and between man and man. And conflict means *loss of harmony*, the loss of aesthetic wholeness.

Yet another dimension of alienation is reification, though it applies mainly to the capitalist mode of production. As commodity production increases, everything including human labour is reduced to exchange value, to money. In consequence, the relation between persons takes on the character of the relation between things. This is clear in every act of buying and selling where the buyer and the seller confront each other not as persons but as possessors of commodities, as representatives of exchange value. Reification in this sense amounts to the *loss of inter-subjectivity.*

Finally, alienation includes an element of mystification. The product, once it has installed itself as an external, hostile force, ends up by *appearing other than what it really is*. Private property, for example, is a product of history; but it appears as natural and eternal, as though flowing from the very essence of man. Similarly, capital which is nothing but a product of labour appears as the real producer, even of the labourer himself. All this results in false consciousness, in *loss of truth*.

Deprivation, mutilation, servitude, conflict, reification, mystification – all have to do with the negation of the human. But every negation is an affirmation. What is affirmed here is that men and women are truly human only when they appropriate what they produce, are whole in relation to the environing universe, determine themselves as free agents, live in harmony with nature and their kind, complete and enrich one another as persons, and are endowed with true consciousness. The concept of alienation, therefore, implies a notion of man's authentic being. Not that Marx believes in a predetermined human essence. Nor is he smuggling in an idealist notion of man through the backdoor, as it were. For what man is called to be is derived from the experience of alienation, an experience that is concrete, historical, verifiable. The *ought* inheres in the *is*; the essence discloses itself in what exists. It is this *ought* that makes Marx's thinking a humanism and an ethical philosophy. Hence it is understandable why those Marxists who repudiate the concept of alienation as a hangover from the idealist phase of Marx's development throw overboard all ethics and reduce Marxism to some kind of natural science. They fail to see that the dialectic of the *is* and the *ought*, of fact and value, of existence and essence, belongs to the core of Marxian thinking.

It is equally the concept of alienation that underpins Marxism as a philosophy of praxis. The experience of the contradiction between what *is* and what *ought to be* is charged with "the categorical imperative to overthrow all conditions in which man is a debased, enslaved, neglected and contemptible being."[4] The brute fact of alienation becomes in individuals the need to change the world. And the more radical the experience of alienation, the more radical is the need to eliminate it.

"A radical revolution can only be the revolution of radical needs."[5]

Alienation affects all levels of human activity: the production of material goods (economy), the production of power (politics), and the production of ideas (culture). In the subsequent chapters, we shall be taking up the different areas of alienation for detailed treatment. Meanwhile, it should be kept in mind that economic, political, and cultural alienations do not run along parallel lines but form a closely-knit system in which economic estrangement determines every other form of estrangement. Marx is convinced that "all human servitude is involved in the relation of the worker to production, and all types of servitude are only modifications or consequences of this relation."[6] Here we have already an early formulation, though couched in the language of alienation, of the materialistic conception of history, according to which "the mode of production of material life determines the general character of the social, political and spiritual processes of life."[7]

Comments & Questions

The concept of alienation is a theme Marxism shares with contemporary existentialism. Both Kierkegaard and Heidegger distinguish between authentic and inauthentic existence. Only he leads an authentic existence who, in freedom, determines himself, thus fathering his own future. Inauthentic are those who move with the anonymous, faceless crowd, going through the daily routine of life from the force of habit. Here existentialism rejoins Marxism which too sees all loss of self-determination on the part of man as estrangement.

Human estrangement forms an important theme in the religious tradition as well. In fact, the roots of Marxism go back via Hegel to the Judaeo-Christian world-view. The single most overriding concern of the Old Testament is with the alienation of man from God. There it finds mythical expression in the story of man's fall from God's favour and his expulsion from paradise. It re-echoes in the theological concept of sin. Estrangement from God carries with it estrangement from nature, society, and oneself. And the goal of the religious quest is a new creation without alienation, which includes the re-creation of social relations.

Similar views can be found also in the Indian tradition In the customary cyclic conception of history the succession of the four *yugas* denotes the progressive estrangement of humanity from an initial state of perfection (*krita-yuga*) culminating in an age of total misery (*kali-yuga*). The Buddhist *Digha Nikaya* describes the origin of the family, private property, and the state as the result of man's fall from a primordial state of pure bliss. *Vedanta* also implies a certain lapse on the part of man from the realm of transcendental truth to that of empirical truth.

It follows that the philosophy of Marx does not form a complete break with all previous thinking, but is heir to the sedimented wisdom of the ages. This fact alone is sufficient reason for us to take Marxism seriously, let alone the corroborative evidence coming from contemporary philosophy. If alienation figures prominently in religion, philosophy, literature, and art, it can only be because it expresses something fundamental to man's historical existence. And that fundamental truth is the recognition that it is in the essence of man to transcend his subjective and objective limitations and march ahead to the fullness of knowing, having and being.

The similarity between the religious and the Marxian conceptions of alienation should not obscure the profound differences between them. The first traces the source of all alienation either to the will of God or to human subjectivity, whether it is the finitude of freedom (Judaeo-Christian tradition), craving (Buddhism) or ignorance (*Vedanta*). The second sees the origin of all alienation in social structures, more precisely, in private property. For the one the most fundamental alienation is from God; for the other, the very notion of that estrangement is the summit of all alienation.

Let me conclude by raising a few problems regarding the Marxian theory of alienation which the reader will have to keep in mind in the course of this study. Marx highlights such alienations of the human subject as derived from perverted social structures. But are there not alienations at a deeper layer of human existence such as loss of meaning, despair, anxiety, sin, guilt, and, above all, death, which seem to be not reducible to objective structures but inherent in the human condition and experienced by all persons in all societies? Is Marx's claim that economic alienation is the birth-place of all other alienations historically verifiable? Did not man in tribal society already experience alienation, though private property had not yet arisen? Besides, how did economic alienation originate in the first place? If it was necessary for human development, would it not also apply to man in communist society? If it did, how is the supersession of all alienation possible? Will not the existential alienations just mentioned persist even after the communist revolution?

(Negations No. 6, April-June, 1983; *Marx Beyond Marxism*, Chapter 4)

The Materialist Conception of History

In the previous chapter, history was dealt with in terms of the dialectical relationship between man and structures. It was explained how, over time, structures become a source of human alienation, needing to be overthrown if human beings are to develop in freedom. Though the perspective of alienation and its overcoming is essential for an understanding of history, it alone is inadequate when it comes to explaining the complexities of the historical process. We must also take into account the dialectical interrelation between social structures themselves. However, the horizontal dialectic between persons and structures and the vertical dialectic between structures form not two but one single process. An example might illustrate the point. When I pedal my bicycle along the road, the pedal moves up and down in unison with my legs. The vertical movement, however, does not propel, me and the machine up into the air. Rather, it generates the horizontal movement. The latter, in turn, helps the former. In like manner, the dialectic of structures interacts with the dialectic of persons and structures to form the one forward movement of history.

It is both difficult and risky to undertake to summarize the Marxian conception of the interrelation between structures. Difficult, because Marx's thinking on this point is riddled with ambiguities and discordant emphases. Even after years of study, one is not sure which interpretation to follow. The task is also risky because one is forced to take a position in regard to Marx, partly or fully agreeing with him or totally rejecting him. In either case, one exposes oneself to attack from those who vehemently hold opposing views. The following interpretation seeks to highlight what is of positive value in the thought of Marx while at the same time showing up its weak points.

Typology of Structures

Structures consist in human practice in so far as it has congealed into more or less stable patterns. They are at once the result and the means of human action on the environment. Now, of all forms of human action the most basic is the one that seeks to produce the means of subsistence – food, housing, clothing, medicine, and so forth. In order to achieve this end, individuals must bring their physical and mental energies to bear on nature either directly or by means of instruments ranging from simple tools to sophisticated machines. In the course of time, the mode of producing one's means of livelihood becomes ossified into traditions that are then handed down from generation to generation. It is this dynamic relationship of human beings to nature that Marx meant by the term, *productive force*. Productive forces are not just a sum of things or items such as raw materials, instruments, and labour power (this latter including scientific and technical know-how).

But production is always a social process involving the co-operation of many. In carrying out the task of producing the means of subsistence, men and women have to enter into relations with one another. These relations of production lay down as to who controls labour power and the means of production and how the product is distributed. No production can take place except within the framework of such social relations. As Marx explains in "Wage-labour and Capital",

> "In the process of production, human beings do not only enter into a relation with nature. They produce only by working together in a specific manner and by reciprocally exchanging their activities. In order to produce, they enter into definite connections and relations with one another, and

only within these social connections and relations does their connection with nature, i.e. production, take place."[1]

The unity of productive forces and relations of production constitutes, for Marx, the economic structure of society. It is not correct to say that the economic structure is made up only of production relations and that productive forces are outside them.

Those who follow this interpretation appeal to Marx's statement in the "Preface to the Critique of Political Economy" that the "totality of these relations of production constitutes the economic structure of society."[2] But the relations here envisaged are those of production, having to do with control over productive forces and apportioning of the product. Besides, elsewhere Marx explicitly states that the "aggregate of the relations in which the agents of this production stand to nature (productive forces) and each other (relations of production), and within which they produce, is precisely society, considered from the point of view of its economic structure."[3]

Understood thus, the economic structure is the base of the social edifice as a whole. All non-economic institutions go to form the superstructure. Under this head come:

1. Political institutions such as civil and criminal law, legislature, judiciary and the bureaucracy,

2. Ideology, meaning forms of consciousness like morality, religion, art, and philosophy.

Here too Marx is not consistent in the use of terms. Sometimes he uses the *ideology* as a blanket term to include also politics, as he does in the famous *Preface* referred to above. I think it more appropriate to consider ideology and politics as two distinct levels of the superstructure, and I shall stick to that use in the articles that follow. Be that as it may, politics and ideology are as much the products of human activity as material goods. In one case the labour involved is mental (spiritual); in the other, material.[4]

The distinction between base and superstructure already contains in germ the materialist conception of history as it implies the primacy of the economic over every other domain of societal life. I shall now proceed to enlarge upon it by stating Marx's position in the form of a set of theses.

Thesis One
> "The economic structure is the real foundation on which legal and political superstructures arise and to which definite forms of social consciousness correspond. The mode of production of material life determines the general character of the social, political, and spiritual processes of life."[5]

Material production and mental production do not run on parallel lines but are "directly interwoven."[6] Now, two things can be interwoven without either enjoying primacy over the other. Hence the term does not tell us anything about the nature of the link involved. That the link is one of origination is clear from Marx's claim that all forms of mental production are "the direct efflux", "the ideological *reflexes and echoes*" of the material life process of individuals."[7] Politics and ideology spring from the structure of material production. If *B* originates from *A*, *A* naturally has primacy over *B*. Hence what is affirmed here is the derivative character of the superstructure in relation to the base. Being products of mental labour, political relations and ideology are different from the economy but bear the birthmarks of their origin in material production. In other words, what set of ideas and relations of power obtain in a society at any given time can be explained from the mode of production prevailing in that society. However, Marx is careful to add, not every detail but only "the general character" of the superstructure is determined by the economic base.

What does determine mean in our context? When I drop my paperweight on the bald head of my friend standing below, I determine the missile to act in a single direction. It falls pat on his benign scalp making him feel sensations that are anything but pleasant. My missile cannot act in any other direction. It cannot fly sideways or upwards. This is physical, unidirectional determination. Quite different is the determination which material conditions exercise over human beings. Here determination means limiting the range of options available to them. It does not mean imposing on them one single option. In a community, for instance, which produces little or no surplus, its members are not free to choose any form of government. Certain options are ruled out such as having a centralized state with a huge bureaucracy because there would be no surplus to maintain them. This does not imply that the economy dictates to the last detail the concrete mode of governing. The form of government chosen will also depend on the influence of other factors. It is in this latter sense, it seems to me, that Marx understands the determining influence of the economy. Of the materialist conception of history, he writes,

> "This does not prevent an economic basis, which, in its principal characteristics is the same, from manifesting infinite variations and gradations owing to the effect of innumerable external circumstances, climatic and geographical influences, racial peculiarities, historical influences from outside, etc. These variations can only be discovered by analyzing these empirically given circumstances."[8]

From the fact that superstructure springs from, and is shaped by, the economy, Marx draws the important conclusion:

> "Morality, religion, metaphysics, and all the rest of ideology as well as the forms of consciousness corresponding to these, thus no longer retain the semblance of independence. They have no history, no development."[9]

Thus, at one stroke, Marx demolishes the position of those who write histories of beliefs, religions and politics without ever caring to relate them to "the material premises of life."

Thesis Two
> "Within the economic structure itself productive forces enjoy primacy over relations of production."

The forces human beings release in order to transform nature and secure the means of livelihood are the source and the determinant of the social relations of production. This is consistently maintained by Marx both in his early and more mature writings: "production ...

presupposes the intercourse (= social relations) of individuals. The form of this intercourse is again *determined* by production."[10] "The aggregate of productive forces accessible to men determines the condition of society."[11] "The form of intercourse determined by the existing productive forces"[12], "the form of intercourse created by this mode of production" [13], "relations of production correspond to a definite stage in the development of their material powers of production."[14] "The form of this relation between masters and producers correspond to a definite stage in the development of the methods of work and consequently of the social productivity of labour."[15], "the (economic) relations and consequently the social, moral and political state of nations change with the change in the material powers of production."[16]

As may be seen from these and similar statements, the key to the understanding of the social system is to be sought in the nature and development of productive forces. In relation to these, even production relations are derivative, just as politics and culture are derivative in relation to the economic base.

Thesis Three

"1. The superstructure, once arisen, can react on the base, 2. In like manner, production relations react to the productive forces."

To begin with the latter part of the thesis, it is obvious that if productive forces create such production relations as are suited to their development, the latter favorably react to the former. Regarding the social relation of domination in class society, Marx says that it "emerges directly out of production itself and in its turn *reacts upon production.*"[17] In the same way, politics, and ideology which emerge from the economic base react on the latter. This finds the clearest formulation in *Theories of Surplus Value*:

> "Man himself is the basis of his material production, as of all products which he accomplishes. All circumstances, therefore, which affect man, the subject of production, have a greater or lesser influence upon all his functions and activities, including his functions and activities as the creator of material wealth, of commodities. In this sense, it can truly be

asserted that all human relations and functions however and wherever they manifest themselves, influence material production, and have a more or less *determining effect* on it."[18]

Since ideas and relations of power are part of the circumstances that affect man, it is clear that they determine his material production just as they are determined by it. This does not mean that Marx gives equal weightage to the action of the base and the superstructure. The determination from below is primary, while the one from above is secondary. In other words, it is the economy that determines the manner in which it is determined by the super-structure.

Thesis Four

> "What triggers off social change is the maturing of contradictions within the economic structure."

If material production determines politics and culture, will there not be perfect harmony in society and, consequently, no possibility of change? Marx's answer is that it is only at the initial stages when a social system has just arisen that equilibrium prevails. In the course of time, contradictions develop starting from the productive forces upwards. Here the dialectical conception of history comes to the fore. The movement of history follows the triadic rhythm of initial equilibrium, disturbed equilibrium or conflict, and the restoration of equilibrium on a higher plane. The following are the major types of contradictions listed in the order of their primacy.

1. Contradiction between productive forces and production relations: Productive forces tend to develop indefinitely as population increases and human needs multiply.

> "At a certain stage of their development, the material forces of production in society come in conflict with the existing relations of production or – what is but a legal expression for the same thing – with the property relations within which they had been at work before. From forms of development of the forces of production these relations turn into their fetters. Then occurs a period of social revolution."[19]

Marx saw the process at work in the breakup of slave and feudal society. Of feudalism, he wrote that, with the development of the then prevailing means of production and exchange, "the feudal relations of property became no longer compatible with the already developed productive forces; they became so many fetters. They had to be burst asunder; they were burst asunder." [20] The same contradiction reappears under capitalism. Here productive forces become ever more collective, ever more socialized, with the majority of people sinking to the ranks of the proletariat, while the means of production become concentrated in a few hands. This results in crises of overproduction, inflation, unemployment. At a certain point, "the monopoly of capital becomes a fetter upon the mode of production, which has sprung up and flourished along with, and under it."[21] Then sounds the death knell of capitalist property relations. In all these cases of social transformation, the contradiction between productive forces and production relations is something that generally takes place, as it were, behind the back of individuals; that is, it is not a consciously controlled process. Only in periods of economic crisis do people become aware of it. Though primarily an objective, unconscious process, this contradiction is the most potent factor of historical change. In the *Communist Manifesto*, Marx and Engels wrote:

> "For many a decade past, the history of industry and commerce is but the history of the revolt of modern productive forces against modern conditions of production, against the property relations that are the conditions for the existence of the bourgeoisie and its rule."[22]

2. Contradiction within the relations of production: What is meant here is the class antagonism between the direct producers and those who appropriate the surplus product, such as arises between slave and master, between serf and lord, between labourer and capitalist. This contradiction too is, at least initially, a merely objective process consisting of a conflict of interests of which the parties concerned may not be aware. Just as today in India many industrial workers think the interests of the bourgeoisie to be identical with their own, though in truth the two sets of interests collide. It is only gradually that workers become conscious of

their *true* interests as opposed to those of the bourgeoisie. Then begins a period of class struggle. The conflict between classes, however, is not something that runs parallel to the contradiction between productive forces and production relations but generated by the latter. For, according to Marx, "of all the instruments of production the greatest productive force is the revolutionary class itself."[23] Their development will sooner or later lead them to rise up against their exploiters. Hence the claim of the *Manifesto* that "the history of all hitherto existing society is the history of class struggles."[24]

3.   Contradiction between base and superstructure: After stating that the development of the productive forces reach a point where they disrupt the prevailing property relations, Marx continues,

> "With the change of the economic foundation the entire immense superstructure is more or less rapidly transformed."[25]

Put differently, the existing political relations and forms of consciousness become obsolete in the context of the changes that have taken place in the economy and they break up under pressure from below. There is, however, a difference between the changes occurring in the economic base and those on the level of the superstructure. The former are intelligible in themselves and "can be determined with the precision of natural science" while the latter "can only be explained from the contradictions of material life, from the existing conflict between the social forces of production and the relations of production."[26]

4.   Contradictions within the superstructure: Marx has never dwelt on this point at any length. *The German Ideology* states that contradictions within the economy can take on various 'subsidiary forms.' Under this head are grouped "contradictions of consciousness, battle of ideas, political struggle, etc."[27] Thinking further along the same lines, one could specify two kinds of contradictions in the superstructure: the one between political relations and ideologies, the other between conflicting ideologies themselves. The first is exemplified in contemporary India by the conflict between bourgeois democracy based on the *equality* of all citizens and the traditional caste culture of *inequality*; the second by

the conflict between traditional culture and capitalist culture. Be that as it may, contradictions on the level of politics and culture also react to those at the base so that prior to every revolutionary upheaval society seethes with multiple contradictions.

At this point in our exposition of the materialist conception of history, the question will naturally arise, if it is the economic structure that determines the course of history, where do human beings come in? Are they not superfluous, mere onlookers passively contemplating the march of history? The answer lies in the oft-forgotten Marxian thesis that follows.

Thesis Five
   "Man himself is the basis of his material production, as of all production he accomplishes."

True, Marx affirms, again and again, the independence of societal structures *vis-a-vis* human beings. In the famous *Preface*, he says, "in the social production which men carry on they enter into definite relations that are indispensable and *independent of their will*."[28] So too in the *German Ideology* Marx and Engels write that productive forces pass through "a peculiar series of phases and stages *independent of the will and the action of the will and the action of man*."[29] If such statements are taken in isolation, one could make out a case that Marx held a form of structural determinism, which relegates human subjects to the sidelines of history. But this independence, he attributes to economic structures, is in relation to particular individuals not to society as a whole. Once an economic system has come into being and has consolidated itself, it gains a certain permanence. Individuals come and go but the system remains. It might persist even when large sections of people are critical of it, unless dissent is organized into collective action. It is only in this, not in any absolute sense, that social structures are independent of individuals. For, Marx also affirms that people are the makers of structures. Productive forces are "the forces of individuals."[30] It is human beings who establish Production relations that accord with Productive forces.[31] These are not only preconditions but also results of human action,[32] partly handed down by tradition, and partly modified by each generation.[33] That Marx did not attribute any absolute autonomy to structures or structural processes, comes out still more clearly in the way he formulates the materialist conception of history. While there are statements to the effect that the base determines the superstructure, there are many others where the stress is on the creative, determining role of human subjects. Writes Marx:

> "Men are the producers of their conceptions, ideas, etc. that is, real, active men, as they are conditioned by a definite development of their Productive forces and of the intercourse corresponding to these, up to its furthest forms."[34]

This must be read in conjunction with those texts where Marx highlights the role of individuals as the creators of history. He writes,

> "The first premise of all human history is, of course, the existence of living human individuals."[35]

Elsewhere he says his aim is to show "men to be at the same time authors and actors of their own history," [36] that history "is nothing but the activity of men in pursuit of their ends."[37]

If these statements are taken seriously, the affirmation that the economy determines every other level of society needs to be qualified. The affirmation is true only if societal structures are taken abstractly and relative to one another; not true in any absolute sense. For all structures - economic, political, and cultural - are, in the end, products of human action. In absolute terms, what is primary are not structures but the human community. Hence the assertion that "man himself is the basis of his material production, as of all production he accomplishes". This accords with our earlier affirmation that, for Marx, the relation between human beings and the environment (nature, structures) is more fundamental than the relation between structures.

An Assessment

Marx's remains the most serious attempt made so far to understand the complexity of the historical process. His greatest contribution is to have shown that history cannot be understood purely in terms of the development of ideas or of the rise and fall of dynasties, without any reference to the economic life of people. He is correct in pointing out the determining effect of the economy on the general character of politics and ideas. The level of development of Productive forces and the nature of class relations that obtain at any given point in time do have a decisive impact on mental production. How futile, for instance, would it be to try to understand *Vedic* religion without taking into consideration primitive pastoral economy or *Tantrism*, without relating it to agricultural practice or the rise of *Saivism* and *Vaishnavism* ignoring caste struggles?

However sympathetically one goes through the writings of Marx, one cannot escape the conclusion that he has erred on the side of economic reductionism. The attempt to derive the superstructure from the base and Production relations from productive forces is likely to meet with resistance from the facts of history. For there is no element of the economy that does not already bear the stamp of definite forms of consciousness and political relations. The choice of the product, the manner in which production is carried out, and the human needs it is meant to satisfy, all are conditioned by culture. Likewise, Productive forces never exist except in the context of a given set of social relations. In other words, the economy that determines the superstructure is itself determined by the latter. The same holds true of Productive forces in respect of relations of production. What empirical observation can verify is reciprocal conditioning by the various domains of social life. However, the manner in which these domains react on one another is by no means uniform. The way economy determines society, is different from the way ideas determine it. The importance of the economy consists in the specific manner in which it shapes other levels of society, not in the fact that it alone is non-derivative, primordial. The materialist conception of history, therefore, should not be set up as a universally valid principle that explains everything. However, reinterpreted along the lines I have suggested, it can serve as a useful tool for the analysis and interpretation of social processes. The important thing is to bear in mind Marx's own warning:

> "Empirical observation must, in each particular case, show empirically, and without mystification or speculation, the connection of the social and political structure with production."[38]

Marx makes a distinction between material and mental (spiritual) production. He has extensively dealt with the former while the latter has scarcely been touched upon. Further reflection on the distinction just mentioned will help us better understand the limits of the materialist conception of history. What material production is, is evident enough. It is human activity geared to transforming nature and thereby procuring the goods people need. Not so easy it is to describe Spiritual production. Here are a few exploratory reflections.

Spiritual production can be twofold: communicative and ideational. (I prefer ideational to ideological as the latter term is often used in a derogatory sense). It is communicative when its object is not nature but other human beings. How do we act upon other persons? When I use force to make someone do what I will, I am not acting upon him in so far as he is a human being but treating him as a mere thing. (The use of force, of course, has been a key factor in the shaping of history. But, we shall leave it out of our purview in the present context.) I act upon him as a human being primarily through speech, understood broadly to include not only the spoken word but also gestures, symbols, and the language of silence. Now speaking is a spiritual activity as it consists of communicating meanings, sentiments, and attitudes. It is spiritual also because what it produces is ideas, sentiments, and, attitudes in the persons spoken to. Spiritual production in this sense is primordial to human beings. We are speaking animals and therefore, social animals. It is through the speech act that we produce social relations. These arise when the members of a community persuade themselves through the spoken word to relate to one another in a specific manner on a more or less permanent basis. The same applies to political relations. The spoken word, in fact, is the most powerful politically productive force.

Humans produce not only material goods and social relations but also ideas. They reflect on what they are and what they do, thereby discovering meanings and values. These they express "in the language, law, morality, religion, philosophy, and art." This is what I call ideational production as distinguished from material and communicative production. It too is a fundamental dimension of human existence, coextensive with the history of mankind. The three forms of production - material, communicative, ideational - differ from one another in terms of the mode of activity (labour, speech, thought, respectively), objects worked upon (things, persons, tradition, respectively) and the product (goods, social relations, ideas, respectively). At the same time, they are closely intertwined.

A little reflection will show that Spiritual production, whether communicative or ideational, is not only a prerequisite but also an inherent factor in material production. By Marx's own admission, human beings cannot engage in material production without projecting in imagination a model of the object desired.[39] But what is projecting a model if not ideation? Similarly, it is only within the framework of definite social relations that they produce material goods. And social relations, as we have seen, are the result of communicative action. This shows that it is not possible to think material production except in conjunction with Spiritual production. But the converse proposition need not be true. One can carry on Spiritual production without at the same time producing material goods. Here is proof that Spiritual production enjoys a certain autonomy in relation to economic life. Marxism has nothing to lose and everything to gain by recognizing the irreducible character and the relative autonomy of non-economic sectors of human life. One significant gain would be the rehabilitation of revolutionary praxis which is essentially communicative -ideational.

(Negations No. 7, July-September 1983; *Marx Beyond Marxism*, Chapter 5)

12

Indian Communism and the Challenge of Cultural Revolution

The Communist movement in India has a long history of popular struggles against exploitation, particularly in West Bengal, Kerala, and Andhra Pradesh. It can proudly point to the hundreds of comrades who have laid down their lives in the cause of the downtrodden and the disprivileged. In the States where it has struck roots, it has helped the labouring classes improve their material conditions and regain self-respect and human dignity. Significant too has been the role it played in bringing about progressive legislation in regard to land-reform, social security, and wages. More, it has greatly contributed to the birth of a people's literature in the various vernaculars. Its influence extends beyond the pale of Party membership to university and academic circles. In short, Communism undoubtedly is a political and cultural force to reckon with, at least where its presence is concentrated.

Nevertheless it is equally undeniable that the Communist movement has not fulfilled the hopes it had raised. It has failed to win the allegiance of the masses in rural India, and this not only in the Hindi speaking areas but also in the southern States, barring Kerala. Even in places like Telengana, where Indian Communism underwent its baptism of fire, there has been a steep decline in its influence. On the intellectual plane, it shows little vitality and creativity. It has made no original contribution to Marxist thought whether in the domain of the social sciences or philosophy. Whatever intellectual life there is within its ranks, is confined to defensive, apologetic responses either to attacks from bourgeois writers or to controversies going on between Communists of different persuasions. How to explain such theoretical sterility and sclerosis of praxis in spite of much unquestioned commitment to the cause of a classless society? How is it that Marxism has not developed into a national cultural movement that can provide an alternative to bourgeois modernity and casteist culture?

Any search for an answer must begin with a critical appraisal of the historical practice of Indian Communists over the last fifty years. It must then proceed to an examination of the theoretical assumptions underlying that practice. In other words, investigation must proceed from practice to Theory. This is the route I have followed, though my study of the Indian Communist movement has been by no means rigorous or exhaustive. In the course of my investigations, it became clear to me that certain theoretical assumptions have prevented Indian Communists from correctly interpreting the Indian reality and transforming it. In what follows I shall discuss some of those theoretical assumptions and try to show how they continue to inhibit, if not distort, Communist practice, particularly in the field of culture. There is, however, no simple causal link between Theory and practice as the latter can be influenced also by other factors, psychological as well as cultural. Hence my line of reasoning is hypothetical in character, subject to further revision and correction. The reflections I offer are to be taken as theoretical groping meant to provoke thought both among Indian Communists and those who are critically sympathetic to them (as the present writer is).

Here it is necessary to make a distinction between formal and operative Theory. An example might clarify the distinction. On the level of formal theorizing I may hold that the Hindu tradition contains negative as well as positive elements. But my actual practice might be based on the assumption that Hinduism is all evil. Here operative Theory represents a fall from formal Theory. In regard to Communism, formal Theory finds its formulation in the classics of Marxism and in the official documents of the Communist Parties. The operative Theory determining day to day practice may either conform to formal Theory or consciously deviate from it. The theoretical assumptions, I am going to discuss now, may belong to either category.

From Dialectic to Dualistic Thinking

As explicitly formulated in the Marxist classics, the dialectic means that all reality, social or natural, tends to generate its own opposite. The relationship between the originally given and the emerging opposite is one of unity in opposition. The ensuing struggle between the two is reconciled on a higher level which integrates the element of truth contained in both. Though Indian Marxists adhere to this understanding of the dialectic, their operative understanding reduces the dialectic to a form of dualism. In any dialectical polarity they seem to see only opposition and not unity. In other words, the opposition is seen in terms of formal rather than dialectical logic. In consequence the resolution of the opposition takes place not through any real synthesis but through the elimination of one term by the other. Thus the world is reduced to a sum of qualities: labour and capital, Materialism and idealism, science and religion. The terms of each couplet are seen as locked in a life-and-death struggle in which the first will inevitably vanquish the second.

This way of perceiving things dovetails with the militarist conception of revolution which Indian Communism has inherited from its insurrectionist past. In the long run it creates a paranoiac psycho-structure among Communists characterized by a compulsive search for, and fear of, one's class or ideological enemy. In this way Communism becomes assimilated to obscurantist religion with its dualisms of God and Satan, heaven and earth, the Sons of Light and the Sons of Darkness, believers and pagans, heaven and hell.

Such dualistic thinking may serve a pedagogical purpose in pre-revolutionary and revolutionary situations where it is necessary to rouse the fervour and militancy of the masses. But were it to become a culture within the Communist movement, it would stand in the way of any fruitful dialogue with opposing tendencies and philosophies. Communists will then fail to see the element of truth in world-views alien to it and in socio-cultural movements arising from other sources. They will also close their eyes to the errors and inadequacies in their own Theory and practice. The result will be sterility and stagnation. If Indian Communism has not assimilated the positive values of the Indian religious traditions and the insights of philosophies like *Advaita*, existentialism, phenomenology, and structuralism, it is possibly because within its ranks dualistic thinking has taken the place of genuine dialectical thinking. This of course, does not apply to every Communist thinker. At least in certain Marxist circles there is an awareness of the need for a positive approach to social sciences[1] and philosophies of non-Marxian inspiration, though the same openness is not shown to religious traditions.

From Humanism to Crass Materialism

Marx understood his philosophy as a synthesis of idealism (which affirmed the active nature of man) and Materialism (which saw man as passively contemplating the world). That is why he termed his philosophy 'fully developed humanism'[2], a humanism that affirms the plenitude of man's being, his free and full development. And it is in human society that Marx saw the working out of the dialectic. Understandably, it is there that dialogue, the root of all true dialectic, takes place, with its three moments of affirmation, negation, and the negation of negation. Engels then extended the dialectic to the realm of inorganic nature. From here it was but one step to the affirmation that the dialectical laws of nature determine social existence as well, or, more crudely, that nature determines the development of society.[3] Thus, by a curious turn of development, the humanism of Marx turned into a form of crass Materialism and the Marxian concept of the specific nature of man as a conscious, self-determining, self-transcending being, essentially different from animals and inorganic nature, was thrown overboard. Here too we see a relapse into dualistic thinking where Marxism as Materialism opposes itself to idealism, as though there is no truth in idealism which it could integrate within its own perspective.

This, at least operative, Theory of crass Materialism, rendered Marxism incapable of entering into dialogue with the Indian cultural tradition. Accustomed as they are to dualistic thinking, Marxist scholars tend to read the matter-spirit dichotomy into the very origins of our philosophical tradition. What they look for in the past, is their chief Ideological enemy of idealism and the ideologically which is Materialism.[4] Great is their joy when they read in the Upanishads that *Brahman* is food, *Brahman* is water, as such statements could be taken to mean that the original Indian thinking was materialistic and that it was only subsequently that it turned idealistic. Greater is still their enthusiasm when they find that there existed in India a fully developed system of Materialism called *Lokayata* which could provide a point of insertion for Marxism in India's past.

On the other side, they write off the entire religious tradition, including that of Buddhism, as idealistic. This whole exercise, Marx would have held in contempt as he had vehemently repudiated the kind of gross Materialism which, in fact, *Lokayata* is.[5] Under the spell of dualistic thinking, Marxists fail to look for the positive elements which the so-called idealistic tradition contains, with a view to integrating them and thereby creatively transcending them just as Marx creatively responded to the entire philosophical tradition from Aristotle to Hegel.

The dualistic bias has stood in the way of Marxists recognizing their Indian forerunners, chief among whom is the Buddha. Despite acosmic, quietist leanings, he anticipated some of the fundamental concerns of Karl Marx. Of all the Indian thinkers, he was the first to call upon man to be a lamp unto himself (Remember the saying of the founder of Marxism that man must move around himself as his own sun), the first to pose the problem of human alienation (though all too exclusively on the subjective level) in the context of the break-up of tribal society, the first to point out the economic basis of violence and social anarchy, the first to institute a radical critique of religion, ritualism and superstitions, the first to repudiate caste inequality and discrimination, the first to envision the disappearance of the State and project a future reign of justice.[6] To be fully at home in the Indian context, Marxists must insert themselves in the original teachings of the Buddha. They must also make their own the 'primitive' socialist motifs in our tribal heritage and in folk religions (the so-called 'little traditions').

Yet another baneful consequence of the materialistic bias is the glorification of science, modeled on the mathematical physical sciences dealing with quantifiable realities. Science, in this sense, is held up as the harbinger of progress and the savior of humanity. So much so that Marxism is itself reduced to a science.[7] This tendency may find justification in some one-sided formulations of Marx himself, such as that the role of philosophy is to codify the general results of the sciences.[8] In the process, it is forgotten that Marxism is not just a science but a total vision of man, nature, and history, that it is also an ethics and a philosophy of hope.[9] Those Marxists, who tend to reduce Marxism to a science, are in fact playing into the hands of the bourgeoisie. For, the science, they glorify, is no different from bourgeois science which capitalism has brought into existence in order to increase the productivity of labour. Besides, the scientization of Marxism makes it incapable of appealing to those in search of a global vision of reality and the ultimate meaning of life. If, nevertheless, Marxism continues to appeal to the youth, it is because in actual practice (on the level of operative Theory) it reinstates the element of faith and hope which its scientism denies.

The vulgar materialistic formulation that matter (nature) determines the spirit makes it impossible for Marxists to explain the phenomena of artistic creation. Following Lenin's Theory of reflection (which is but crass Materialism applied to cognition), they can, at the most, say that art must reflect the social reality. They can also investigate the class basis of artistic production. But, within the framework of the reflection theory of knowledge, they cannot understand the nature of art as a new creation that brings into being something unique and original and, as such, does not represent anything that already is. In order to grasp the meaning of art, one must leave the terrain of gross Materialism and recapture the original Marxian conception of man, as one whose creative imagination projects ever new models to be embodied in subsequent practice.[10]

The Architectural Model and the Downgrading of Culture

Orthodox Marxism holds that it is the economic structure that determines the superstructure, meaning politics and ideology. It is, of course, admitted that, once arisen, politics and ideology can react on the base. In this perspective, the economic base is primary while the superstructural realities are derivative, in any case, not equiprimordial with the base. Even this, to me, one-sided formulation can be a useful heuristic tool in the analysis of society. However, it can only reveal partial truth as it denies culture and politics the autonomy they enjoy. Further, by implying that changes in the base will automatically transform the superstructure, it devalues cultural action. Culture is seen as something hovering above economic life as though the latter is without any cultural component.

In reality, culture is an integral factor in economic production, inasmuch as the greatest of all Productive forces is the proletariat whose technical know-how, sense of values, and aesthetic sensibilities determine the quantity as well as the quality of the product. Similarly, the circulation and consumption of products presuppose appropriate needs, attitudes, and values in the mass of people. No entrepreneur will invest money in producing chewing gum or lipstick for villagers. That is why the transition from one mode of production to another is not possible without a prior cultural transformation. This holds true of political systems as well.

Bourgeois democracy, for instance, cannot function if people have not assimilated the notion of the equality of citizens and accepted the legitimacy of legislative, executive, and judicial institutions. If so, the transformation of the structures of production and power, in any society, is not possible without a critical minimum of change in \e consciousness of people. This is all the more so in a country like India where capitalism and bourgeois democracy, let alone socialist ideas, did not organically originate from the womb of tradition. If Indian Marxists id not face up to this challenge with the seriousness it deserved, one possible reason is their economic interpretation of culture.

The same interpretation acted as a break on cultural action also for another reason. Where culture is seen as privative, it tends to become no more than a means to action on the economic and political front, an instrument class struggle. This involves a distortion in one's assessment of culture. Cultural phenomena, like philosophy, ethics, art and literature, represent man's self-understanding and world-understanding at a given historical juncture. They are not things that man *has* but what he *is*,[11] a specific mode of being human. To reduce culture to an instrument of wealth or power is to degrade in himself to the level of a means to an end.[12] The estrangement of culture, is greater still when it is called on to legitimate not so much genuine proletarian struggle as the ever changing tactics of a vanguard party, its quest for power. Culture cannot be made to order even when the order were to emanate from a revolutionary party. Could this not be one reason, among many others, why the Communist parties have not been able to keep the loyalty of intellectuals and artists, why there is a dearth of creative thinking and cultural flowering within the Communist movement?

Indian Marxists, in their preoccupation with objective social structures, seem to forget that structures are but the stable patterns according to which human subjects relate to one another. They seem to assume that, in the development of society, structures and their interaction mean everything and human persons mean nothing, as though the latter are no more than mere by-products of social processes.[13] Even eminent personalities of history are seen as mere products of their times, and this in spite of Marx's own clear assertion that if circumstances make man it is no less true that it is man who makes circumstances. Here is another instance of dichotomic thinking which opts for one term of a polarity (structure) into which the other (person) is absorbed. What this amounts to is a denial of the freedom of man. Or, more precisely, Marx's concept of freedom as the conquest of necessity is replaced by Engel's (Hegelian) notion of freedom as the recognition of necessity. True, the material conditions of life provide man with the possibilities for action, but it is far from true that they predetermine him to choose any one possibility against the others. In fact, it is in the freedom of man that Marx locates the source of aesthetic creation, i.e. production that is its own end, that is not determined by needs.[14] The same is true of all cultural production. It is not structures that formulate theories and philosophies, set norms and goals of action, and construct models for the future. These are the work of human subjects struggling to transcend themselves and their conditions of existence. And freedom as self-transcendence is founded in human subjectivity. Because Marxists tend to ignore the problems of subjectivity, they have little to say on the specificity of cultural production. For the same reason, they have little sympathy for literary men who deal with problems of ennui and despair and sin and guilt and death, and label them apologists of bourgeois individualism.

The Class Interpretation of History

The *Communist Manifesto* opens with the words,

> "The history of all hitherto existing society is the history of class struggles."

This is a variant formulation, this time in terms of the relations of production, of the materialist conception of history. It is also the one most commonly appealed to by Marxists. Admittedly, no one will deny the role of class struggle in history. But, when it is projected as the only key to the understanding of historical processes or is crudely interpreted, it can distort one's analysis of concrete situations and frustrate the attempt to formulate a correct strategy of action.

Marx made a crucial distinction between *class-in-itself* and *class-for-itself*. Class-in-itself is class defined objectively to mean all those who share the same position in the mode of production. Class-for-itself is class defined subjectively, to mean those who, besides sharing the same position in the mode of production, are also conscious of their interests as opposed to the interests of other classes and organize themselves for struggle.[15] Only in proportion as the proletariat becomes a class-for-itself, can it become an agent of socialist revolution. This is a historical process to be brought about through planned human intervention and not just a product of objective social factors. Indian Marxists tend to see the development of class consciousness as a necessary process. What is more, what they think will necessarily happen is seen as already realized, thus wishing the possible into the actual. From the official documents of Communist Party of India (Marxist), CPI(M), for instance, one would get the impression that the working class in India is already charged with revolutionary consciousness. The same consciousness is also attributed to people as a whole.[16] This is the language of triumphalism, which is the reverse side of fatalism. Thus, by a curious reversal, preoccupation with objective necessary processes passes over into its opposite, a subjective interpretation of historical reality, which cannot stand the test of empirical observation. The proletariat as a class-in-itself may, and often does, develop not revolutionary but reformist consciousness. This is because the economic and political structures, within which human beings function, have a tendency to create in them a psycho-structure suited to the reproduction of the same structures, so much so that the proletariat begins to think that its own interests coincide with those of the bourgeoisie. In other words, the working class lets itself be integrated into the culture organic to capitalism and bourgeois democracy. This process is further reinforced by the systematic manipulation of consciousness carried on by the media and the educational system.

There is then no necessary, unilinear development from *class-in-itself* to *class-for-itself*. All that can be reasonably argued is that, if the proletariat becomes conscious of its true interests, it can play a greater role than any other class in overthrowing capitalism, since it constitutes the main productive force and can be more easily organized. The vanguard role of the working class is conditional not absolute. The tendency to argue from objective class position to subjective class consciousness has also led Marxists to maligning the petit bourgeoisie. As a class that both engages in labour and employs wage labour, it is represented as vacillating, opportunistic, now siding with the bourgeoisie, now with the proletariat. There is some truth in this assessment. But, it is by no means the whole truth. For, class position itself can make the petit-bourgeoisie more susceptible to revolutionary ideas than than any other class. Engaged as they are in productive labour, the petit bourgeoisie have some experience of the human alienation inherent in commodity production. Besides, they enjoy a certain economic independence from the bourgeoisie and a minimum of leisure and access to education which enables them to address themselves to the contradictions of society. In fact, they have played a significant role in all twentieth century revolutions including the Indian Independence Movement. Lenin was indirectly saying the same thing when he said that, the proletariat can acquire revolutionary consciousness only from outside,[17] i.e. through the mediation of the party of revolution whose members are generally of petit bourgeois origin. In fact, does not this class form the bulk of the membership of the Indian Communist parties and their front organizations?[18] If so, neither is the petit bourgeoisie necessarily vacillating nor is the proletariat consistently revolutionary. Here too, the weakness of Indian Marxists consists in not testing the classical formulations of Marxism against empirical investigation.

Here, it is useful to distinguish between the immediate, corporate interests and the long-term, real interests of the various classes. The immediate interest of each class is to safeguard its respective rights within the status quo. This is true also of the proletariat. Its immediate interest consists in security of employment, higher wages and better working conditions. Marx's statement that the working class has no particular interest to safeguard, does not fully reflect social reality particularly in India, where even a low paid regular job marks a definite economic advancement. The real, objective interest of the working class however is to overthrow the capitalist system itself, which had deprived them of the conditions of their labour. This real interest coincides with the genuine long-term interests of all other classes, including the bourgeoisie. For these too can realize their full and free development only in a genuinely socialist society. It is this convergence of real interests of all classes that makes it possible for the members of the non-proletarian classes to attain to revolutionary consciousness. Whether this possibility will ever become a reality depends not only on objective crises in the system but also on the historical initiative of critical intellectuals and the Parties of revolution using all the cultural means available to bring about the hegemony of socialist ideology. This means, further, that the working class can be said to have acquired genuine revolutionary consciousness only when it seeks to liberate not only itself but also all other classes.[19] In other words, it must develop a universal consciousness as opposed to merely trade-union, corporate consciousness. Class struggle, therefore, is directed against the capitalist system, not against individual capitalists or the petit bourgeoisie. It follows then that when we take seriously the cultural definition of classes and the cultural prerequisites of the struggle for socialism, the stereotype pitting of one class against another on the basis solely of their objective role in production, proves inadequate and misleading.

The tendency to look at society exclusively in terms of class has led the Communist parties to neglect many important terrains of social struggle within the pale of 'civil society' as redefined by Gramsci [20] to mean all institutions of a private character demarcated on the one hand, from economic and, on the other, from state-political institutions. Such are the family, the caste, the temple (church, mosque), the school, the political parties and the media. To these may be added organizations representing the interests of specific strata in society like women, the youth, the unemployed, and the intellectuals. These institutions and organizations are not directly related to the production of goods or to the production of law and order. Nevertheless they fulfill an essential role in producing the kind of human subjects necessary for the capitalist system (workers, engineers, executives, technicians) and for bourgeois democracy (government officials, parliamentarians, judges, policemen, army men and citizens). At the same time, they enjoy a certain autonomy in relation to the economic and state-political sectors.

They produce human subjects in so far as they instill in individuals from childhood onwards the kind of reflexes, attitudes, values, and ideas without which the social system cannot be reproduced. Hence no social revolution is possible without radically transforming these institutions and organizations in such wise that they become vehicles of a counter-culture. Unfortunately, the Communist Parties have not seriously addressed themselves to this task, largely because they have not realized the importance of the psychological, cultural preconditions for social revolution . The only area of civil society where they are active is that of political parties.

They have, of course, their own front organizations for women, youth and students, but they tend to be assigned a supportive role in relation to electoral politics and trade-union work as may be judged from their failure to project a youth culture or a sexual humanism superior to the traditional and the bourgeois. Indian Communists have yet to come out with any serious critique of the educational system, let alone formulating an alternative model. Even their criticism of religion and caste, is on a low key though it is very much on their agenda. This is all the more unfortunate since caste and religion are responsible for neutralizing class consciousness among the exploited sections and thereby undermining class struggle itself.

The struggle for socialism, then, must extend beyond class struggle whether on the economic or political front to the various sectors of 'civil society'. It is only the conjuncture of, and interaction between, multiple struggles - of the working class against the bourgeoisie, of people against the bureaucracy, of women against male domination, of the youth against gerontocracy, of students against the educational system, of intellectuals against curbs on freedom of expression, of critical believers against religious obscurantism, of the Harijans against caste discrimination, of the tribals against Hinduization and bourgeoisification and so on - that will usher in a socialist revolution. Nor need all struggles be led by the Communists. There will be many that draw inspiration from sources other than Marxism such as Gandhism, religion and folk tradition.

Tactics Versus Strategy

If Indian Communists have not met the challenge of cultural revolution, it is due not only to their class-reductionism but also to certain theoretical premises which distorted their reading of the Indian situation. Chief among them is the two-stage theory of revolution, which holds that the bourgeois-democratic revolution - revolution against imperialism and feudalism and for the independent growth of capitalism - must be completed before socialist revolution can be accomplished. Underlying the theory is the more general premise that "no social order ever disappears before all the Productive forces for which there is room in it have been developed."[21] Though it was Marx who formulated this principle, he was careful not to invest it with universal validity for all peoples. He was critical of those who tried to "metamorphose my historical sketch of the genesis of capitalism in Western Europe into a historic-philosophic theory of the general path, every people is fated to tread, whatever the historical circumstances in which it finds itself, in order that it may ultimately arrive at the form of economy which ensures, together with the greatest expansion of the productive powers of social labour, the most complete development of man. But I beg his pardon. (He is both honouring me and shaming me too much.)"[22] This was sufficient warning to the Indian Communists to chalk out their own path of transition to socialism . But dogma prevailed. And reality was made to fall in line with it.

Be that as it may, having committed themselves to the two-stage theory of revolution, Indian Communists (Here I confine myself to the CPI(M) came to the assessment that the Indian government cannot complete the bourgeois-democratic revolution and, consequently, it was necessary to replace it with a popular democratic one, based on the alliance of the working class with the petit-bourgeoisie, the peasantry small, middle as well as rich, and non-monopoly bourgeoisie. That this reading did not conform to the Indian reality has been ably demonstrated in a recent study by Bipan Chandra.[23] My concern here is limited to showing how the self-imposed task of completing the bourgeois-democratic revolution has condemned Indian Communism to cultural impotence.

The very first lesson that every communist learns is that capitalism is essentially exploitative and dehumanizing. But now he is told that his target of attack is not capitalism as such but monopoly capitalism which is in league with imperialism. This itself is enough to confuse any-Communist worker. For, is it not in the Essence of capitalism to turn monopolistic and be integrated into international capitalism? Is not promoting national capitalism, while opposing its monopolistic development as meaningless, an exercise as willing the tree and not wanting its fruits? More importantly, will not such a policy involve succumbing to the culture organic to capitalism -the culture of private interest, competition, aggressiveness, consumerism and the monetization of human values? Here lies the reason why, despite their avowed opposition to bourgeois culture,[24] Indian Communists are unable to form a cultural front against it, why they have not taken any initiative in mobilizing public opinion against 'the cult of violence in films, the commoditization of sex by advertising agencies, the use of the media for commercial advertising, the engineering of consciousness for partisan ends, the glorification of bourgeois legality, and the degrading of votes, voters, and elected representatives into marketable items.

Have Indian Communists at least put up a cultural front against traditional culture? Struggle against the remnants of 'feudal' relations of production and against caste and religious obscurantism, is very much on their agenda. It is also a fact that Communist presence has helped weaken the hold of caste in states where they are a decisive political force. However, since the switch-over to electoral politics, there has been, it seems to me, a weakening of the radical stance against traditional culture. This is understandable, since the constraints of electoral politics call for compromises with casteist and communal forces. How can the Communist Parties organize an all out onslaught on caste, so long as they look upon the rich capitalist peasants as a progressive force and as possible allies in the fight against feudalism and imperialism, though the latter are as much steeped in caste culture as traditional peasants? This is particularly the case in places where the leadership of the local Communist Party and of its peasant organization comes from the intermediate castes who are today the main oppressors of the Harijans.

The lesson is clear. Within the framework of the tactical alliances in view of establishing a People's (National) Democracy it is not possible for Communists to initiate the cultural revolution the country needs.

Further, where tactics enjoys primacy over strategy, Marxism ceases to be an ethical philosophy and becomes an ideology in the derogative sense of the term. The recognition on the part of Marx that Capitalism is alienating, carried with it "the categorical imperative" to overthrow it and create a new social order in which human beings will exercise control over the economy, be subject to no structure over and above them in the form of a state, and be free to think their own thoughts and dream their own dreams. It is this goal of a humanized world that confers legitimacy on all subversive-constructive action. Whatever contributes to the birth of the new society of free and fully developed individuals, is necessarily moral. This is what makes Marxism, pre-eminently, an ethical theory. But it ceases to be so when the place of the final goal is taken by immediate ends which have no causal link with that goal or might even impede its realization. Violence, intimidation, money-power, demagogy, and false electoral promises, might prove effective in securing votes but may in no way contribute to the creation of a classless society. Though the Indian Communist Parties are more principled in their politics than any other Party, with the adoption of the immediate goal of People's (National) Democracy, they have sacrificed their original ethical grandeur to politics of expediency. In the bargain, they have also lost their appeal to the idealism of the youth.

Dictatorship or Socialism

The completion of the bourgeois-democratic revolution will signal the beginning of the socialist revolution, aimed at overthrowing capitalism and ushering in a transitional stage when the proletariat (the majority of people) will exercise coercion over the bourgeoisie (the minority). In further defining the dictatorship of the proletariat, the founders of Marxism used the Paris Commune of 1871 as model, which "Sought to realize the primacy of direct over indirect democracy, made the elected representative responsible to, and revocable by, the electorate, replaced the standing army with a people's militia, decreed equal wages for all government servants from the highest to the lowest.[24] Barring the notion of the post-revolutionary use of coercion against the bourgeoisie, what is envisaged here is dictatorship of the proletariat with a human face.

But what actually came into being in the Soviet Union, in the wake of the October revolution, was a monstrous distortion of it. What was to be dictatorship of the proletariat over a recalcitrant bourgeois minority, became the dictatorship of the Party over the proletariat and, eventually, of one man (Stalin) over the Party and the people as a whole.[26] Though private property, and with it capitalism, was abolished, under the new dispensation all genuine democratic institutions were neutralized, and the masses depoliticized into mere providers of passive information while all active decisions were vested in the higher echelons of the Party bureaucracy - all of which resulted in the emergence of a privileged ruling stratum with a vested interest in maintaining the status quo of institutionalized repression.[27]

To say that all this was due to personality cult or to the paranoiac psychos of a Stalin is but deluding the public. What is called for is identifying the historical-structural causes and the theoretical promises that gave rise to Stalinism - the cultural backwardness of the Soviet Union, the reincarnation of the Czarist bureaucracy as Soviet bureaucracy, the requirements of primitive socialist accumulation, the inevitable militarization of the Party in the context of civil war and external aggression, the notion that the proletariat must first capture power (political revolution) and then proceed to the task of social revolution, and the Leninist idea of the Party as the sole bearer of revolutionary consciousness. An adequate understanding of these factors would have helped Indian Communists evolve an original, indigenous strategy of socialist reconstruction. Instead, large sections of Indian Communists have been half-hearted and ambivalent in their criticism of the Soviet experiment. While, rightly, rejecting the insurrectionist strategy of revolution, they still hold on to the theoretical premises, which led to the Stalinist distortion. The Communist movement has everything to gain and nothing to lose by radically revising the notion of the dictatorship of the proletariat. It is to be recognized that, for a revolution to be truly socialist, it must be accomplished by the people and not for the people by any political party, that state political revolution must come as the culminating point of a long process of social and cultural revolution, that the post-revolutionary regime must be seen as the radicalization of bourgeois democracy and not its negation. Then, the question of coercion against the bourgeoisie after the revolution becomes irrelevant. In this perspective, the term, dictatorship of the proletariat, loses all theoretical legitimation,[28] as has been recognized by a number of Communist Parties elsewhere. Such a thoroughgoing self-criticism on the part of the Communist Parties will, at one stroke, remove the psychic barrier separating them from the intellectuals and the masses. It will, likewise, enhance the democratic credibility of the Communist movement and enable it to enter into creative dialogue with the Gandhian tradition and the emerging radical wing among believers, and articulate itself with all progressive cultural forces in the country.

An Ersatz Religion?

The concept of revolution in stages, each of which is meant to be a qualitative lead, involves relegating the goal of a classless society (which I, following the practice of Marx, refer to, interchangeably, as socialism or Communism) to an indefinite future. As the relevance of any one stage for realizing the final goal is problematic, for all practical purposes, that goal lapses into mythical, meta-historical time. It thus acquires the character of an object of religious hope, somewhat like the notion of heaven in traditional religions. In this way, what was a secular project becomes a quasi-religious extrapolation. Since the goal does not directly determine contemporary practice, the former tends to become but another opiate of the masses. The mythicization of the goal brings about, also, a corresponding change in the self-awareness of the Party. It splits into two selves - one secular; the other quasi-religious. In actual fact, the Party may have only a limited following and may be very much localized. But, in its mythical self-awareness, it transcends all limits and extends to gigantic proportions. One is reminded of the theophanies of the *Puranas* as when Siva's severed *linga* suddenly grew into cosmic proportions, reaching up to the heavens above and the primal waters below. Similarly, in the consciousness of Communists, the Party becomes co-extensive with the proletariat, then with all left and democratic forces and, finally, with the oppressed people all over the world. With that, the Party assumes the character of an Absolute, the defense of which is equated with the defense of all that is good and true on earth. This, in turn, generates a quasi-religious attitude to the Party, its leaders, and their teachings. More, there sets in a process of the ritualization of revolution, as though by way of compensation for the reformism of actual practice. Demonstrations, slogan-shouting, strikes, electioneering - all takes on a double meaning, one instrumental and the other ritual-symbolic. Simultaneously, there emerges within Party ranks a sectarian language - which delight in polemics, apologetic, labeling, anathematizing and triumphalism. This is how Parties become churches, each with its own hierarchy, magisterium, dogmas, rites of initiation and excommunication. Such estrangement of Communism, into a pseudo-religion, can be overcome only when the link between present practice and future goal (socialism) is restored, that is, when the challenge of socialist revolution is taken up right earnestly.

Our analysis shows how certain theoretical premises, uncritically accepted, gave birth to a Communist practice which could not creatively respond to the socio-cultural challenges posed by the Indian situation. Once this truncated practice got routinized, it, in turn, served to legitimize the theory that inspired it. Thus theory and practice tended to reinforce each other, forming aninvoluted circular movement incapable of becoming spiral-dialectical.[29]

A breakthrough from out of this incestuous circularity to a genuinely revolutionary Marxism is not likely to come from the side of practice. For, partisan practice of a certain type creates, over time, vested interests in its own reproduction. The breakthrough has to take place on the plane of theory. The time has come for Marxist intellectuals to squarely face the challenge of subjecting their theoretical assumptions, including those coming from the founders of Marxism, to a ruthless critique in the light of their historical experience and with reference to the contemporary Indian cultural situation. The choice before them is - change or stagnate!

(Negations No. 13, January–March 1985; *Marx Beyond Marxism*, Chapter 6)

13

The Goals of Revolution

Where there exist oppressive structures of exploitation, revolution becomes a moral task. As such it derives its justification primarily from its goal. Freedom *from* oppression must become freedom *for* the fullness of being. Else it is empty and may give rise to newer forms of servitude. Moreover, it is only in light of the goal that a suitable methodology of revolution can be worked out. The methods must be such as to create the necessary pre-conditions for the new society to be ushered in. Where they are out of harmony with the end in view the latter remains a utopian dream. Hence the relevance of this paper on the goals of social revolution in India. Here a few preliminary reflections on revolution, in general, may be found useful.

What is Revolution?

Revolution may be described as the radical and rapid transformation of a social system into a new one more in harmony with the dignity and the true destiny of man. By 'social system' we mean the complex of actional and value structures. Actional structures refer to patterns of social behaviour that are relatively permanent and more or less organized. These have their motivational support in the corresponding system of values, i.e. differentially ranked objects of socially conditioned desire. The transformation of actional structures, therefore, is conditional upon and accompanied by a change in value structures. Since the values prevalent in any given society reflect the self-understanding of man, their mutation implies also a mutation in the human potential. In other words, in changing the structures of society, man changes his own being and consciousness. It is this coincidence of the transformation by man of the environment and his own self-transformation which for Karl Marx constituted the core of revolutionary practice.[1]

To be termed revolutionary, the intended transformation has to be radical. In other words, what is aimed at is a change not merely *in* the social system but *of* the system. For instance, a mere increase in wages would not constitute a revolutionary change in the capitalist system. It would only be a reform within the system. Not so if a qualitative change in the form of adequate worker participation in ownership and management is effected. For, in this case, the change is disruptive to the system. Besides the element of radicalism, revolution implies also the element of rapidity. The rapidity in question is up to a point conditional upon the presence of objective factors like the development of the media of communication, the extent of the socialization and organization of the masses, etc. But more decisive are the subjective factors related to consciousness and freedom. The objective need for revolution must become also a subjective (felt) need. The intensity with which society experiences the conflict between the existing social system and its own emergent self-understanding largely determines the speed of change. What is crucial here is the role of the elite who give articulate expression to the inarticulate aspirations of the masses. Revolution, therefore, is not something that happens to society as a result merely of the confluence of socio-historical forces but is a process consciously and deliberately initiated by man.

Revolution as a social process engineered by the historical initiative of man is never an end in itself. It is essentially oriented to the realization of a new social goal, to the creation of a society in which man can be more fully man. The definition of this goal cannot be left to phantasy or merely to creative imagination. It must be based on a method that would do justice to the total destiny of the human community. What follows is a tentative approach to the formulation of such a method.

Defining Goals: A Heuristic Analysis

Goal Horizons

The experience of a revolutionary situation is essentially prospective. Rooted in the present it projects into the future horizons of the possible. An analogy taken from the interpersonal relationship may prove illuminative. When a boy and girl are in love, their experience has an inner core of joy and communion in the present. But the present is not experienced as rounded off and complete in itself. Rather it tends to the future, to what is *not-yet* but is hoped for. It projects a triple horizon: First there is the horizon of the immediate future in the form, perhaps, of a subsequent rendezvous. But beyond the immediately possible, they also look forward to the day when they will get married, have a home and settle down in life. This we might call the mediate horizon of their love. The prospectiveness of their love does not stop even here. Embedded in the experience of the present, is the dimension of fullness (I am *all* yours) and of eternity (I am *for ever* yours). This forms the ultimate horizon of their love. The mediate and the ultimate horizons are not deduced from the actually experienced but are co-given in the original expedience itself. The future is already immanent in the present; the present contains in germ the contours of the future. We find a similar horizontal structure also in the experience society has of a revolutionary situation.

The proximate goal-horizon of revolution is what can and should be realized in the not distant future to redress the evils of the existing system. In concrete, it coincides with the overthrowing of the oppressive power structures. But this by itself does not exhaust the inner dynamism of revolutionary consciousness. One pulls down in order to build up, uproots in order to plant. The abolition of an existing system is viewed as the necessary condition for the creation of a new social order in which man will come to his own as the maker of history. This forms the *mediate goal* of revolution. Implicit in the collective urge to create a new society is also the horizon of the *ultimate goal* conceived in terms of the total perfection of the human community, freed not only from the fact but also from the possibility of alienation. Here we have the teleological dimension of revolution.

The ultimate goal conceived as integral and indefectible humanization is not something added to the revolution from outside. It is immanent in the logic of the revolution itself. For it is precisely the hope in the absolute future that can adequately explain the unconditional character of the ethical imperative calling for revolutionary commitment. It is implicitly and existentially affirmed even by those who in theory deny its validity, in so far as even they affirm the absolute value of man as an end in himself. Far from diverting him from his task here and now, the vision, however vague, of an ultimate goal goads man on to action and invests his sacrifices with meaning and value. It is significant that even the Marxian conception of revolution implies belief in an ultimate goal. For Marx conceives the communist society as the *definitive* resolution of the antagonism between man and nature, and between man and man.[2] This means transcending not only the fact but also of the possibility of alienation. In this sense, the classless society is a properly religious concept and is the object of religious hope. The absoluteness, however, of this goal is compromised in so far it is envisaged also as the beginning of the authentic history of man as the creator of his own future. The man of the classless society still remains a quester after his own fuller identity. In contrast, Christianity professes hope in an absolutely absolute future which is truly the end and the summing up of history. Its belief in the 'new heaven and the new earth' is the most articulate expression of the ultimate horizon of all social evolution and revolution.

Of the three goals of revolution indicated above, the mediate one needs to be focused upon more clearly since it has special relevance for the formulation of a methodology of revolution. Our reflections thus far already imply that the shape of the new society can be determined only on the basis of the possibilities contained in the revolutionary situation itself. In our attempt to project the future on the basis of the present the dialectic of transcending employed by Hegel and Marx serves as a useful methodological tool.

The Dialectic of Transcension

Transcension (Aufheben) in dialectical language has a three-fold dimension of meaning: suppression, preservation, and sublimation. To arrive at a conceptual model of the new society, we should first *suppress* (negate) the alienations of the present. This presupposes a scientific analysis of the existing structures of exploitation and alienation. For instance, a critical analysis of the human alienation implied in wage labour is necessary for us to project a new mode of organizing labour which does not alienate. However, it would be wrong to stress only the aspect of negation. Revolution does not mean destroying the achievements of the past and creating a new society out of nothing. A future that is totally discontinuous with the past will itself be another form of alienation since it would frustrate man's historical identity. Revolution must therefore also *preserve* and carry over into the future the positive values realized in the present. But since these values exist today in an alienated and therefore limited manner, preserving them for the future should mean *sublimating* them, i.e. realizing them on a higher plane in the new society. The social character of labour, for example, which is characteristic of capitalist production, will have to be maintained in the new society but outside the framework of private property.

Suppression, preservation, and sublimation are not so much three separate stages as three 'moments' or dimensions of the same dialectical process. "It must further be noted that they are not only laws of thought but also laws of being. In other words, they must be verified in the objective, historical process of revolution itself. The dialectic of transcension, therefore, could be of help also in defining more clearly the methodology of revolution.

The Dialectic of Theory and Practice

Using the dialectic of transcension we could arrive at a conceptual model of the new society. But this model should not be invested with absolute validity. It is a theoretical *project* and is therefore essentially provisional. It is conditioned by, and born of, our contemporary practice and consequently bears the birthmarks of its origin. It needs to be revised and corrected in the light of our future practice, revolutionary as well as post-revolutionary. In translating the project we have in mind into reality, we are likely to discover that the latter does not fully fit into our theoretical framework. This may happen either as a result of the emergence of entirely new forms of alienation or as a result of the explosion of new productive forces (computerization, cybernetic revolution, etc.) This would call for a revision of our project. The revised project, in turn, becomes the basis of subsequent praxis. It follows from this that the dialectic of transcension needs to be supplemented with the dialectic of theory and practice. Only such a dialectical approach to the understanding of the new society can steer clear, on the one hand, of social stagnation at the level of practice, and of dogmatism and ideological fixation, on the other. Only thus can the transcendence of man be safeguarded and society kept open to its absolute future that is God.

The New Society

As is clear from the methodology suggested above, any projection of the new society must be based on an adequate analysis of the existing structures of alienation in our country. Such an analysis is however beyond the scope of this paper. We shall confine ourselves to certain basic forms of alienation at the socio-economic, political, and cultural levels. Even here we shall have to exclude from our purview the dehumanizing structures and attitudes we have inherited from feudalism. A limited analysis like this cannot be expected to provide us with a detailed project for the future. It can at best help us derive certain structural principles for the construction of the future.

Socio-economic Structure

The most glaring aspect of economic alienation in India is the appalling misery and want of the masses. By far the majority of the Indian population is denied the satisfaction of their basic needs in terms of goods (food, clothing, housing, etc.) and services (medical, educational, cultural, etc.). This is clear from the fact that 40 percent of the rural population and 50 percent of the urban live below the nationally desired minimum of annual per capita consumer expenditure which is estimated to be Rs.324 for the rural area and Rs.486 for the urban area at 1968-69 prices.[3] Still more shocking is the realization that economic want is not a static quantity but is on the increase. We are also told that the condition of the bottom 20 percent rural poor has over the past decade more or less remained stagnant, whereas that of the bottom 20 percent urban poor has definitely deteriorated.[4]

If this is true, it is evident that the fundamental structural principle that should shape the new society is that of *equitable distribution* of the national wealth. An economic system that robs the worker of his product mutilates him. For what is the product if not the extension in time and space of the personality of the producer? Besides, only a society in which basic human needs are met can release the creative energies of the masses and bring into existence a truly democratic culture.

It would, however, be wrong to think of welfare in the new society purely in terms of consumption. And this for the following reason: Though in terms of felt need the satisfaction of the craving for goods and services merits high priority, what is objectively most dehumanizing is the fact that the masses have little control over the economic system. It is not they who decide what to produce, how to produce, or for whom to produce. The working class is reduced to being mere accessories to the means of production. Their labor-power itself is degraded to the level of a marketable commodity. The poor peasants who form the backbone of rural India are equally the victims of economic domination. They are drawn into the orbit of capitalist agriculture which lets only the fittest survive. Further, the little marketable surplus they produce is subject to the law of supply and demand prevailing in the agricultural market, which in turn is controlled by financial and industrial interests in the urban sector. Not even the white-collar workers and the petty bourgeoisie are free from the tyranny of the market. Those who are are the big landlords and capitalists. In them is concentrated not only wealth but also its inevitable concomitant, power. But even in their case freedom is largely an illusion. For they too are subject to a necessary law of production for its own sake.

Freedom from the law of economic necessity must, therefore, be an essential feature of the new social order. But how is it to be achieved? Not by an equal distribution of the means of production. For, while such distribution may be feasible in respect of agriculture, it is impracticable with regard to the means of industrial production where there is a question of huge enterprises. Besides, mere distributionism would mean not the abolition of private property with its ideology of private interest and competition but rather its universalization. Nor can the rule of necessity be overcome by resorting to total nationalization. State capitalism will only accentuate economic servitude by universalizing wage labour, in so far as *all* citizens will be reduced to the position of employees of the state. The only way to steer clear of the universalization of both private property and wage labour is socialization.

Socialization as a structural principle demands that society as a whole at various levels of its organization determine the ownership and use of its productive forces. In a fully socialized economy, one could envisage three types of property: 1. Personal property (not bourgeois private property) of which ownership, as well as use, is determined by society as a whole. 2. Communitarian property, i.e. property directly owned and administered by the local community. 3. State property which is directly administered by the representative stale. The apportioning of the means of production among individuals, communities, and the state will have to be determined on the basis of the objective nature of productive forces and the subjective option of the people themselves.[5] The essential thing to bear in mind is that transition from the reign of necessity to the realm of freedom is only possible where the people control and shape their economic destiny.

But socialization in itself tells us little of the content of freedom devolving upon the community. For one could envisage a society which, in full freedom, sets up production itself as the highest value. In that case, there will still be alienation in so far as man would exist for production, instead of production being subordinated to the good of man. Here, the experience of the more 'developed' countries gives us a warning. Maximization of production does not automatically mean the maximization of human wellbeing. It can even bring about worse modes of human alienation in the form of the denial of subjectivity and of the reduction of all needs to the need for 'having' or possessing. Man is greater than what he has or produces or consumes. He is also one who loves, hopes, and tends to the horizon of absolute meaning and value. Hence in the new society, economic values should be subordinated to man's social, cultural, and moral values. Such a concern for the hierarchy of values will have practical consequences even for economic planning. For instance, a ceiling on production may sometimes be necessary to ensure the total wellbeing of the community of producers. Our aim, therefore, should not be to catch up with the gadget civilization of the West but to build up a model of society reflecting our specific understanding of the hierarchy of values. Socialization should, therefore, serve *humanization.*

In an economic system in which the community freely determines its own economic destiny and in which the human person is affirmed as an absolute value, production and consumption will cease to be factors that divide man from man, groups from groups. Nature and the product of work will then become the bond between men, the concrete embodiment of human togetherness. Work will then become the primary factor that builds up the community. In such a society there will no longer be any basis for class antagonism based on economic interests?

Political Structure

As in the case of the economy, so too here we shall start with a consideration of the more basic alienations so that through their negation we shall arrive at the structural principles that should be embodied in the new society. Taking the country as a whole we are confronted with the constant tensions and conflicts of interests between the constituent states. So long as the citizens of India cling to their option in favour of a single national political authority, it is important to stress *solidarity* as a structural principle. Solidarity should find its structural concretization in the form of a central authority, which is all the more necessary when it comes to defense and foreign relations. But solidarity should not be understood in terms of social and cultural uniformity. Each constituent state has its own social and cultural identity which needs to be preserved. The resurgence of regional cultures in modern India contains a warning against envisaging the future of the country in monolithic terms. Besides, such cultural diversity as exists can be a principle even of national cohesion and integration. For, as in the case of biological evolution, so too in the development of peoples, *union differentiates* (Teilhard de Chardin), and *difference unifies*. Hence it is necessary to supplement the principle of solidarity with that of *federalism*. If the first principle demands that the development of the whole nation be the necessary condition for the development of any one constituent state, the second demands that the development of each state be the condition for the development of the nation as a whole.

There is in India a still more acute form of political alienation. It consists of the concentration of power at the highest levels of decision-making and of execution both in the States and in the Centre. The steady expansion of the public sector and the formulation and execution of planning from above affecting every area of societal life are so many indices of centralism. And where power becomes concentrated, democracy is in danger. For the state becomes an institution set up over against the people whose effective participation in decision-making, planning, and execution of plans is reduced to the minimum. Such a government may be *for* the people but it is in no real sense *of* and *by* the people. Besides, where political power becomes autonomous *vis a vis* the people it can easily be made subservient to the interests of the privileged classes. This is precisely what has happened in India. The Government which professes to stand for the common good is actually promoting the interests of the privileged classes.[6] Hence the need to subordinate the centralization to the principle of *subsidiarity*. This means that what any lower unit of society is capable of doing should not normally be taken over by the higher unit. For example, what the village community can do should not normally be done by the district organization or by the state. The new political community we envision must, therefore, be characterized by the decentralization of authority and by the effective participation of the masses in the legislative, executive, and judicial power. The function of the state in this new order of things will not be to rule by dictates from above but to synthesize and coordinate the various initiatives coming from below. This will naturally bring about a reduction in the strength of the bureaucratic machinery and make it more sensitive to the will of the people. The Panchayat Raj, shorn of its structural and functional inadequacies, could become the main axis of such a political order.

In the new social order, conceived along these lines, there will not be any sharp distinction between the economic and the political communities. The village, for instance, will be a truly political community. So too solidarity, federalism, and subsidiarity will also be principles governing all levels of social organization. The realization of such a political order is conditional upon the existence of the right type of political consciousness among the masses and of an elite committed to, and representative, of the popular will. This brings us to the problem of culture in the new society.

Cultural System

By cultural system, we mean the system of goals, values, norms, and ideas prevalent in society. Goal refers to the shape of the future which a given society wants to realize; value, to any socially desired good i.e. one to which people, in general, attach importance; norms, to the patterns of behaviour prescribed for the realization of goals and values; and ideas, to the world-view characteristic of any people. Our view of the socio-economic and political structure of the new society already implies a cultural system. Leaving out goals, norms, and world outlook, we shall now try to focus on some of the fundamental values which should be incorporated in the structures of the new society. True to our methodology we shall begin with an analysis of the alienations inherent in our present culture.

The system of values disseminated by our schools and colleges is of capitalist origin. It finds a convenient vehicle in the media of communications like the radio, the press, films, and literature. It is percolating steadily even to the lower stratum of society. It has become so much a part of our consciousness that we seldom challenge it. We shall examine some of these bourgeois values with a view to defining the value system of the future.

The one value that occupied primacy of place in contemporary India is 'money'. It is not just one value but the value of all values. It is the source of status and power. It can save or damn, create or destroy, make, or unmake. But the universality of its power is an effect nothing but the reduction of all human needs to the need for possessing, of man's being to 'having', of spirit to matter, of quality to quantity. In the new society, not money but the very fact of being human and man's service to the community will be a source of status in society. Another bourgeois value much hymned by all and sundry is 'freedom' understood as the chance one has to do what one likes (to own, to produce, and to consume) unhindered by any other. Of this freedom, the natural corollary is private interest and competition. Here 'the other' is viewed as the limit of one's possibilities. In the future society, on the contrary, 'the other' far from being the limit of one's possibilities will be the necessary condition for the possibility of transcending one's limits. Equally bourgeois in content is the value of 'justice' which consists of giving each one his due. If for instance employer and the employee get their due in terms of profit and salary respectively, we would call it a just order of things. This sort of justice presupposes and never calls into question the injustice inherent in the system itself of salaried labour. In a socialist order, on the contrary, justice will be the quality of the social structure which restores to each man his dignity as the creator of history.

Yet another value which our newspapers and politicians never tire of stressing is 'stability'. But it is often forgotten that what stability there exists today is the result of either inherited fatalism or organized repression. The stability of the new society will have to be qualitatively different inasmuch as it would leave room for creative instability by recognizing the right to dissent. Cultural alienation is manifest also in the bourgeois cult of 'efficiency' judged in terms of quantitative output. Thus the efficiency of our educational institutions is measured by the standard of first classes secured and trophies won. Capitalists measure their efficiency in terms of units produced irrespective of the quality of the product; the government in power measures its strength in terms of the votes secured or seats won, however unfair be the methods employed; the authorities in charge of family planning evaluate their success in terms of the number of loops inserted, of condoms distributed and of babies unborn, unmindful of the moral coercion exercised over the ignorant masses. The cult of capitalist efficiency can be overcome only in a society in which efficiency is demoted to the status of instrumental value, in which quantitative production is geared to enhancing the *quality* of human existence, in which man will be the measure of all things. One could go on widening the range of this analysis. What has been said is enough to show that the new system of values which is to animate the socio-economic and political structures of the future will have to be qualitatively different from the one that prevails today. What we have to strive for is a new humanism that respects the personal, social, historical, and creative dimensions of man.

We have thus far tried to delineate a few of the salient features of the new society. Our aim was not to paint a concrete picture of things to come but to suggest some approaches to the solution of the problem on the basis of partial use of the methodology we proposed in the beginning. A more adequate morphology of the future can be worked out only within the framework of inter-disciplinary collaboration between competent economists, sociologists, political scientists, and theologians, who in their turn will have to listen to those others actively involved in socio-political action. The present paper is only an invitation to launch such a venture.

(Religion and Society, vol. xx, No.1, March 1973, pp.51-61; *What the Thunder Says*, Chapter 1)

14

Revolution: For What? By Whom?

I thought of critically evaluating the traditional Marxist approach to social revolution in the light of the Asian situation. I felt such criticism might help us discover, at least lead us on the way to discovering, the right approach for us in Asia. We cannot ignore the traditional left movement in India and then work out a solution on our own.

Revolution – Its Goal

First of all, about the goal towards which we are all moving or rather towards which we want society to move — this goal is often referred to as the classless society. You may also call it Socialism or Communism or whatever you like. Whether you are a Marxist or an independent thinker, you will agree on certain points regarding the nature of this goal we are striving towards.

Economic Process

From the economic point of view, what is the goal? Here one must distinguish three elements: one is the socialization of ownership. All property must be socialized, which does not mean nationalized. Nationalization is one form of socialization. Socialization means ownership must vest in the people. It does not necessarily mean in the state. The state is not the people. The second element is control over the production processes. People must control the production process, especially the decision making at all levels of production. The choice of technology, the organization of labour, the setting of goals - in all these matters people must have a say. And, finally, the third element would be the equitable distribution of the product. Usually, it is this third aspect that is emphasized. The socialization of ownership too is sufficiently stressed. But, control over the production process is not sufficiently emphasized when we speak of future society.

I think, even for Marx, more important than equitable distribution was people's control over the economy. At present, it is the economic process that controls people. In a genuinely socialist society, people will have to control the economic process. That means people must be able to realize freedom in relation to the economy. If the economy controls you, you are not free. Therefore, even where Marx speaks of transition to a classless society, the stress, in my view, is on human freedom. Freedom was the central concern to Marx. Thus far, about the economic visage of the type of society we want to create. I do not think that any reasonable person can disagree with this project.

Political Decision Making and Implementation

Now let us come to the political aspect. In any political system, we have a two-fold process: one is the process of decision making. You elect your representatives, and they make decisions. The other is the process of implementing decisions. The two-fold process must be under the control of the people, it should not become independent of people, as is happening, to a large extent, in our country. Here the political decision making and implementation processes have become a sort of autonomous. People are drawn into this process only at the time of elections every five years or so. During the intervals, people are depoliticized. And that works to the advantage of those who have been elected as people's representatives. If the mass of people are depoliticized, what does that mean? It means the elected representatives and the bureaucracy have all power concentrated in their hands, and that suits them well. It helps them fill their pockets and enjoy the fruits of power.

So the present kind of political system functions only by depoliticizing the people. This is happening also in the Soviet Union. The masses have been depoliticized, with political power concentrated in the Party and in the government apparatus. As for people, their role is to work and to produce. So, politically what does socialism mean? It means people's control over decision making and implementation at all levels — from local to national level.

Cultural Freedom

But, socialism means more than that — more than restructuring the economy and the system of decision making and implementation. It means also cultural freedom. In the present society, not all have the freedom to think, to question, to express themselves, and to engage in creative activity. The right to think and the right to self-expression are again concentrated in the dominant classes and castes. Marx's statement that the ruling ideas of any age are the ideas of the ruling classes is largely true of the Indian situation. The mass of people does not have the right to think their own thoughts - thoughts which spring up from their own souls, from their own experience. They are made to think the thoughts that percolate down from the ruling classes and castes. They think by proxy. The entire educational system and most cultural institutions are at the service of the privileged classes who use them to make the masses think as they think, feel as they feel. So, our present society is characterized by cultural unfreedom. What common people really think matters little.

The newspapers may say "public opinion is in favour of that", "public opinion is in favour of this." What is this public opinion? If you are an editor or a journalist you find out the opinion of your friends, of people of your own class, who are likely to agree with you, who like you, share the benefits of the existing system, and you call it public opinion. What a few people — the editor, his friends, and those whom he meets at parties — think, is presented in the newspapers as public opinion. In reality, it is not public opinion. It is not the opinion of the 680 million people of India.

So, in terms of culture what does socialism mean? It means the right for human beings to have their own thoughts and feelings, and their own ways of expressing them. It means also the right to dissent. It means not to have ideas and beliefs imposed on them from outside. This aspect of cultural freedom has not been explicitly dealt with by Marx. It is implicit in his analysis of religious ideology. That human beings have to get free of ideas, concepts beliefs, and myths imposed on them by the ruling classes, was central for Marx. Unfortunately, when we speak of a classless society, we often forget this fact. Economic and political freedom is to some extent kept in mind, but cultural freedom is often forgotten.

I think all of you will agree that the socialist goal as explained above is acceptable and is worth living for and struggling for. I do not think there can be any controversy over it.

Yet, if you ask Party members, what is socialism and what do you understand by the future society, very often they evade an answer. That is my experience. Their mind is focused on immediate problems. But Marx never did that. He was a dialectical thinker. When he analyzed capitalist society, he saw that society as pregnant with its own future, as containing within itself its own opposite. So, both in his early and later writings, the socialist horizon, the classless society, is invariably there and often we find repeated references to it. He could not study the present without indicating the possibilities for the future contained in it. But today, Marxists fight shy of speaking about the future. And that is highly significant, it is symptomatic.

The Goal Mythicized

Symptomatic of what? It signifies, in my view, that the concept of a classless society has been made into a myth, into something like a religious belief. Myth has its own time. Mythical events relating to gods and goddesses do not take place in our time. They are beyond history. And naturally, what is beyond our historical time is not of much relevance for us, for our praxis; just as, for the vast majority of

Christians, heaven is a mythical concept, is outside history and has no immediate relevance for praxis. There is no link between heaven and earth. It is in your consciousness as a mythical reality. Similarly, the very concept of a classless society has been reduced to a myth. With that, the link between praxis today and the goal ahead has been broken; the bond joining them has been snapped. Why has this bond been snapped? (I am just thinking aloud. I am not giving a formal talk, nor am I proposing dogmas). This link has been broken mainly because of revolutionary impotence.

When you do not want to change society, you forget about the goal. You do not want to change society because existing conditions confer many privileges on you. Since at heart, you are not committed to change, you relegate the classless society to beyond history, make it into a myth. So, the myth of classless society is born of revolutionary inertia and impotence.

Here is another reason: if you do not reduce classless society to a myth, but accept it as your goal of historical praxis, then it will make inconvenient demands on you, which you may not be prepared to meet. Suppose we form a Party of revolution and say we want to create a new society, in which human beings will be able to think and act in freedom, what a contradiction it would be if within our own Party we are not free to think. If some 'omniscient' leader is imposing his views on us, then this whole vision of a classless society will indeed become very inconvenient. People would say, "Well, you want a society in which human beings would be free but, you yourselves are not free. In your own group, in your own Party, you have no freedom". Again, as a Party of revolution, we believe that people must control the political decision-making process. But within our own Party, is the decision-making process controlled by all the members, or, is it again centralized in some superior authority? So, a real commitment to the goal of a classless society makes demands — uncomfortable demands — and the only escape from them is to reduce that goal to a myth.

Just as, if we really believe that this world has to be changed through our action into the Kingdom of God (the Kingdom of God is for Christians, the final goal of history — an age of freedom), then it makes tremendous demands on us. But, if we lose all hope of changing society or have a vested interest in maintaining the status quo, the future will be reduced to a myth. Myth does not make any demand. For Jesus Christ, there was a clear link between his own life and his hope in the Kingdom of God. He believed in the Kingdom of God, the age of full freedom. Hence, he contested the powers that were and was killed. He was killed because he believed in the Kingdom and protested against injustice. The political powers of his day got rid of him. But today, do we hear of bishops being crucified? No. It is impossible because they have broken the link between hope and praxis. The kingdom of God has long since been mythologized. So, they can conveniently wallow in the flesh-pots of Egypt.

Once the goal is mythologized, there arises a problem. The Party of revolution has no object for concrete praxis. There is no immediate, feasible goal for collective action. But people committed to social change will say, "Give us an immediate goal, something feasible we can work for". Hence, it becomes necessary to find a goal which can be an object of praxis. And for Communists, the feasible goal came to be the Dictatorship of the Proletariat. With that, the classless society was eclipsed. And revolutionaries began to focus their eyes on the Dictatorship of the Proletariat. The amusing thing is, eventually even proletarian dictatorship became mythicized. So, revolutionists had to look for another goal. The CPI found it in 'National Democracy' and the CPI (M) in 'People's Democracy'. You ask any party member, "What are you working for?" He will not answer: "the classless society." I doubt whether today he will mention even Dictatorship of the Proletariat. He would say, "We are working for people's democracy". I would not be surprised if soon even this modest goal is made into a myth, and revolutionaries settle down to fighting for *clean* democracy as distinguished from *dirty* democracy. Probably this is already happening.

So, the greater the revolutionary impotence of a party, the greater is the tendency to mythologize one goal after another and finally opt for the politics of expediency. And you are content with minor changes, with short-term reforms. The original goal has been jettisoned long ago. So, we have a Party of revolution which is not for revolution. We have a movement that does not know where it is moving. Therefore, even the claim that it is a movement sounds hollow. Are we moving at all? If we have no goal, we are not moving. We are just static.

The Dictatorship of the Proletariat: Fact or Fiction?
Leaving aside this process of mythologization, let us reflect a bit on the Dictatorship of the Proletariat. What is this dictatorship of the proletariat? It means that after the revolution the proletariat, which by supposition is the majority of people, will exercise dictatorship over the minority of the bourgeoisie that is still there. The dictatorship of the proletariat is supposed to be the transitional stage leading to the classless society of the future. Behind this conception is Marx's understanding of history as governed by class struggle. He believed that as capitalism develops, there will be a clear polarization of people into two classes: on the one hand, the bourgeoisie, those who own the means of production and employ wage labour and on the other, the proletariat, those who do not own any means of production and are forced to make a living by selling their labour power. Marx believed that of the intermediate class — the petty-bourgeoisie — the majority will sink to the level of the proletariat, while a minority will climb up to the level of the bourgeoisie. Thus, we have two major poles: the majority constituted by the proletariat over and against a minority of the bourgeoisie.

This was a mere projection on the part of Marx and did not conform to the historical reality in Europe at the time when he and Engels wrote the *Communist Manifesto* (1848). During that period, the proletariat was only a minority. Therefore, he was not speaking about what existed actually in Europe at that time. He was but extrapolating on the basis of his understanding of contemporary capitalism. Now, has history proved

Marx right? We can see the proletarization of the petty-bourgeoisie in India even today. To some extent what Marx envisaged is happening. But at the same time, we see the emergence of the new intermediate class created by capitalism itself. Any new industrial invention, even a television or refrigerator, brings into existence a new service class. And the service class is multiplying. The polarization as Marx had forecasted has not taken place and it is doubtful whether it is really going to take place.

Co-option of the Proletariat

Marx envisaged a proletariat exploited and immersed in misery. But, what has actually happened elsewhere and perhaps even in India is something different. Of course, there is a numerical growth of the proletariat in India. But, as the proletariat develops, it also develops distinctions among themselves — distinction on the basis of salary, status, and loyalty. You can see the clear distinction between workers employed by the multinationals and those employed by small entrepreneurs — a clear difference in salary, in status, in the scale of values and attitude to life. Then again, as the proletariat grows, there is also an increase in intellectual labour; clerks, technicians, executives, and so on. These are highly paid. A top executive in a factory, by definition, belongs to the proletariat and is on a par with the lowest worker in the factory; for he does not own the means of production, he is selling his labour power for wages. But he may be drawing a salary of Rs.2,000, may be getting a house allowance, and be provided with a car. His level of consumption is high, his social contacts are so different from those of the lowest employees in the factory - the blue collared workers — which shows that the proletariat is today not a homogeneous entity.

There is a very clear demarcation between intellectual and manual labour and between different categories of manual labour. This creates a problem regarding the emergence of the proletariat as a revolutionary class. Mark believed that the proletariat from its birth is a revolutionary class, a radical class, a class with radical chains, a class whose interest consists of overthrowing the capitalist system. It is a class that has no private interest to safeguard, a class that has nothing to lose and everything to gain by a revolution. But, is that the actual situation?

In India today, the organized proletariat comes to only about 6 million out of a total of about 29 million. This small minority is already becoming something like a labour aristocracy receiving higher wages, enjoying higher status in society, enjoying the security of work and so many other privileges. Some of them have to pay income tax. Even those who may be getting only say Rs.6 per day have at least the security of a job. Security of job places them in a far superior position compared to the vast majority of people in rural India, whose monthly income is a meager Rs.30, who do not enjoy any security at all. Therefore, the organized proletariat has to lose much by a revolution. This, of course, is much more true of Europe where even an ordinary worker has his own house, his own swimming pool, his own television set, and car. He has everything to lose by revolution. So, we find a growing differentiation within the proletariat itself, and naturally, this adversely affects their revolutionary consciousness. Many of them just do not want a revolution.

If you are a married person having two children and you get an income of Rs 500 a month, it is heaven for you compared to what your parents had to go through. All that you want is security. Your children must be able to go to school. So, if you could get an additional Rs 10 per month, all the better. Therefore, it looks as though the proletariat, as it improves its own economic position, gets reconciled with capitalism. And this integration of the working class into the capitalist system is facilitated by their exposure to the media. Marx did not and could not foresee the extent to which workers would be exposed to the mass media - the television, the radio, newspapers, cinema, and so on. The mass media are controlled by the bourgeoisie. So too, the educational system. They use the educational system and the media to integrate the proletariat into the capitalist value system. They have developed highly sophisticated techniques for it — a technology of engineering people's consent, of manipulating people's sensuousness. Even the subconscious has been perfected by the bourgeoisie so that, even without your knowledge, you get integrated into the system. This is often done deliberately and consciously.

Another thing which Marx did not see clearly because of the limitations imposed by his theoretical presuppositions and by his actual preoccupations was the extent to which day-to-day work in a factory can change one's system of values. Suppose, you are a young girl who has come to the city from a village. In the village, you lived in an entirely different setup, in the context of caste rules of pollution and social segregation. You had to conform to so many taboos and restrictions. You could speak to your relatives, but you could not speak to a stranger. And in the village, you would not dare befriend a Harijan, or deal with him as an equal. Now that you are in the city and are employed in a factory, you are in a different cultural milieu. In the factory you cannot observe caste rules; you may have to obey a Harijan foreman or eat with people of other castes.

Work in the factory demolishes your village culture and instills in you new values like private interest, efficiency, and competition. You have to produce more than others. Your wages may depend on that. You have to obey higher functionaries. You have also to practice self-discipline. At home when you milked the cow you could let the milk fall directly into your mouth if you so wished. If you are working in a biscuit factory, you cannot take the biscuits and eat them as they come out of the machine. So, simply by working in a factory, you assimilate the values of capitalist production. Therefore capitalist culture is disseminated not only through the media, schools, and religious organizations, but also through the system of production. Your reflexes become reshaped. All this Marx did not pay attention to. He did not deal systematically with this entire problem of culture and ideology. But for a few stray remarks here and there, there is in his writings no sustained analysis of those problems. We have, therefore, to make our own analysis and draw our own conclusions. We cannot just go by what Marx said. We have to go beyond him.

So, I have been trying to show that the very concept of the proletariat as the revolutionary class has to be rethought in our context. I am not saying that the proletariat cannot be revolutionized. I am simply indicating certain facts of life. What is happening today is that workers are being integrated into the system. We should not develop a mythical conception of the proletariat. We have to be true to historical reality. It is highly problematic whether the proletariat is a revolutionary class, especially in the Indian context.

I was posing this problem of the revolutionary character of the industrial proletariat so that it might help us find an alternative approach to radical social change. I do not deny the possibility of radicalizing the urban proletariat, at least sections of them. But, I believe the focus in the future will have to be on the rural poor.

I think the Communist Parties had originally a much better appreciation of the Indian situation and of the rural poor. If you take Telengana struggle and other peasant movements, the Communists have played a significant role. They were in those days very close to the people. Their subsequent neglect of the rural working class is due, partly to the dogmatic bias in favour of the industrial proletariat as the revolutionary class and partly to a shift in the policy of the Communist Party. Around 1957-58, the Communist Party took a definite turn in favour of parliamentary politics of power. With that, electioneering, the setting up of candidates, and the capturing of power became its main concern. And party members themselves will tell you that it was one of the reasons why they neglected the rural sector.

Revolution - In Search of An Agent

From my criticism of the Marxist theory of revolution a major question arises. Who is the agent of revolution? If the industrial proletariat in India are being integrated into the system, then who will bring about a revolution? The problem is, we have an objective need for revolution, but no agent of revolution. The vision of revolution is looking for an agent, somebody to bring it about. There is no real agent of revolution.

The agent cannot be the existing political parties — if revolution is taken in the sense I explained earlier — in the threefold sense of economic, political and cultural transformation. Parties only aim at capturing power, not a total transformation. And here we have to evaluate in the light of our historical experiences so far. Not even the Communist Parties can be the agent of revolution unless they undergo a very radical self-criticism and totally reorient themselves. Today, they are very much part of the Establishment. So, the only agent we can think of is the *people*.

Now, who are the people? By people I mean, all the exploited people, all those exploited by the system. And the dominant system in India is capitalism. The exploited as a whole will have to bring about revolution. But, we can rely more on those sections which have not been integrated into the capitalist culture. In India, this means the rural poor who form the vast majority of our people: the landless labourers, the small peasants, and the unorganized proletariat.

People as agents of revolution must be defined not only in terms of exploitation but also in terms of alienation. In any system, you can easily distinguish between the exploited and the exploiters. The capitalist is the exploiter, worker the exploited. The landlord is the exploiter; the landless labourer is the exploited. You can say the merchant is the exploiter; the small peasant who brings his marketable surplus for sale is the exploited. Here we can more or less easily make a distinction. But, when we come to the problem of human alienation, these distinctions do not apply. Because, as Marx clearly states in his early writings, the exploiter is also alienated.

Under capitalism, not only the working class but also the capitalists are alienated. Alienated in the sense of being dehumanized; of not being able to develop one's faculties, creativity, and freedom. Capitalism smothers, and destroys humanity; not only of the working class but also of the employing class; not only of the landless but also of the landed; not only of the ruled but also of the rulers. Members of the bureaucracy too are alienated. Their creativity is denied. Imagine a bureaucrat sitting in his office from morning till evening, doing drab, dreary work.

Exploitation is not a common ground uniting all interested in overthrowing capitalism. But, alienation is. Here Marx makes a distinction. He says that the proletariat experiences alienation as powerlessness, while capitalists experience alienation as power. The capitalist is alienated because, once capitalism has developed and starts moving on its own foundation, he is subjected to its law. He is also governed by the market and is unfree in a certain sense. But, his unfreedom is compensated by so many other benefits. At least he is accumulating surplus value. In his own factory, he can take decisions concerning production. There are other compensations too. If you are thoroughly depressed and dehumanized and you hate the drudgery of routine and meaningless, administrative work, you can always take a holiday. So, capitalists experience their alienation as power. Therefore, it is not likely they will say: "Let us get rid of capitalism, it is alienating." But, there may be individuals among them who are conscious of the alienating character of capitalism, who are particularly sensitive to it. In fact, I know of people who have left the I. A. S. as they found their work alienating and meaningless.

When we speak of people as the agent of revolution, the term would include not only the exploited but also the alienated that are aware of their alienation and are prepared to fight the system.

Kinds of Struggle

Monopolistic Struggle

We can think of three different kinds of struggle. The first is the monopolistic struggle for revolution, which is the line of the Communist Parties. They claim to have a monopoly on revolution. They do not even like people like me, using the word 'revolution'. They may not like even my reading Marx just as formerly Catholics did not like non-Christians reading the New Testament and interpreting the message of Jesus. Catholics will say: "The New Testament is our property, we have a monopoly of it, you non-Catholics, have no right to speak about it". Likewise, the Communists claim the monopoly of all revolution. They think of the proletariat as the vanguard of revolution and in front of the proletariat they place the Party, and in front of the Party, they place the Party leaders. Behind the proletariat come the rural proletariat and the rest. The whole procession under centralized command marches forward to Delhi to bring about the collapse of capitalism. Decisions are taken by the top Party functionaries to be disseminated to all the ranks from Kashmir to Kanyakumari. Thus, we march forward. This is the monopolistic, streamlined process of revolution. I have my own doubt whether this is really a workable proposition, whether this is not a myth that we have to maintain because without myths we cannot live.

Competitive Struggle

Then there is the competitive struggle for social change. The political parties are already engaged in a sort of competitive struggle. If power is a cake, the various parties are striving to have a piece of it. Through manipulating the masses, they hope to secure a share in power. This is a competitive struggle at the political level. Trade Unions engage in competitive struggles at the economic level. Here the cake is the national surplus. Different sections of the working class are fighting for a larger share of the national surplus.

In the two cases I have mentioned, the competitive struggle is carried on by a minority. Political parties are not the people. Their membership is small. Trade Unions too, represent only a minority, a fraction of the working population.

The competitive struggle can become universal, with every group trying to get a bigger and bigger share of power or of economic goods. This means the war of all against all. We can foresee the industrial proletariat organizing struggles against capitalists, landless labourers against landlords and rich peasants, landlords against capitalists, rich peasants against landlords, small peasants against big peasants, college students against teachers, teachers against the management, management against the government and so on and so forth. Fishermen will organize struggles in one place, beedi workers in another place, quarry workers somewhere else. Each group will be concerned with its own interest without aiming at the creation of a better society for *all* human beings.

This kind of universal struggle is already taking place. And, I doubt whether the struggles organized by action groups go beyond this stage of the war of all against all.

I am not unhappy with such a development. So far struggles were limited to the trade unions and the political parties. Now, the unorganized workers too, are drawn into struggles. They too will get some benefits. It is not a bad thing if due to action groups these sorts of struggles have increased. Such struggles are better than no struggle at all.

Truly Socialist Struggle

So, we have two major types of struggles: monopolistic and competitive. Now, both monopolistic and competitive struggles are in keeping with the nature of capitalism. The competitive struggle is keeping with competitive capitalism. It is a struggle against capitalism carried on within the framework and according to the culture of capitalism. The monopolistic struggle is struggle assimilated into monopoly capitalism. In either case, we are within the capitalist system. Therefore, we need a new kind of struggle which is neither competitive nor monopolistic. That is a socialist struggle. Socialist struggle does not eliminate struggles by different groups, communities, and deprived sections of the population. It will be aimed at not only meeting the immediate needs of people but also bringing about radical changes in society as a whole. Each group engaged in the struggle will be concerned about all other groups in society. Its perspective is broader. Suppose you are a quarry worker, there is nothing wrong in seeking to meet your immediate needs; but, you must not stop at that. You must also take into consideration the well-being of other groups in your own area that may be more disadvantaged than you. Therefore, you must join hands with them. You must also have a certain perspective on the type of society you want to build. Thus, you go beyond competition. You join hands with other people and engage in struggles in such a way that others also benefit from them, whether in terms of bread or freedom.

In the Indian context, there cannot be uniform struggles that can be sort of dictated to by centralized leadership. Why? Because of the uneven persistence of traditional culture and the uneven development of capitalism. There are so many variations in terms of caste and class composition. No two villages are alike, no two districts are alike. We may have a village where all are poor, another village where there are landlords employing bonded labour, a third where rich peasants and wage labourers form the majority, and so on. Therefore, socialist struggles in the future will have to be pluralist.

How can competitive struggles become really socialist struggles? The solution is obvious. We need to re-educate the masses. If the masses are not re-educated they will lapse into a mere competitive struggle. A real socialist re-education of the masses is necessary so that groups will not fight for their own sectional interests but, will have in mind the interest of the community as a whole. Only through such education will people arrive at a clearer perception of the type of society they want to bring into existence. I am glad that a lot of activist groups are engaged in that kind of education. Actually, I attach much more importance to it than even to struggles. In the long run, socialist education may prove more capable of delivering the goods than illprepared struggles. Of course, the struggle itself is education. You cannot divorce one from the other.

The second means is training leadership from the oppressed classes themselves. This is so obvious that there is no need to enlarge upon it. In the future, we should emphasize training persons from the same village, from the same panchayat and so as far as possible in their own setup. So, after the training, they can carry on as a team and support one another. Of course, trained social activists will need an organization. I think it is best to leave it to the groups to develop the kind of structures needed. Only they can decide how they must work together, how they can co-ordinate their activities at the district level or at the state level.

(Talk given at the East Asian Partnership for Building of People's Movements, held at Madras, August 1981; *What the Thunder Says*, Chapter 6)

15

Consciousness and Reality in Marxism

The Scope and the Approach

Marxism may be understood in two different senses: In the broad sense, it means the thought of Marx and all the currents of thought which draw inspiration from it. In the narrow sense, it refers to the original thinking of Marx himself, leaving out the subsequent developments it has undergone. It is in this latter sense that we understand the word in this paper. Here again, our aim is to understand Marx not so much through his interpreters as through his own writings. For this, it is necessary to conduct an exegesis of the original sources with a view to discovering their true meaning. This, in turn, calls for a certain intellectual sympathy for the basic philosophical concerns of Marx, which however does not dispense us from the task of critical evaluation. If this paper errs, it would be rather on the side of positive appreciation than of negative criticism.

In this paper, we are not dealing with the formal laws of thought (Logic), but with consciousness itself as a mode of *being*. In other words, our aim is to delineate the main features of the Marxian ontology of consciousness in the broader framework of his philosophy.

Genesis of Marxian Epistemology

Marx's thinking on consciousness was shaped by his confrontation with the idealism of Hegel, on the one hand, and with French and Feuerbachian Materialism on the other. In his *Phenomenology*, Hegel explained the progressive march of the Spirit to higher and higher forms of consciousness. The lowest form of consciousness is *sensuous certitude* which naively accepts the data of the concrete world. The next is *self-consciousness* which consists in *finding oneself in the other*. It means the integration of the external objects into the consciousness of the subject. The last and the highest moment is *Absolute Knowledge*, where the Spirit reaches complete possession of itself and understands the word as the product of its own creativity. In this scheme of thought, the real subject of the whole process is consciousness. The world of objects is nothing but the self-estrangement, the exteriorization of consciousness. Against this central thesis of Hegel, Marx maintained that the real subject of objectification is not consciousness but the concrete man of flesh and blood. It is man who progressively creates himself through work. Consciousness is a function of this auto-generation of man in history. It is only the predicate, not the subject.[1] While Marx rejected Hegel's idealism, he retained from the latter the following key ideas: 1. The unity of thought and reality. 2. The dialectical development of history. 3. The possibility of the progressive rationalization of the real.[2] These ideas, in fact, form the cornerstone of Marxian philosophy.

In arriving at these conclusions, Marx was greatly aided by his study of Feuerbach and the nineteenth-century materialists. It was, in fact, Feuerbach who showed him conclusively that the subject of history is not abstract consciousness but the concrete man. He is regarded by Marx as the real founder of materialism in so far as he considered the social relations among men the ground-principle of theory.[3] However Marx's acceptance of Feuerbach is not without reservations. For the latter, along with other materialists, considered reality merely as the object of contemplation, and not as the object of action, nor as action itself.

> "The main shortcoming of materialism up to now (including that of Feuerbach) is that the object, the reality, sensuousness, is conceived only in the form of the object or of perception, but not as sensuous, human activity, as practice, not subjectively."[4]

In other words, Marx rejects materialism inasmuch as it fails to grasp the dynamic nature of reality as shaped by man, inasmuch as it does not recognize the dialectical character of history. Thus in distancing himself from materialism, he comes closer to Hegel.

The conclusions reached by Marx from his critical evaluation of idealism and materialism may be summed up thus: 1. The real subject of history is the concrete man. 2. Reality is a process that is essentially dialectical i.e. moving up to higher and higher forms by resolving immanent contradictions 3. Consciousness is a function of this dialectical movement of history.

The Dialectic of Consciousness and Reality

Unity in Tension

Marx understands the relation between consciousness and reality in dialectical terms. To grasp his thought, it is useful, to begin with, an inquiry into what he means by reality. The German word he uses is *wirklichkeit*. He explicitly relates the noun *wirklichkeit* to the verb *wirken*, which means 'to act', 'to work.'[5] To exist really (*wirklich*) means to operate, to produce materially. Hence the noun *wirklichkeit* means 'that which consists of action' or 'actuality'. Reality is actuality. It is a dynamic process, a becoming, not a passive, quiescent state. More precisely, it is praxis i. e. 'sensuous human activity'.[6] But the activity of man is essentially related to nature and to other men. All work is a self-objectification of man in nature.[7] Man humanizes himself in humanizing nature. This process of humanization is above all a social process, not merely in the sense that all work is a 'working-with' and a 'working-together' but also in the sense that through work, man produces society. To refashion nature is to create ever new bonds between man and man. It is to create society. Hence society is not only the subject but also the object of human activity.[8] It follows from this that for Marx reality signifies the concrete historical process in which human society reproduces itself in recreating nature. It also follows that he is not concerned with reality in the scholastic sense of *being*. Even where he uses the term *being,* what he means to say is 'social life.'[9]

How does reality stand in relation to consciousness? It is clear that reality as the process of man's self-creation already presupposes the mediation of consciousness. This is borne out also by the Marxian definition of praxis as sensuous activity.[10] Sensuousness includes consciousness and need.[11] Consciousness, therefore, is not something outside the pale of reality. Reality not only includes consciousness but also is ontologically continuous with it. For, "being conscious cannot be anything other than conscious being, and the being of man is their real life process."[12] In other words consciousness is nothing but a qualitatively specific mode of being. It is the concrete life-process of man become transparent to itself. What is man existentially, socially, that he is aware of?. In the words of Marx,

> "My relationship to my surroundings is my consciousness. For the animal, its relation to others does not exist as a relation. Consciousness is, therefore, from the very beginning a social product and remains so as long as men exist at all.[13]

But the unity between consciousness and reality reveals also a tension. For the function of consciousness is not exhausted by its being immediately related to ma's self-creation, nor by merely mirroring reality. Consciousness can return to its birth place which is the inwardness of man, and express itself in more or less articulate forms. It can thus construct complex ideas, hypothesis and theories. It can even create illusory worlds of its own that are in conflict with reality. This shows that it can assume forms that are relatively independent of reality. These evolved forms of consciousness need not necessarily imply creative activity. In this sense, we may speak of a difference between consciousness and reality. Hence the affirmation of Marx.: "... thought and being are indeed different, yet at the same time in unity with each other."[15]

The unity in tension between consciousness and reality will become still clearer when we critically examine the epistemological determinism that is commonly attributed to Marx. According to this view, Marx considered consciousness as totally determined by material conditions, where the adjective material is understood in the metaphysical sense. Marx's rejection of the contemplative materialism of Feuerbach already gives the lie to this interpretation. Let us now consider the classical text where Marx discusses the relationship between conciseness and reality:

> "To begin with, the production of the ideas and images of consciousness is immediately interwoven with the material activity and the material intercourse of men, the language of real life. Imagination thought, the spiritual intercourse of men - these appear as the direct outflow of their material behavior. The same holds true of the spiritual production as is realized in the language of politics, law, ethics, religion, metaphysics etc. of a people. It is man who produces their conceptions, ideas, etc. i.e. actual, acting men as conditioned by a definitive stage in the development of their productive forces and the corresponding relationships. Being conscious can be nothing but conscious being, and the being of men is their actual life process. Even the foggy ideas in the brains of men are the necessary sublimations of their life-process that is material, empirically verifiable, and bound up with material presuppositions. Ethics, religion, metaphysics, or any other ideology for that matter and the corresponding forms of consciousness, do not have any longer even the appearance of autonomy. They have no history, they have no development. Rather it is men who develop their material production and their material intercourse, and change, along with this reality of theirs, also their thought and the products of their thought. It is not consciousness that determines life, but life that determines consciousness."[16]

The basic thesis enunciated here implies neither materialistic nor economic determinism, and that for the following reasons: Firstly, as is clear from the immediate context, Marx is here criticizing the theory of consciousness put forward by Hegel. The latter made consciousness the real subject of history and reduced the concrete man and the concrete nature to the position of predicates. It is this absolute primacy and autonomy of consciousness which Marx is here vehemently denying. He is not denying that consciousness has a constructive role in the self-creation of man in history. What he rejects emphatically is the hypostatization and apotheosis of abstract consciousness. Secondly, when Marx says that consciousness is determined by material conditions, the adjective material does not mean *related to brute, unconscious matter*. He uses the word as a synonym for 'concrete', 'objective', 'existential'.[17] This is clear also from the fact that he considers reality (being = praxis = life-process etc.) as already mediated by consciousness. Hence what Marx wants to convey is nothing more, nothing less, than the truth that it is men who determine their consciousness, who create their own ideas, theories, and ideologies. The thought of Marx, therefore, steers clear both of idealism and of mechanistic materialism.

Though Marx denies autonomous creativity to abstract consciousness, he is equally emphatic that consciousness as a *principium quo* has a determining, creative role in relation to man's social, historical existence. It is thanks to consciousness that man is capable of creating *universally* in contradistinction to animals which create only according to certain particular well-defined patterns.[18] It is consciousness that makes him free in relation to the world of his creation.[19] It is again consciousness that enables him to project ideally ever new models to be realized.[20] This creative role is verified even in the case of theory which is a complex form of consciousness. Theory, once it has percolated to the masses, becomes the spiritual weapon for revolution.[21] It follows from this that reality not only determines but also is determined by consciousness. This is but another manner of stating the truth that it is man who determines both his consciousness and his reality.

Immanence and Transcendence

The unity in tension between consciousness and reality unfolds itself not only in the dimension of space but also, and above all, in the dimension of time. Consciousness, in so far as it mirrors reality and forms one of its essential components, is immanent in the concrete 'here and now'. But in so far as it anticipates intentionally the contours of the future, it is the principle of transcendence. Marx explains this by comparing human activity to that of animals:

> "The animal is in immediate unity with its vital activity. It does not differentiate itself from the latter. It is its vital activity. Man, on the contrary, makes his vital activity the object of his volition and consciousness. His is conscious vital activity. Conscious vital activity distinguishes man immediately from the vital activity of animals. It is this that makes his activity free activity... Of course, animal also produces. They construct nests, dwellings, as in the case of bees, beavers, ants etc. But they only produce what is strictly necessary for themselves or their young. They produce only in a single direction, while man produces universally. They produce only under the compulsion of direct physical needs, while man produces when he is free from physical needs and only truly produces in freedom from such need. Animals produce only themselves, while man reproduces the whole of nature... Animals construct only in accordance with the standards and needs of the species to which they belong, while man knows how to produce in accordance with the standards of every species and knows how to apply the appropriate standard to the object. Thus man constructs also in accordance with the laws of beauty.[22]

These words show conclusively that Marx views consciousness as the principle of man's transcendence over the immediately 'given'. Endowed with consciousness, man can overcome the tyranny of the present, of existing conditions. He can make his own the standards of every species, and form universal laws of beauty and harmony. In short, he is potentially everything. History is the actualization of this original potentiality. Man is a being who consciously transcends himself throng work, and thus makes his own history. Marx gives us an indication as to the concrete manner in which man creates his future:

> "But what distinguishes the worst architect from the best of bees is this, that the architect raises his structure in imagination before he erects it in reality. At the end of the labour process, we get a result that already existed in the imagination of the labourer at its commencement..."[23]

Man can, in imagination, project models to be subsequently translated into reality through work. The 'project' once realized awakens new ideas in man, which in their turn induces him to project yet other and more perfect models. This dialectical process is the mainspring of history.

Consciousness in Alienation

The dialectical unfolding of consciousness and reality we have described thus far is constitutive of man as he ought to be. But what ought to be is only partly realized at the present stage of historical development, since the essence of man exists today in an alienated form. Today man is alienated from nature and from other men: from nature, because the product of his work has assumed the character of an alien force that oppresses and ruins him both materially and spiritually; from other men, because society is dived into classes that are in conflict with one another. This existential alienation is reflected also in the realm of consciousness.[24] We shall now briefly indicate the main forms of alienation affecting human consciousness.

Alienation as Fixation

Authentic consciousness should enable man to transcend existing conditions of life and fashion his own future. But when alienated, it tends to freeze human development at any given stage. It does so by providing justification and moral sanction for the maintenance of the status quo[26], and by constructing its own 'universal theory' to explain away the actual miseries of life.[27] Theoretical alienation manifests itself in ideologies of stagnation.

Alienation as Fragmentation

The disintegration of man at the practical level brings about also a disintegration of consciousness. Thus in religion - which is the theoretical alienation par excellence - the consciousness of the believer splits into two: a profane consciousness of real misery, and an illusory consciousness of heavenly bliss. A similar disintegration is found also at the level of social consciousness. The individual as a citizen finds in the political community, the State, the realization of his universal, social essence since the State is supposed to stand for the common good. But in actual, bourgeois society his consciousness is conditioned by self-interest and private gain. Here again, his belief that social essence is realized in the state is an illusion, since the latter is, in reality, the guardian exclusively of the private interests of certain classes. Thus his social consciousness branches off into two - into an illusory consciousness of the common good and a real consciousness of self-seeking.

Alienation as Illusion

Our remarks on the division of consciousness shows that theoretical alienation creates its own world of illusion. This needs further elucidation. The alienated man shows his protest against his actual condition of misery by constructing an imaginary world of self-fulfillment. This 'world ' becomes for him his 'universal existence'[29] the reality of heaven'[30] and the realization of his true essence.[31] In every respect, it is diametrically opposed to the real world. If the latter is misery, disunity, and impoverishment, the former is happiness, unity and fulfillment. This shows that even alienated consciousness retains the power of creating projects. What differentiates it from authentic consciousness is the fact that the former constructs projects in the order of phantasy only. These illusory projects either leave the concrete world as it is; or prevents its reconstruction by acting as the opium of the people.[32]

Towards Universal Consciousness

The supersession of alienation at the level of reality carries with it also the supersession of alienation at the level of consciousness. Before we proceed further, it is necessary to define what we mean by *the supersession of alienation.* 'Supersession' does not fully express the thought of Marx. The word he uses in German is *Aufheben,* which means not only 'to suppress' but also ' to preserve', 'to carry over', or ' to sublimate'.[33] This implies that alienation, whether in the realm of thought or of being, is not pure dis-value, pure negativity. Alienation contains also positive truths and values, though in a distorted form. The supersession of alienation, therefore, eliminates not the values and truths but their distorted realization. Religious alienation provides us an illustration. The believer projects the image of a creator who exists in virtue of his own essence. This is a distorted representation of the truth that man is his own creator. Consequently, the supersession of religious alienation does not mean the elimination of the idea of a creator. It means only the elimination of the idea that the creator is other than man himself. This said, it remains now to describe briefly the new consciousness that emerges as the result of revolutionary praxis.

The consciousness of the new man will reflect at the wealth of his cosmic, social, and historical existence. With the supersession of private property, man will rejoin nature and the product of his work. He will appropriate nature not only materially through consumption but also spiritually and aesthetically.[34] It will be a conscious integration of the universe in man. The appropriation of the world of objects will bring about also a corresponding unfolding of his subjective sensuousness, of his hearing, seeing, willing, loving etc.[35] It will lead to a veritable resurrection of man.

The definitive reconciliation of man with nature implies also his reconciliation with other men. With the elimination of class struggle and class exploitation, the narrow sense of 'mine' and 'thine' will give place to an all-embracing consciousness of the communion of all men "in which the free development of each is the condition for the free development of all."[36] Man will then see in his fellowmen his own 'nature.'[37] Each individual will thus become "the whole, the ideal whole, the subjective existence of society as thought and experienced."[38]

Finally, the supersession of alienation will usher in the real subject of history, man. Man will realize that he is his own creator, that history is " an act of generation, which is *known* and which *consciously* transcends itself as an act of generation."[39] Only in communism shall man know that he owes his existence to himself (Durchsichselbstsein). With that, the question regarding the existence of God will have become practically impossible.[41]

An Evaluation

An adequate evaluation of Marx's thinking on the subject under discussion would call for criticism of his whole philosophy, which is beyond the scope of this paper. We shall confine ourselves to a cursory statement of the main merits and demerits of Marx's position regarding consciousness and reality.

Marx has made an abiding contribution to philosophy by stressing the sociological bases of human consciousness. He has proved that consciousness is essentially historical, and carries the birth-marks of the age in which man lives. He has exploded the pretensions of certain types of 'philosophia perenis' which tend to absolutize historically conditioned ideas and theories. It is also to his credit that he made "true praxis the condition for effective and positive theory"[42] and the criterion of its ultimate validity. A theory that is divorced from practical involvement in concrete life may be true at a certain level of abstraction but is of little relevance to the destiny of man. In other words, though logically true, it becomes ontologically false. Marx has also shown that theory should not only emerge from praxis but also return to it, and become an instrument for changing the world.[43] Knowing must lead to fuller being. We can, therefore, agree with Marx when he says:

> "The time must come when philosophy will get in touch with the real world of its time and establish a reciprocal relationship with it, not only internally through its content, but also externally, through its phenomenal manifestation as well."[44]

The basic demerit in Marx consists in his too one-sided emphasis on the social existence of man and the corresponding form of consciousness to the neglect of metaphysical anthropology. He even seems to equate the socio-historical activity of man with his ontological auto-generation. Similarly, he has failed to analyze the metaphysical alienation of man which consists of the ambivalence of freedom. Such analysis would have revealed to him that the definitive supersession of socio-economic alienation is not possible without the definitive supersession of man's metaphysical alienation. The supersession of the latter alienation, in turn, cannot be brought about purely on the basis of man's own resources. The believer, therefore, is justified in positing God as the condition for the possibility of the definitive supersession of all alienation, as the condition for the possibility of the realization of the classless society. Hence, Marxism by an inner logic looks to God as the ultimate guarantee of its own "realization".

(*What the Thunder Says*, Chapter 10)

Dialectic of the Psycho-structure and the Social Structure

There is a heightened awareness among social activists and theoreticians about the need for a scientific analysis of society. This is a welcome step forward from the days when attention was focused more on the symptoms than on the root causes of social ills. But where it lacks a global perspective of human existence or ignores other branches of knowledge, structural analysis can even becloud our perception of reality. This is particularly the case when social structures are seen as autonomous *vis-a-vis* social actors. Change is then attributed not so much to the historical initiative of human beings as to the working out of contradictions within or between structures. Thus analysis itself provides an excuse for inaction and apathy.

Further, the kind of social analysis made at seminars and study-sessions tend to ignore dissenting behaviour, for the simple reason that it doesn't fit into some preconceived analytical framework, which is tragic. For dissenting behaviour is precisely what signals and provokes change. What is revolution but organized dissent?

One must hence never stop with the analysis of structures. Equally important is the study of structuration i.e. the process whereby structures come into being and are continually reinforced. This means turning one's attention from structures to persons, from the object to the subject.

Structures are nothing but stable, generalized patterns of behaviour. As such, they can persist only so long as individuals spontaneously conform to them. This presupposes that they have already acquired the corresponding psycho-structure, meaning an interrelated whole of relevant drives, reflexes, perceptions, and values. The psycho-structure expected of a sales-girl is not the same as that required in a factory worker. Monarchy calls for one kind of psychic make-up in citizens; democracy for another. This leads to the further question, How is the appropriate psycho-structure created in the members of a society? In other words, how are they constituted into subjects?

Vulgar Marxism will see in the economy the main, if not the sole, determinant of the psycho-structure. That participation in the economic process shapes our attitudes and values, none would deny. But the role of the economy should not be overrated. Generally, the individual psyche will have assumed its distinctive features long before it begins to consciously participate in economic life. The most formative agent in this regard is culture. The ideas and beliefs, enfleshed in symbols, myths, rituals, and aesthetic creations and vehicled through institutions like the school, the temple, and the family, mould minds and hearts much more radically than material production and consumption. The impact of culture reaches down to the very roots of man. And the roots of man are, in a sense, in the unconscious.

This brings us to the role of the unconscious in the constitution of the subject. It is not as though individuals are born into the world like so many empty shells into which society may pour whatever content it may please. Each person is heir to a specific psychic potential in the form of unconscious instincts and drives: the sexual drive seeking expression in mating or sublimating, the instinct of self-preservation geared to the consumption of goods, the death-instinct which translates itself into conscious striving to dominate both self and the world. To these ones might add the urge for togetherness and community. The psycho-structure of each person takes shape in the interaction, from early childhood, between his inherited psychic potential and the socio-cultural influences from outside. If cultural forms like myths and symbols have the power to penetrate the unconscious *self-beneath-the-self* and release the subterranean, volcanic forces of creation and destruction locked up within it, it is because they are themselves largely the product of the unconscious.

Is the human being then nothing but a product of the environment and the unconscious? By no means. He is eminently one who creates himself in freedom. If circumstances change him, it is no less true that he can also change circumstances. Though subject to unconscious forces, he has it in him to take charge of the same forces and harness them to the creation of the future. What is more, he has the terrifying power to negate all structures, all reality, even his own being in the world.

Certain conclusions follow: To begin with, no worthwhile strategy for the Indian revolution can emerge if we ignore the dialectic of psycho-structure and social structure, on the one hand, and the dialectic of the conscious and the unconscious, on the other. Second, any social revolution must begin with the revolution of the unconscious, individual, and collective. To bring that about the most effective means is cultural action. Third, while recognizing the need for the analysis of social structures, we must be wary of all approaches that reduce persons to structures, ignoring human creativity and freedom.

(Editorial, Negations No. 2, April-June 1982; *What the Thunder Says*, Chap. 7)

How Not To Be a Revolutionary

"A revolutionist is a man signed with death. He has neither personal interests nor business, neither personal feelings nor connections, nothing he could call his own, not even his name. Everything in him is governed by one single interest, by one single thought, by one single passion: the revolution. In his innermost being, not merely in *words* but also in *deeds*, he has broken with all that concerns public order and the civilized world - its laws, conventions, customs as well as morality. The civilized world is his inexorable enemy. And if he still continues to live in it, it is only to fully destroy it — He knows only one science, the science of destruction. He has only contempt for public opinion. He despises and hates the prevailing social morality in all its motives and expressions. In his eyes, only that is moral which contributes to the victory of the revolution; immoral is everything that hampers it. Day and night, he should have only one thought, only one goal: inexorable destruction. With calm deliberation and without respite should he work for this goal and be prepared himself to come to ruin and with his own hand bring ruin on everything that stands in the way of this goal."

Thus wrote Sergej Gennadievic Necaev (1847-1882), one of the precursors of the Russian revolution, in his *The Catechism of the Revolutionist*. The portrait of a revolutionist, he has painted is at once beautiful and tragic. Beautiful for the singleness of purpose, the intensity of commitment, and the selflessness-unto-folly it conjures up. Nonetheless, it is tragic. For the kind of revolutionism, Nicaev preaches rests on an absolute negation and, for that reason is self-defeating. It wills the end but not the means. It would construct the future but not before it has destroyed the tools handed down by generations gone by. In the end, it will swallow up the revolutionist himself. He will negate his youth, his love, his sentiments, his friendships, and his joys. And what if the hoped for revolution fails to happen?

Disillusioned and frustrated, he might end his life or, as often happens, find a convenient escape in some form or other of religious sentimentalism.

Of quite different mettle is the genuine revolutionist. For him, revolution is not only negation but also affirmation, not only abolition but also preservation. It seeks to build the future on the possibilities offered by the past; it carries over into the morrow whatever is humanizing here and now. This is increasingly being recognized by social thinkers and activists, particularly in Asian and African countries.

(From the Editorial, Negations No. 7, July-September 1983; *What the Thunder Says*, Chap. 8)

Notes

ABBREVIATIONS

'Bonaparte'   = "Eighteenth Brumaire of Louis Bonaparte"

'Critique'   = "Contribution to the Critique of Hegel's Philosophy of Right"

'Family'   = *Holy Family*

'Ideology' GI   = *German Ideology*

'Jewish'   = "On the Jewish Question"

'Manuscripts'   = "Economic and Philosophical Manuscripts"

'Poverty'   = *Poverty of Philosophy*

"Preface"   = "Preface to: A Contribution to the Critique of
Political   Economy"

'Theories'   = *Theories of Surplus Value*

'Theses'   = "Theses on Feuerbach"

Chapter 1

1. McLellan 1976, p. 6. **2.** Ibid, p. 7. **3.** Ibid, p. 11. **4.** See Findlay 1958 **5.** 'Manuscripts', in Marx 1963, p. 212. **6.** Feuerbach 1957, p. 184. **7.** 'Manuscripts' in Marx 1963, p. 199. **8.** 'Theses', in Marx 1970, p. 84. **9.** Ibid, **10.** Ibid. **11.** Ibid **12.** Calvez 1956, p. 84. **13.** Ibid, p. 85. **14.** Ibid.

15. Bauer 1938, Part I, Vol. I, p. xxiii. 16. Marx-Engels 1975, p. 14-15. 17. 'Manuscripts'in Marx 1963, p. 217, footnote. 18. Ibid, p. 214. 19. Ibid, p. 212. 20. Ibid, p. 214. 21. Ibid, p. 210. 22. 'Critique', Marx 1963, p. 43. 23. Ibid, "Communism of the Rheinischer Beobachter", Marx-Engels 1975, pp. 74-75. 24. 'Manuscripts'in Marx 1963, p. 165. 25. Ibid. 26. Ibid, pp. 165-167. 27. Ibid, p. 44. 28. Ibid.

Chapter 2

1. Karl Marx, "Leading, Article in No. 179 of Koelnische Zeitung" in Marx-Engels 1975, pp. 32-33. 2. Ibid, p. 35. 3. Ibid, p. 36. 4. 'Jewish', Marx 1963, pp. 7-12. 5. Ibid. 6. Ibid, p. 14. 7. Ibid, p. 15. 8. Ibid, p. 17. 9. Ibid, p. 20. 10. Ibid, p. 31.

Chapter 3

1. 'Manuscripts', Marx 1963, p. 156. 2. Ibid, pp. 132-133. 3. Marx-Engels 1976, p. 43. 4. 'Manuscripts' in Marx 1963, p. 156. 5. 'Preface', Marx 1970, pp. 67-68. 6. McLellan, 1971, p. 120. 7. 'Theories', Marx 1970a, p. 113. 8. Marx 1973, p. 278. 9. 'Manuscripts', Marx 1963, p. 122. 10. Ibid, pp. 122-123 11 Marx 1977, Vol. I, pp. 153-163; 179-193. 12 McLellan 1971, pp. 99-100. 13 Ibid. 14 'Manuscripts', Marx 1963, p. 123. 15 Ibid, p. 124. 16 Ibid. 17 Ibid, pp. 124-125. 18 McLellan 1971, p. 133. 19 Ibid, p. 142. 20. 'Manuscripts', Marx 1963, p. 126. 21. Ibid, p. 126. 22. Ibid, p. 127. 23. Ibid, p. 129. 24. Ibid. 25. Capital, London, Vol. I, p. 46. 26. Ibid, p. 48. 27. 'Manuscripts', Marx 1963, p. 192. 28. Ibid, pp. 189-193. 29. Marx 1973, p. 146. 30. Ibid, pp. 450-456. 31. 'Manuscripts', Marx 1963, p. 122. 32. Capital, London, Vol. II, p. 685. 33. Ibid, Vol. I, pp. 45-46. 34. 'Manuscripts', Marx 1963, p. 125. 35. 'Jewish', Marx 1963. p. 39. 36. 'Manuscripts', Marx 1963, pp. 132-133. 37. 'Jewish', Marx 1963, p. 37. 38. 'Manuscripts', Marx 1963, pp. 189-192. 39. Capital., London, Vo. I, p. 53. 40. Ibid. 41. Ibid, p. 54.

Chapter 4

1. 'Manuscripts', Marx 1963, pp. 202-203. 2. 'Theses', Marx 1970, p. 84. 3. Ibid, p. 83. 4. Marx 1970, p. 243. 5. Gl, Marx 1970a, p. 80. 6. Karl

Marx, "Drafts for Civil War in France", in McLellan 1971a, pp. 209-210. **7.** 'Ideology', Marx 1970a, p. 71 **8.** 'Critique', Marx 1963, p. 58. **9.** Marx 1970b, p. 243 **10.** Marx 1977a, Vol. II, pp. 845-846. **11.** 'Bonaparte', Marx 1970a, p. 196. **12.** 'Ideology', Marx 1970a, p. 71. **13.** McLellan 1971a, p. 110. **14.** Marx-Engels 1970, p. 237. **15.** 'Poverty', McLellan 1971b, p. 205. **16.** Ibid. **17.** 'Critique', Marx 1963, p. 53. **18.** Ibid, p. 54. **19.** Ibid, p. 52. **20.** 'Family', in Avineri 1969, p. 142. **21.** 'Manuscripts', Marx 1963, p. 176. **22.** Marx 1973, p. 304. **23.** Karl Marx, Letter to Bolte (1871), in Avineri 1969, p. 145. **24.** Ibid **25.** 'Poverty', Marx 1970a, p. 244. **26.** 'Manuscripts', Marx 1963, p. 201. **27.** Ibid, p. 161. **28.** Ibid, p. 163. **29.** 'Ideology', Marx 1970a, p. 110. **30.** 'Manuscripts', Marx 1963, p. 181. **31.** Marx 1973, pp. 487-488. **32.** Ibid. **33.** 'Bonaparte', McLellan 1971b, p. 207.

Chapter 5

1. 'Manuscripts'. Marx 1963, p. 155. **2.** Ibid, p. 208. **3.** Ibid, p. 207. **4.** Ibid, p. 208. **5.** Ibid, pp. 126-127. **6.** Ibid, p. 128 **7.** Ibid **8.** Ibid, pp. 160-161. **9.** Ibid, p. 160. **10.** Ibid, p. 161. **11.** Ibid, p. 168. **12.** Ibid, p. 159. **13.** Ibid. **14.** Ibid, p. 160. **15.** Ibid. **16.** Ibid, pp. 157-158. **17.** McLellan 1971a, p. 71. **18.** 'Manuscripts', Marx 1963, p. 157. **19.** McLellan 1971a, p. 149. **20.** 'Manuscripts', Marx 1963, p. 154. **21.** Ibid, p. 158. **22.** Marx 1973, pp. 172, 287, 706. **23.** Ibid, pp. 162, 487, 496. **24.** 'Manuscripts', Marx 1963, p. 160. **25.** Ibid, p. 164. **26.** Ibid, pp. 164-165. **27.** Ibid. **28.** Ibid, p. 128. **29.** Ibid, p. 127. **30.** Marx 1977a, Vol. I, pp. 169-170. **31.** Marx 1973. p. 158. **32.** Ibid, p. 649. **33.** Ibid, p. 156. **34.** Ibid **35.** Ibid, p. 650. **36.** Ibid, p. 652. **37.** Ibid, p. 158. **38.** Capital Vol. Ill, Marx 1970a, pp. 259-260. **39.** 'Manuscripts', Marx 1963, p. 128; McLellan 1971a, pp. 75, 142, 148. **40.** McLellan 1971a., pp. 45-46. **41.** Marx 1973. p. 297. **42.** Ibid. **43.** Ibid, pp. 611-612. **44.** 'Manuscripts', Marx 1963, p. 175. **45.** Ibid, p. 126. **46.** Ibid, p. 158. **47.** Ibid, pp. 166-167. **48.** Ibid, p. 160. **49.** Ibid, p. 203. **50.** Marx 1977a, Vol. I, pp. 53-54. **51.** 'Manuscripts', Marx 1963, pp. 129-130.

Chapter 6

1. 'Theses', Marx 1963, p. 82. **2.** 'Manuscripts', Marx 1963, p. 164. **3.** 'Ideology', Marx 1970a, p. 253. **4.** 'Manuscripts', Marx 1963, p. 155. **5.** Quoted in "Religion as Superstructure and Infrastructure" by Enrique E. Dussel, Mexico, 1977 (Unpublished paper) **6.** Marx-Engels 1975, p. 275. **7.** 'Manuscripts', Marx 1963, p. 206. **8.** Ibid, pp. 158-159. **9.** 'Critique', Marx 1963, p. 50. **10.** Ibid, p. 52.

Chapter 7

1. Plato, Sophist, 263 **2.** 'Manuscripts' in Marx 1975, pp.385-386. Wherever clarity or fidelity to the German original required it, I have modified the translation. **3.** Ibid, p. 396 **4.** Ibid, p.398 **5.** Ibid, pp.388-389 **6.** Ibid, p. 384 **7.** Ibid. **8.** Ibid, p. 386 **9.** 'Theses', Marx 1975, p. 421-422 **10.** 'Manuscripts', Marx 1975, pp. 386-87 **11.** Ibid. **12.** Ibid., p. 389 **13.** Ibid., p. 395 **14.** Ibid., p. 396 **15.** Ibid., p.381 **16.** Marx 1977b, p. 29 **17.** 'Manuscripts', Marx 1975, p. 398 **18.** 'Theses', Marx 1975, p. 421-422 **19.** 'Manuscripts', Marx 1975, p. 389 **20.** F. Engels, "Ludwig Feuerbach and the end of Classical German Philosophy", in Marx-Engels 1970a, p. 609.

Chapter 8

1. See Marx 1973, pp. 100-108; also, afterword to the second German edition of *Capital,* Vol. 1, pp. 26-29 **2.** 'Manuscripts', Marx 1975, p. 355 **3.** 'Jewish', Marx 1975, p. 241 **4.** Marx 1977b, Vol. 1, pp. 76-87 **5.** 'Manuscripts', Marx 1975, pp. 332, 341 **6.** Marx 1977b, Vol. 1, pp. 181-192 **7.** Ibid, p. 300 **8.** Marx 1973, p. 101 **9.** Ibid, pp. 101-102 **10.** Marx 1977b, Vol. 1, p. 28 **11.** 'Manuscripts', Marx 1975, pp. 351, 390 **12.** Ibid. **13.** 'Theses', ibid, pp. 421-422 **14.** 'Manuscripts', ibid, p. 326 **15.** 'Theses', Ibid, p. 422 **16.** Ibid. **17.** Ibid. **18.** Ibid. **19.** 'Manuscripts', Ibid, p. 364

Chapter 9

1. 'Manuscripts', Marx 1975, pp. 357, 391 **2.** Ibid., pp. 385-386 **3.** Ibid., pp. 324, 329 **4.** Ibid., pp. 324-327 **5.** Marx speaks of the resurrection of nature in socialist society, Marx 1975, pp. 349-350 **6.** Ibid., p. 351 **7.** Ibid., p. 328 **8.** Marx-Engels 976b **9** Marx 1977b, Vol. I, p. 174 **10.**

'Manuscripts', Marx 1975, p. 327 **11**. Ibid, pp. 389-390 **12**. Ibid., p. 391 **13**. Ibid., p. 331 **14**. Ibid., p. 350 **15**. 'Theses', Marx 1975, p. 423 **16**. Notes on James Mill, Marx 1975, p. 265 **17**. On base and superstructure, see 'Preface', Marx 1975, pp. 424-26 **18**. Marx 1977b, Vol. III, p. 820 **19**. 'Manuscripts', Marx 1975, p. 328 **20**. Ibid., p. 351 **21**. Marx 1977b, Vol. III, p. 820 **22**. 'Manuscripts', Marx 1975, p. 386 **23**. Ibid., p. 328 **24**. Ibid. **25**. Ibid., p. 348

Chapter 10

1. 'Manuscripts', in Marx 1975, p. 398 **2**. Ibid, p. 348 **3**. Ibid, p. 386 **4**. 'Critique', intro., p. 251 in Marx 1975 **5**. Ibid, p. 251 **6**. 'Manuscripts', Marx 1975, p. 333 **7**. 'Preface', Marx 1975, p. 424

Chapter 11

1. Karl Marx, "Wage-Labour and Capital", in Marx 1970a, p. 155 **2**. 'Preface', Marx 1970a, p. 67 **3**. Marx 1977b, Vol. III, p. 818 **4**. Marx-Engels 1976b, p. 42 **5**. 'Preface', Marx 1970a, p. 67 **6**. Marx-Engels 1976b, p. 42 **7**. Ibid **8**. Marx 1977b, Vol. III, p. 791 **9**. Marx-Engels 1976b, p. 42 **10**. Ibid, p. 37 **11**. Ibid, p. 49 **12**. Ibid, p. 57 **13**. Ibid, p. 61 **14**. Ibid,p. 67 **15**. Ibid,p. 112 **16**. Marx, "Theories of Surplus Value"('Theories'), Vol. III, p. 430 **17**. Marx 1977b, Vol. III, p. 791 **18**. 'Theories' in Marx 1970a, p. 113 **19**. 'Preface', Marx 1970a, pp. 67-68 **20**. Marx-Engels 1973, p. 48 **21**. Marx 1977b I, p. 715 **22**. Marx-Engels 1973, p. 49 **23**. Marx 1970b, p. 196 **24**. Marx-Engels 1973, p. 40 **25**. 'Preface', Marx 1970a, p. 68 **26**. Ibid, **27**. Marx-Engels 1976b, p. 83 **28**. 'Preface', Marx 1970a, p. 67 **29**. Marx-Engels 1976b, p. 54 **30**. Ibid, p. 91 **31**. Marx 1970b, Marx 1970a, p. 108 **32**. Marx-Engels 1976b, p. 91 **33**. Ibid, p. 62 **34**. Ibid, p. 42 **35**. Ibid, p. 37 **36**. 'Poverty' in Marx 1970a, pp. 76-77 **37**. 'Family' in Marx 1970a, p. 78 **38**. Marx-Engels 1976b, p. 41 **39**. Marx 1977b I, p. 174

Chapter 12

1. Panikkar 1980, p. viii **2**. 'Manuscripts', Marx 1975 Penguin 1975, p. 154 **3**. Though Namboothiripad rejects mechanical materialism, he lapses into a form of crass materialism when he says that it is material nature that shapes the thought and ideas and that identical laws operate in nature and society, Naboo 1963, pp. 17, 46 **4**. for this approach see chatto 1959 **5**. 'Theses':1 and 3, in Marx 1970a **6**. For relevant texts, cf. "The Indian Religious Traditions" in Kappen 2019, Chapter 1. **7**. A useful discussion of this problem may be found under the titles "Bernstein and the Marxism of the Second International" in Colleti 1972, pp. 229-236 **8**. Marx-Engels 1965a, p. 91 **9**. See the studies in Fromm 1966 **10**. Marx 1977b, Vol. 1, p. 174 **11**. In the 'Manuscripts', Marx speaks of nature as man's material and spiritual inorganic body. This applies in fact to all cultural products also. Marx 1975, p. 126 **12**. The instrumentalist notion of art continues to be projected as the quintessence of marxist aesthetic theory. See Namboothiripad 1981. p. 91 **13**. Namboothiripad 1983, p. 16 **14**. Marx 1977b, Vol. 3, p. 820 **15**. Marx, Eighteenth Brumaire of Louis Bonaparte" in Marx-Engels 1970b, pp. 170-171 **16**. See, for instance, the program of the Communist Party of India (Marxist) adopted at Madurai Congress in 1972 (malayalam version), Revised fourth edition, p. 39 **17**. Lenin, "What is to be done?" in Lenin 1975, p. 152-153 **18**. A positive answer is given by CPI(M) in regard to West Bengal in its 'report on organisation' adopted by the plenum of the cental committee, Howrah, 1978, no. 57 **19**. Marx 1975 **20**. Gramsci 1971, p. 12 **21**. 'Preface', Marx 1970a, p. 68 **22**. "Reply to Mikhailovsky (1877)" in Mclellan, 1971, p. 137 **23**.Bipin Chandra, "A Strategy in Crisis - the CPI Debate 1955 - 1956" in Chandra 1983, pp. 259-400 **24**. The Madurai Programme of the CPI(M), no. 114 **25**. Marx, "Civil War in France" in Marx-Engals 1970b, pp. 287-289 **26**. See Elleinstein 1976, and Mandel 1979 **27**. For an authoritative statement on Euro-communist position, see Carillo 1977 **28**. In a challenging analysis, which contains many valid insights, P. C. Joshi attributes to Indian Communists the error of considering theory as subservient to a praxis, already distorted by the ideology of the dominant classes. See "Reflections on Marxism and Social Revolution in India", in Panikkar 1980. While there is some truth in this assessment, in my view, the more fundamental error consisted in subordinating practice to an imported theory that had already been invested with the status of a dogma. Nor can I fully agree with his view that the original character of Marxism was distorted under conditions of colonial and semi-feudal backwardness (p. 183), as though the original Marxism itself did not have to be subjected to criticism.

Chapter 13

1. 'Theses', Marx 1963 p. 53 2. Marx 1963, p. 155 3. Dandekar 1971, pp. 124-26 4. *Ibid*, p. 33 5. See below under *Political Structure*. 6. Myrdal 1968, Vol. II, pp. 930-931

Cnapter 15

1. "Kritik der Hegelschen Dialektik und Philosophie Ueberhaupt" (KHD) in *Buecherei Des Marxismus- Leninismus* (BML), vol. 41, pp. 69-98. 2. Ibid, pp. 73-98 3. Ibid, pp. 75-76 4. Marx, *Thesen Ueber Feuerbach*, BML, Vol. 29, p. 593. 5. Marx-Engels 1965, pp. 36-37 6. Marx, *Thesen Ueber Feuerbach*, BML, Vol. 29, p. 593 7. Marx, "*Oekonomisch-philosophische Manuskripte*" (abv: MSS), BML, Vol. 42, p. 105 8. Ibid, p. 129 9. Marx, *Die Deutsche Ideologie* (DI), BML, 29, p. 22 10. Marx, *Thesen Ueber Feuerbach*, BML, Vol. 29, p. 593 11. MSS, BML, 42, p. 136 12. DI, BML, Vol. 29, p. 22 13. Marx-Engels 1965, pp. 41-42 14. MSS, BML, Vol. 42, p. 128 15. Ibid, p. 131 16. DI, BML, Vol. 29, pp. 22-23 17. Marx, "*Zur Kritik der Hegelschen Rechtsphilosophie*" (KHR), BML, Vol. 41, p. 27: here Marx refers to the proletariat as the material weapon for revolution! 18. MSS, BML, Vol. 42, p. 105 19. Ibid, p. 104 20. Marx, Marx 1977b, Progress Publishers, Moscow, 1977, Vol.1, pp. 177-178 21. Marx, Moscow 1977, KHR, BML, Vol. 41, p. 27 22. MSS, BML, Vol. 42, pp. 104-105 23. Marx, Moscow 1977,vol. 1, pp. 177-178 24. Marx, "*Zur Judenfrage*" (JF), BML, Vol. 41, pp. 31-34, 40 25. Ibid, p. 10 26. KHR, BML, Vol. 41, p. 11 27. Ibid. 28. JF, BML, Vol. 41, p. 38 29. MSS, BML, Vol. 42, p. 135 30. KHR, BML, Vol. 41, p. 11 31. Ibid. 32. Ibid, pp. 11-12 33. KHD, BML, Vol. 41, p. 89 34. MSS, BML, Vol. 42, pp. 135, 161 35. Ibid, pp. 133-134 36. Karl Marx and Frederick Engels, *Selected Works,* Moscow: Foreign Languages Pub; 5th edition (1962), Vol. 1, p. 54 37. MSS, BML, Vol. 42, p. 137 38. Ibid, p. 131 39. KHD,

BML, Vol. 41, p. 86 **40.** MSS, BML, Vol. 42, p. 138 **41.** Ibid, p. 139 **42.** Ibid, pp. 147-148 **43.** KHR, BML, Vol. 41, p. 27 **44.** Marx's article on press censorship, in Rheinische Zeitung, 14 July, 1842, in Marx-Engels, *Werke*, Berlin, 1956, Vol. 1, pp. 97-98.

Bibliography

Avineri, Shlomo (1969), *The Social and Political Thought of Karl Marx*, Cambridge

Bauer, Bruno (1938), *Kritik der Geschichte der Offenbarung*, Berlin

Calvez, Jean-Yves (1956), *La Pensee de Karl Marx*, Editions Du Seuil, Paris

Carillo, Santiago (1977), *Eurocommunism and the State*, Lawrence and Wishart, London

Chandra, Bipan, ed.(1983), *The Indian Left - Critical Appraisals*, Vikas Publishing House

Chattopathyaya, Debiprasad (1959), *Lokayata, A Study in Ancient Indian Materialism*, People's Publishing House

Colletti, Lucio (1976), *From Rousseau to Lenin*, Monthly Review Press, London

Dandekar, V M and Nilakantharath (1971), *Poverty in India*, Bombay

Elleinstein, Jean (1976), *The Stalin Phenomenon*, Lawrence and Wishart, London

Feuerbach, Ludwig (1957), *The Essence of Christianity*, ed. George Eliot, Harper Torchbooks, New York

Findlay, J N (1958), *Hegel - A Re-examination*, Oxford University Press, New York

Fromm, Erich, ed.(1966), *Socialist Humanism*, Double Day, New York

Garaudy, Roger (1972), *The Alternative Future*, Simon and Shuster, New York

Gramsci, Antonio (1971), *Selections from Prison Notebooks*, Lawrence and Wishart, London

Lenin (1975), *Selected Works*, Progress Publishers, Moscow

Mandel, Ernest (1979), *From Stalinism to Euro-communism*, KLB, London

Marx, Karl (1955), *The Poverty of Philosophy*, Progress Publishers, Moscow
- (1970a), *Selected Writings in Sociology and Social Philosophy*, ed. TB. Bottomore and Maximilien Rubel, Penguin Books

- (1970b), *Poverty of Philosophy,* Progress Publishers, Moscow

- (1972), *Theories of surplus values,* Moscow

- (1975), *Early Writings,* Penguin Books

- (1977a), *Capital,* Everyman's Library, Dent, London

- (1977b), *Capital,* Progress Publishers, Moscow

- (1963) *Early writings,* ed. T B Bottomore, CA Watts and Co., London

- (1973), *Grundrisse: Foundations of tne Critique of Political Economy,* Penguin Books

Marx-Engels (1970a), *The Holy Family,* Progress Publishers, Moscow

- (1970b), *Selected Works,* Progress Publishers, Moscow

- (1973), *Manifesto of the Communist Party,* Progress Publishers, Moscow

- (1973), *Manifesto of the Communist Party,* Progress Publishers, Moscow

- (1975), *On Religion,* Progress Publishers, Moscow

- (1976b), *The German Ideology,* Progress Publishers, Moscow

- (1965a), *The German Ideology,* London

McLellan, David (1971a), *Marx's Grundrisse,* Macmillan, London

- (1971b), *The Thought of Karl Marx: An Introduction,* Macmillan, London

- (1976), *Karl Marx: His Life and Thought,* Paladin, Frogmore

Myrdal, Gunnar (1968), *Asian Drama,* New York

Namboodirippad, E. M. S. (1966), *Economics and Politics of India's Socialist Pattern,*

- (1983), *Marxisathinte Prasakthi Innu* (Malayalam), Chintha

- (1981), *Kerala Charithravum Samskaravum, Oru Marxist Veekshanam,* (Malayalam), Chintha Publishers, Trivandrum

Panikkar, K. N. (ed.) (1980), *National and Left Movement in India,* Vikas, New Delhi

Sebastian Kappen's Books

- *Jesus and Freedom* (1977), intr. Francois Houtar, Orbis Books, Maryknoll, New York, Edition 2: Notion Press, Chennai, 2019

- *Marxian Atheism* (1983a), self published, Bangalore.

- *Jesus and Cultural Revolution - an Asian Perspective* (1983b), BILD, Bombay

- *Jesus Today* (1985). AICUF, Madras

- *Liberation Theology and Marxism* (1986), Asha Kendra, Punthamba

- *The Future of Socialism and Socialism of the Future* (1992), Visthar, Bangalore.

Posthumous Publications

- *Tradition Modernity Counterculture – an Asian Perspective* (1994), Visthar, Bangalore.

- *Spirituality in the New Age of Recolonisation* (1995), Visthar, Bangalore

- *Hindutva and Indian Religious Traditions* (2000), ed. Sebastian Vattamattam, Edition 2: Notion Press, Chennai, 2019

- *Divine Challenge and Human Response* (2001), ed. Sebastian Vattamattam, CSS, Tiruvalla

- *Jesus and Society* (2002a), ed. S Painadath S. J., ISPCK, Delhi.

- *Jesus and Culture* (2002b), ed. S Painadath S. J., ISPCK, Delhi

- *Towards a Holistic Cultural Paradigm* (2003), ed. Sebastian Vattamattam, CSS, Tiruvalla

- *Marx Beyond Marxism* (2012), ed. Sebastian Vattamattam, Voice Books, Manjeri.

- *Ingathering – Autobiographical Writings and Selected essays* (2013a), ed. Sebastian Vattamattam, Jeevan Books, Bharananganam

- *What the Thunder Says – A poem and selected Essays* (2013b), ed. Sebastian Vattamattam, Jeevan Books, Bharananganam

Books in Malayalam

- *Viswasathil Ninnu Viplavathilekku* (1 9 7 2), e d it i on 3: Pusthaka Prasadhaka Sangham, Kozhikode, 2019

- *Nalathekku Oru Laingika-sadacharam* (1973), Edition 3: Pusthaka Prasadhaka Sangham, Kozhikode, 2019

- *Paristhithi Samskruthi* (1988), (Co-author: Sebastian Vattamattam), Edition 2: Ascend Books, Kottayam, 2014

- *Marxian Darsanathinu Oramukham* (1989), tr. of Marx Beyond Marxism by Sebastian Vattamattam, Edition 2: NBS, Kottayam, 2012

- *Kalasrushtiyude Uravidam* (1991), tr. of Martin Heidegger: Der Ursprung Des Kunstwerkes, DCB, Kottayam

- *Pravachanam Prathisamskruthi* (1992), Yatra Publications, Kottayam

- *Socialisathinte Bhavi* (1993), Manusham Publications, Ettumanoor

- *Akraistavanaya Yesuvine Thedi* (1999), Current Books, Kottayam, 2005

- *Irupathonnam Noottandinoru Prathisamskruthi* (1991), tr. of Tradition Modernity Counterculture, Yatra Publications, Kottayam

- *Yesuvinte Mochanam Sabhakalil Ninnu* (2012), Dr. Bishop Paulose Mar Paulose Foundation, Thrissur

- *Daivathinte Maranavum Manushyante Jananavum*, (2015), tr. of Marxian Atheism, Media House, Calicut

About the Editor

Sebastian Vattamattam is a retired professor of mathematics and a writer. In Malayalam he has authored the books: *Ecology and Culture* (with Fr. Kappen), *Language and Power, Unconscious Travels of Language – From Freud to Lacan, Ideology and Symbolic Revolution, Sigmund Freud*. His books in English are *Book of Beautiful Curves* (Math) and *What Dreams Tell Us – Lacanian Interpretations*. Vattamattam has compiled, edited, and published many books of Fr. Kappen.

Contents of the Six Volumes

Volume I

Part 1: Jesus and Freedom
Preface of the First Edition

Part 2: Essays

Volume II

6. An Atheism of Ambivalence

Part 2: Essays

7. The Dialectical Method I

8. The Dialectical Method II

9. Man - A Dialectical Being

10. Alienation and the Dialectic of History

11. The Materialist Conception of History

12. Indian Communism and the Challenge of Cultural Revolution

13. The Goals of Revolution

14. Revolution: For What? By Whom?

15. Consciousness and Reality in Marxism

16. Dialectic of the Psycho-structure and the Social Structure

17. How not to be a Revolutionary

Volume III

Part 1: Jesus and Cultural Revolution
Foreword

1. The Dialectic of Culture and Prophecy

2. Jesus: the Prophet of a Counterculture

3. The Decline of Prophecy

4. Countercultural Movements in India

5. Jesus and Transculturation

6. Communities for Countercultural Action

Part 2: Essays
7.   The Prophet of Hope

8.   Towards Theandric Fullness

9.   The Not-yet and the Already

10. The Future: A Gift and a Task

11. A Manifesto of Freedom

12. Freedom for the Body

13. Salvation as Wholeness

14. Man, Woman and the Human

15. Either God or Money

16. The Temptations of a Radical

17. The Abolition of Power

18. The Pure and the Impure

19. Mercy, not Sacrifice

20. Faith versus Ideology

21. Attuning Oneself to the Divine

22. Discipleship as Contestation

23. The Spirit Brooding over a Wasteland

24. A Quest That Never Ended

25. Power in Powerlessness

26. Let Jesus be

27. Historizing and Historiology as Prophecy

28. The Cost of Discipleship

Volume IV

Part 1: Liberation Theology and Marxism

Part 2: Essays

Volume V

Volume VI

Part 1: Tradition Modernity Counterculture
Preface

Part 2: Essays